Palgrave Macmillan Studies in Banking and Financial Institutions

Series Editor: **Professor Philip Molyneux**

The Palgrave Macmillan Studies in Banking and Financial Institutions are international in orientation and include studies of banking within particular countries or regions, and studies of particular themes such as Corporate Banking, Risk Management, Mergers and Acquisitions, etc. The books' focus is on research and practice, and they include up-to-date and innovative studies on contemporary topics in banking that will have global impact and influence.

Titles include:

Mario Anolli, Elena Beccalli and Tommaso Giordani (*editors*)
RETAIL CREDIT RISK MANAGEMENT

Rym Ayadi and Emrah Arbak
FINANCIAL CENTRES IN EUROPE
Post-Crisis Risks, Challenges and Opportunities

Rym Ayadi and Sami Mouley
MONETARY POLICIES, BANKING SYSTEMS, REGULATORY CONVERGENCE, EFFICIENCY AND GROWTH IN THE MEDITERRANEAN

Caner Bakir
BANK BEHAVIOUR AND RESILIENCE
The Effect of Structures, Institutions and Agents

Alessandro Carretta and Gianluca Mattarocci (*editors*)
ASSET PRICING, REAL ESTATE AND PUBLIC FINANCE OVER THE CRISIS

Dimitris N. Chorafas
BASEL III, THE DEVIL AND GLOBAL BANKING

Dimitris N. Chorafas
HOUSEHOLD FINANCE
Adrift in a Sea of Red Ink

Dimitris N. Chorafas
SOVEREIGN DEBT CRISIS
The New Normal and the Newly Poor

Stefano Cosma and Elisabetta Gualandri (*editors*)
THE ITALIAN BANKING SYSTEM
Impact of the Crisis and Future Perspectives

Joseph Falzon (*editor*)
BANK PERFORMANCE, RISK AND SECURITISATION

Joseph Falzon (*editor*)
BANK STABILITY, SOVEREIGN DEBT AND DERIVATIVES

Juan Fernández de Guevara Radoselovics and José Pastor Monsálvez (*editors*)
CRISIS, RISK AND STABILITY IN FINANCIAL MARKETS

Juan Fernández de Guevara Radoselovics and José Pastor Monsálvez (*editors*)
MODERN BANK BEHAVIOUR

Franco Fiordelisi and Ornella Ricci (*editors*)
BANCASSURANCE IN EUROPE
Past, Present and Future

Josanco Floreani and Maurizio Polato
THE ECONOMICS OF THE GLOBAL STOCK EXCHANGE INDUSTRY

Jill M. Hendrickson
FINANCIAL CRISIS
The United States in the Early Twenty-First Century

Otto Hieronymi and Constantine Stephanou (*editors*)
INTERNATIONAL DEBT
Economic, Financial, Monetary, Political and Regulatory Aspects

Paola Leone and Gianfranco A. Vento (*editors*)
CREDIT GUARANTEE INSTITUTIONS AND SME FINANCE

Ted Lindblom, Stefan Sjögren and Magnus Willesson (*editors*)
FINANCIAL SYSTEMS, MARKETS AND INSTITUTIONAL CHANGES

Ted Lindblom, Stefan Sjögren and Magnus Willesson (*editors*)
GOVERNANCE, REGULATION AND BANK STABILITY

Gianluca Mattarocci
ANOMALIES IN THE EUROPEAN REITs MARKET
Evidence from Calendar Effects

Bernardo Nicoletti
CLOUD COMPUTING IN FINANCIAL SERVICES

Özlem Olgu
EUROPEAN BANKING
Enlargement, Structural Changes and Recent Developments

Fotios Pasiouras
GREEK BANKING
From the Pre-Euro Reforms to the Financial Crisis and Beyond

Daniela Pîrvu
CORPORATE INCOME TAX HARMONIZATION IN THE EUROPEAN UNION

The full list of titles available is on the website:
www.palgrave.com/finance/sbfi.asp

Palgrave Macmillan Studies in Banking and Financial Institutions
Series Standing Order ISBN 978–1–4039–4872–4

You can receive future titles in this series as they are published by placing a standing order. Please contact your bookseller or, in case of difficulty, write to us at the address below with your name and address, the title of the series and the ISBN quoted above.

Customer Services Department, Macmillan Distribution Ltd, Houndmills, Basingstoke, Hampshire RG21 6XS, England

---

Financial Systems, Markets and Institutional Changes

Edited by

Ted Lindblom
Professor of Business Administration, University of Gothenburg, Sweden

Stefan Sjögren
Associate Professor of Business Administration, University of Gothenburg, Sweden

and

Magnus Willesson
Senior Lecturer, Linnaeus University, Sweden

palgrave
macmillan

First published 2014 by
PALGRAVE MACMILLAN

Palgrave Macmillan in the UK is an imprint of Macmillan Publishers Limited, registered in England, company number 785998, of Houndmills, Basingstoke, Hampshire RG21 6XS.

Palgrave Macmillan in the US is a division of St Martin's Press LLC, 175 Fifth Avenue, New York, NY 10010.

Palgrave Macmillan is the global academic imprint of the above companies and has companies and representatives throughout the world.

Palgrave® and Macmillan® are registered trademarks in the United States, the United Kingdom, Europe and other countries

ISBN: 978–1–137–41358–1

This book is printed on paper suitable for recycling and made from fully managed and sustained forest sources. Logging, pulping and manufacturing processes are expected to conform to the environmental regulations of the country of origin.

A catalogue record for this book is available from the British Library.

Library of Congress Cataloging-in-Publication Data

Financial systems, markets and institutional changes / edited by Ted Lindblom, Stefan Sjögren, Magnus Willesson.
pages cm.—(Palgrave Macmillan studies in banking and financial institutions)
Includes bibliographical references.
ISBN 978–1–137–41358–1
1. Financial institutions. 2. International finance – Government policy. 3. Monetary policy. I. Lindblom, Ted, 1956– II. Sjögren, Stefan. III. Willesson, Magnus.

HG173.F5184 2014
332—dc23 2014019730

Contents

List of Figures ix

List of Tables x

Preface xii

Notes on Contributors xiii

1 Institutional Change and the Design of Financial Systems 1
Ted Lindblom, Stefan Sjögren and Magnus Willesson

2 The Road to a Viable Euro Zone and the Preconditions for Becoming a More Optimal Currency Region 9
René W. H. van der Linden

2.1 Introduction 9
2.2 The rationale of the euro area from different perspectives 12
2.3 Preconditions for fulfilling the role of a monetary union 14
2.4 Preconditions for becoming an optimum currency area 19
2.5 Flaws of the EMU design and misdiagnosis of the euro crisis 22
2.6 Five pillars for a viable monetary union in the euro area 25
2.7 Structural reforms and the controversy between growth and austerity 26
2.8 From a fiscal compact to a fiscal union 29
2.9 A permanent rescue fund as a fiscal backstop 31
2.10 The European banking union 32
2.11 The ECB as a lender of last resort 35
2.12 Concluding remarks and recommendations 37

3 Gross Imbalances, Liquidity Shortage and the Role of the Federal Reserve 43
Pierluigi Morelli, Giovanni B. Pittaluga and Elena Seghezza

3.1 Introduction 43

3.2 Demand for US dollar swap lines 44
3.3 The supply of swap lines from the Fed 48
3.4 A discussion of the results 53
3.5 Conclusions 55

4 Firm-based and Institutional-based Determinants of the Bank Debt Maturity: New Evidence for Developed Countries 61
Eleuterio Vallelado, Paolo Saona and Pablo San Martín
4.1 Introduction 61
4.2 Determinants of the maturity of bank borrowing 63
4.3 Data and variables 69
4.4 Results 72
4.5 Conclusions 74

5 The Financing of Italian Firms and the Credit Crunch: Findings and Exit Strategies 80
Elisabetta Gualandri and Valeria Venturelli
5.1 Introduction 80
5.2 The evolution of financial systems and the financial structure of non-financial companies in Europe 81
5.3 The crisis and the credit market in the euro area 86
5.4 Italian firms: financial constraints and the credit crunch 89
5.5 The exit strategies 96
5.6 Conclusions and recommendations 102

6 Does the Team Manager Earn More than His Coached Players? Analysis of the Earnings of Italian Asset Management Companies, and their Portfolio Companies, in the Field of Private Equity 110
Elisa Giaretta and Giusy Chesini
6.1 Introduction 110
6.2 Literature review 111
6.3 Research hypotheses 116
6.4 Data description and methodology 117
6.4.1 Data description 117
6.4.2 Methodology 119
6.5 Results 121
6.6 Conclusions 126
6.6.1 Discussion and implications 126
6.6.2 Limitations of the research and directions for future analyses 128

7 Does 'Political Bias' Undermine the Korea Investment Corporation? 132
Andrea Paltrinieri, Flavio Pichler and Stefano Miani
7.1 Introduction 132
7.2 A brief literature review on SWFs' investment strategies 136
7.3 The Korea Investment Corporation's framework 137
7.4 Data and methodology 140
7.5 The KIC's investment strategies 142
7.5.1 The analysis of benchmark and strategic asset allocation 142
7.5.2 The analysis of geographical asset allocation 145
7.5.3 The 'internal political bias' analysis 146
7.6 Conclusion 148

8 Regulating High-frequency Trading: An Examination of European, US and Australian Equity Market Structures 152
Giusy Chesini and Elisa Giaretta
8.1 Introduction 152
8.2 Literature review 154
8.3 Market factors contributing to the rise of high-frequency trading (HFT) 156
8.4 Main risks and proposed policy measures to mitigate them 161
8.5 Regulatory measures around the world: the state of the art 166
8.5.1 Supranational level organizations 167
8.5.2 European directives 170
8.5.3 US regulation 172
8.5.4 Australian regulation 173
8.5.5 Other regional regulation in Europe 174
8.5.6 A regulatory comparison concerning different market structures 178
8.6 Conclusions 183

9 Islamic and Conventional Exchanges: A Performance Analysis and Governance Perspectives 188
Josanco Floreani, Andrea Paltrinieri, Maurizio Polato and Flavio Pichler
9.1 Introduction 188
9.2 Literature review and theoretical framework 190
9.3 Description of the sample 193
9.4 Data and methodology 197

9.5 Main results 200
9.5.1 Descriptive statistics 200
9.5.2 Analysis of variance and differences in means 204
9.5.3 Regression results 206
9.6 Strategic implications 208
9.7 Conclusion 211

Index 217

List of Figures

2.1 Government deficits and general government debt of EMU members in 2012 15
2.2 Government deficits of EMU members in 2009 and 2012 18
2.3 Wage and productivity developments in the EMU between 1999 and 2012 21
2.4 Five pillars for a viable monetary union 26
2.5 Nominal unit labour costs and the current account balance of Germany and the PIIGS countries between 2000 and 2014 28
5.1 Lending by borrower sector 87
5.2 Interest rates on bank loans to firms 88
5.3 Bank lending flows/GDP 90
5.4 Corporate investment trends in Europe 90
5.5 Access to credit of Italian firms in relation to firm size 94
5.6 Proportion of credit-rationed firms 94
5.7 Interest rates on loans in relation to firm size 95
6.1 Limited partnership 112
8.1 Fidessa Fragmentation Index from 2008 to 2013 157
8.2 The decline in the average trade size in the regulated markets 159
8.3 Summary of market factors contributing to the rise of HFT 160
8.4 HFT market share in the US and in Europe 167
8.5 The new liquidity landscape in Europe 178
9.1 Trading values and listed companies (CAGRs) 196

List of Tables

3.1 Drawing of swap lines by the Fed 46
3.2 Descriptive statistics 46
3.3 OLS estimate of the demand for swap lines 46
3.4 Short-term claims of US banks on OECD economies 47
3.5 Timeline of dollar swap announcements 49
3.6 CDS prices and swaps operations (sample of 42 banks) 50
3.7 EGARCH estimate of the spread between bank CDS and sovereign CDS (eurozone) 52
4.1 Description of the corporate governance legislations across countries 67
4.2 Descriptive statistics and test of mean differences among the variables by legal system and application of corporate governance legislation (CGR) 70
5.1 Financial intensity ratio: non-financial corporations' financial liabilities/GDP 82
5.2 Financial surplus/deficit of non-financial corporations 83
5.3 Non-financial corporations: breakdown of liabilities 84
5.4 Percentage of firms reporting 'access to finance' as their principal concern 92
5.5 SMEs' need for bank loans 93
5.6 Availability of bank loans 93
5.7 Trends in lending in relation to creditworthiness of firms, in Italy 95
5.A1 Breakdown of liabilities of European firms by size class 104
5.A2 Instruments and actions for the creation/reinforcement of financing channels for SMEs, other than bank loans 106
6.1 Typical income statement for Italian AMCs 114
6.2 Distribution of private equity-backed companies in the years studied 118
6.3 Descriptive statistics of Italian AMCs and portfolio companies in the period 2008–2011 119
6.4 Probit model 122
6.5 OLS regressions – dependent variables: TAS, EQU, INT and NET 124
6.6 OLS regressions – dependent variables: FEE, INT/E, NET/E and FEE/E 124

6.7 OLS regressions – dependent variables: INT/A, NET/A, FEE/A and PRO 125
6.A Variable definitions and data sources 129
7.1 The top twenty SWFs for assets under management (June, 2013) 134
7.2 Benchmark for asset class (December 2007–December 2012) 142
7.3 KIC strategic asset allocation (December 2006–December 2012) 143
7.4 KIC geographical asset allocation (December 2010–December 2011) 146
7.5 Korea Investment Corporation performance 147
8.1 Main pieces of regulation concerning HFT 176
8.2 Regional regulation concerning HFT 177
8.3 The main characteristics of market structures 182
9.1 Sample characteristics: Conventional (CEs) and Islamic (IEs) stock exchanges 195
9.2 Revenue composition 197
9.3 The variables 198
9.4 The matrix of correlations 200
9.5 Islamic and conventional stock exchanges: a comparison 205
9.6 t-statistic test 206
9.7 Regression results 207
9.A Relevant measures of performance 213

Preface

Financial Systems, Markets and Institutional Changes comprises a selection of chapters originally presented as papers at the annual conference of the European Association of University Teachers of Banking and Finance – Wolpertinger 2013 – which was held in August 28–31, 2013 at the School of Business, Economics and Law, Gothenburg University, Sweden. The Wolpertinger 2013 was open for papers in all areas of banking and finance and this volume includes high-quality contributions focusing on financial markets and firms' financing.

As editors, we would like to thank all the contributors to this volume for their contributions and their efforts in keeping up the time schedule. We are also grateful to all the referees who acted as reviewers to the chapters published in this volume – the blind peer review process significantly improved the quality of each contribution. We also want to thank all the conference participants for their active discussions during seminars, for contributing to a constructive atmosphere and for introducing new perspectives on challenges to future studies in banking and finance.

Special thanks to Palgrave Macmillan and Philip Molyneux (Series Editor for Studies in Banking and Financial Institutions) for the opportunity to edit the book and to the staff at Palgrave Macmillan, especially Aimee Dibbens (Commissioning Editor Finance) for helpful comments and guidance.

Finally, as conference organizers, we would like to thank Dr Martin Andersson, General Director of Sweden's Financial Supervisory Authority, for giving an opening speech at the conference. We are also very grateful to the Bertil Danielsson Foundation, VINNOVA and the School of Business, Economics and Law at the University of Gothenburg for financial contribution to the conference and Ragnar Söderbergs stiftelse for research grants to Magnus Willesson.

Notes on Contributors

Giusy Chesini is Associate Professor of the Economics of Financial Intermediaries at the University of Verona, Italy, where she specializes in the structure and regulation of international financial markets. Her main research topics include the stock exchange industry, the evolution of financial systems, banking and risk management. She often participates in Italian and international conferences and she has written numerous papers and books on the above subjects.

Josanco Floreani has graduated in Economics at the University of Udine, Italy in 1999. He received a PhD degree in Corporate Sciences at the University of Udine in 2005. He is currently a lecturer in Banking and Finance. His research fields mainly relate to the securities and exchange industry. He is co-author of various publications on topics which address issues related to the industry structure, measurement of performances and value for securities exchanges and regulation.

Elisa Giaretta is a PhD student in Business Administration and Management at the Faculty of Economics of the University of Verona. She is a researcher in the 'Polo Scientifico e Didattico di Studi sull'Impresa', an academic centre focused on the analysis of Italian enterprises. She is also a member of the Italian Association of Scholars of Economics and Management of Financial Institutions and Markets (ADEIMF), an organization of scholars interested in the area of financial studies, in Italy. Research topics include asset management companies, private equity and venture capital. She has participated in Italian and international congresses on these subjects.

Elisabetta Gualandri is Full Professor in Banking and Finance at the 'Marco Biagi' Department of Economics of the University of Modena and Reggio Emilia, where she is a member of CEFIN (Center for Studies in Banking and Finance) and of Softech-ICT (Center for Industrial Research). She graduated from the University of Modena and obtained a MA in Banking and Finance at the University College of North Wales. She is currently Director of the European Association of University Teachers in Banking and Finance, a member of ADEIMF (Italian Association of Teachers in Banking and Finance), of AIDEA (Italian Academy of Business Administration and Management), and of Suerf (The European Money and Finance Forum). She served as an auditor of Banca d'Italia from 2007 to 2012, when she was appointed to the board of Banca Popolare dell'Emilia Romagna. Since 2013, advisor of the EC for Horizon 2020, Access to Risk Finance Group. Recent research topics include regulation and supervision, financial crisis, the financing of innovative SMEs and public intervention programmes.

Ted Lindblom is Professor of Business Administration at the School of Business, Economics and Law, University of Gothenburg, Sweden. His current research mainly concerns corporate finance and banking. In the corporate finance area he particularly focuses on corporate governance, capital budgeting and financial structure decisions. In banking his emphasis is on banking strategies, pricing, profitability and risk management under different market conditions and regulatory frameworks. He has authored and co-authored several articles and books on these issues.

René W. H. van der Linden is Lecturer in Economics, Banking & Finance and European integration at the InHolland University of Applied Sciences in Amsterdam/Diemen, The Netherlands. He was previously with the Erasmus University Rotterdam and the Amsterdam Academy for Banking and Finance, a collaborative venture between InHolland and the Free University of Amsterdam. He has published several papers on the Chinese economy and banking system and is co-author of the textbook *European Business Environment: Doing Business in the EU* (2010).

Stefano Miani is Full Professor in Banking and Insurance at the Department of Economics and Statistics, University of Udine. Recent research topics include pension funds and pension systems, the regulation and monitoring of insurance companies and the regulation of financial markets and intermediaries.

Pierluigi Morelli works at the Research Department of the Italian Bank Association (ABI) where he is responsible for the econometric model of the Italian economy and of the Italian banking system. He graduated in Statistics and Economics at the University of Rome 'La Sapienza' in 1988. From 1988 to 2009 he worked at the Centro Europa Ricerche (CER). As Research Director of the CER Monetary and Banking sector, he was in charge of the econometric models of the Italian economy, of the banking sector, and of pension expenditure. He has published numerous articles on monetary economics, banking, social security and environment.

Andrea Paltrinieri is Research Scholar in Financial Markets and Instruments at the University of Verona. Research topics include the evolution of financial systems, stock exchange mergers in the emerging markets, asset management and institutional investors, with a particular focus on sovereign wealth funds.

Flavio Pichler is Associate Professor in Banking and Finance at the University of Verona. Research topics include the theory, regulation and supervision of financial systems, the economics of insurance, banking and risk management.

Giovanni B. Pittaluga is Full Professor of Economics at Genoa University, Italy. Previously he was Associate Professor of Monetary Economics at Università Cattolica del Sacro Cuore, Milan (1991–1994) and an economist in the Research Department of the Bank of Italy (1983–1988). He has been responsible for the budget of Regione Liguria (2000–2002 and 2005–2010). He is the author of books and articles in international journals in the area of monetary economics. His research interests include central banking, banking, inflation, international political economy and economic history.

Maurizio Polato is Full Professor of Banking and Finance at Udine University. His research fields mainly relate to the securities and exchange industry. He has written on issues related to the structure of the industry, measurement of performance and value for securities exchanges and regulation.

Pablo San Martín is Assistant Professor of Finance at Universidad Católica de la Santísima Concepción, Chile. He obtained his PhD at the Universidad de Valladolid (Spain) through a BecasChile scholarship programme for PhD studies. His research and publications are associated with corporate finance, specifically capital structure and corporate governance.

Paolo Saona is Assistant Professor of Finance at Saint Louis University, Madrid, Spain. He received his PhD at Universidad de Valladolid, Spain, and his MBA and BSc in Business at Austral University of Chile. His work has appeared in *Applied Economics, Review of Managerial Science, Emerging Markets Finance and Trade, International Journal of Banking, Accounting and Finance, Spanish Journal of Finance and Accounting, Academia Revista Latinoamericana de Administración, Cuadernos de Economía y Dirección de Empresa, Abante, Research Management,* and the *International Review of Business and Finance,* among others. His research fields include corporate finance, corporate governance, and financial systems. He has also served as a reviewer for international journals such as the *Financial*

Review, Review of Managerial Science, Emerging Markets Finance and Trade and *INNOVA*.

Elena Seghezza is Assistant Professor at Genoa University, Italy. She previously worked as an economist at the Department of Economic Affairs of the Italian Government and at the Organization for Economic Cooperation and Development (OECD). She has a PhD in International Economics from the Graduate Institute of International Studies, Geneva. She has published several articles on political economy, interest groups, inflation and international trade.

Stefan Sjögren is Associate Professor at the Department of Business Administration at the School of Business, Economics and Law, University of Gothenburg, Sweden. He obtained his PhD at Gothenburg University in 1996. His research interests are across a broad range of corporate finance including capital budgeting, international finance, valuation, deregulation and, efficiency measurement. His research interests also cover venture capital and the valuation of ideas.

Eleuterio Vallelado is Professor of Finance at the Universidad de Valladolid, Spain. He obtained his PhD at the Universidad de Valladolid and an MBA from the Stern School of Business, New York. He was a Fulbright Scholar from 1989 to 1991. He served as Vice Chancelor of Strategic Planning from 2006 to 2008 at University of Valladolid. He has published widely in corporate finance, banking and behavioural finance areas. His current research focuses on banking strategies, behavioral finance, the relevance of institutional setting on corporate finance, and corporate governance, compensation and models of financial system.

Valeria Venturelli is Associate Professor in Banking and Finance at the 'Marco Biagi' Faculty of Economics of the University of Modena and Reggio Emilia. She is a member of CEFIN (Center for Studies in Banking and Finance) and Softech-ICT (Center for Industrial Research) where she teaches Financial Markets and Private Banking at both undergraduate and graduate level. She received her PhD in Financial Markets and Institutions from the Catholic University of Milan. Her main research interests are the economics of banking and other financial institutions and valuation methods. She is author of several articles in leading academic journals. She has acted as a consultant to various public institutions and consulting firms.

Magnus Willesson is Senior Lecturer at Linnæus University, Växjö, Sweden and obtained his PhD from University of Gothenburg. His current teaching includes banking, financial institutions and markets, strategic risk management and corporate finance. His research mainly focuses on the management of risk, efficiency of banks and banks' adoption of regulatory frameworks. He is the author of a number of journal articles and book chapters covering subjects as risk taking and risk management in banks, banking efficiency, operational risk in banks and banks' and adoption of the Basel II and Basel III accords. He has also contributed to several international publications on cost efficiency and pricing of payments.

1
Institutional Change and the Design of Financial Systems

Ted Lindblom, Stefan Sjögren and Magnus Willesson

Financial Systems, Markets and Institutional Changes includes contemporary studies on different institutional settings and how these affect firms' ability to borrow money, as well as how the latest financial crisis has affected the relationship between firms that borrow and banks that lend. The book also addresses issues related to the globalization of the financial market. One such issue concerns the imbalances between different regions in the EMU, which raises the question of whether this is as an optimal currency union and also puts new requirements on an international lender of last resort (ILLR). Recent technology development, along with high-frequency trading, and the growth of Islamic banking, are two other examples of institutional changes that forms new actors and new markets. We will in this introductory chapter take the opportunity to discuss each contribution from another perspective, perhaps different from the original purpose of the author(s) in their specific chapter. We have observed that the chapters all have similarities in that they describe, analyse and exemplify how the financial system endogenously adjusts to institutional changes.

The analytical framework used in this introductory text rests on the ideas described and elaborated upon by Merton and Bodie (2005). In their conceptual work, Merton and Bodie lay the foundation for what they refer to as 'functional and structural finance' (FSF) in which they try to synthesize three different theoretical foundations or theories. The authors propose a new way to integrate the three broad and, to a greater or lesser extent, conflicting perspectives of the neo-classical, the neo-institutional and the behavioural theories. Instead of viewing these perspectives as competing abstractions of the complex reality, the FSF paradigm aims at integrating the core understanding from each perspective. Broadly described it is an attempt to adopt an analytical framework that views institutions as endogenously shaped and formed as a response to exogenously given functions. A particular institution exists, when exchanging goods and capital, as a response to existing transaction costs and behavioural distortions.

The basic neo-classical theory, with atomistic actors acting on a perfect market, has been criticized for not providing an adequate model for identifying inefficient structures and therefore delivers only limited guidance to decision-makers. However, behavioural theories emphasizing the human factor as important when analysing market failures have offered some answers, albeit not without criticism. The most recent financial crisis is said to constitute an example of how aspiration, overconfidence and perceptions affect mortgage markets. This is, however, not a new phenomenon: Keynes (1936) argued that booms and busts are a result of sentiment, pessimism and other psychological factors.

The neo-institutional theory advocates that organizations are 'caged' by institutional isomorphism (DiMaggio and Powell, 1983). Organizations can sanction or even actively support the current institutional structure. One example is again related to the mortgage market where organizations, such as too-big-to-fail banks (TBFBs), involved in the issuance, securitization and rating of assets, gave authorization to the existing regulatory regime and a cultural acceptance of, as it turned out, excessive borrowing.

The FSF paradigm can be viewed as an attempt to enrich the neo-classical theory by including behavioural distortions and institutional theories to allow for better understanding of how organizations, and not atomistic players, are endogenously formed in order to minimize market distortion.

How about regulation? If organizations can reform, or if the construction of a new organization is a result of a 'invisible hand', which minimizes the costs of behavioural distortions or transactions, the neo-classical market solution should be a reasonable approximation of the second-best outcome. However, the recent financial crisis has called for a lot of regulatory changes. Many blame the deregulation of the financial services markets in the US about a decade ago. In 1999 the Congress enacted the Gramm–Leach–Bliley Act (also referred to as the Financial Services Modernization Act), which allowed commercial banks to engage in investment banking. What followed were ever-increasing, larger banks, which eventually ended up as TBTF banks. Today, we can hear voices advocating a much tougher regulation of the financial markets. This has many similarities with what happened after the financial crisis in the late 1920s, which finally lead to implementation of the Glass–Steagall Act of 1932.

The functional and structural finance theory of Merton and Bodie (2005) has the neo-classical perspective as a point of departure. If market failures, which violate the idea of an invisible hand, occur the reasons for these failures can be argued to be institutional rigidities, technological inadequacies, or dysfunctional behavioural patterns. However, as technology progresses and institutions strive for reduced transaction costs, the neo-classical theory can still produce a fair prediction of the future. Even individual irrationality can be offset by institutions. As an example, the authors use the market for life insurance to explain that the long-run market equilibrium will not reflect individuals' underestimation of their life expectancy whenever competing insurance firms enter the market. In this book we can provide the reader with eight other examples.

The rest of the text in this introductory chapter consists of brief summaries of each contribution. These summaries are to some extent based on the chapter abstracts and, thus, 'co-authored' with the contributors to this book. Our aim is to describe the content of the chapters and, at the same time, highlight the importance of the research carried out by the different contributors by placing them in the context of a functional and structural finance theory, of which the ambition and overall purpose is to synthesize the three different perspectives of neo-classical, neo-institutional and behavioural theories.

The neo-classical theory constitutes the basic foundation for many areas. One such area is the theory of optimal currency unions. In **Chapter 2**, René W. H. van der Linden discusses the EMU as an optimal currency union and describes how one of the key sources of stress within the EMU is the divergence of competitiveness and external imbalances between its 'core' and 'periphery' members, whereby the single monetary policy as 'one size fits all' has proved to be an illusion or 'one size fits none' problem. On one hand the euro has boosted trade, credit flows and foreign direct investments (FDIs) within the EU. On the other hand, the single currency has also become an economic trap and the resulting recession has created a disaffection in several EMU members, which has enhanced the different views of both its advocates and critics. The author concludes that the architects of the EMU definitely hoped that the emergence of a single currency would create the conditions for an optimal currency area (OCA). However, the EMU has created externalities that require fiscal transfers between member countries to compensate for a lack of exchange-rate adjustments and to offset regional divergences and temporary imbalances. The interconnectedness between banks and governments shows that the central bank should broaden its mandate without interfering with its monetary policy aims. Although the OCA theory does not explicitly refer to a banking union, it is obvious that a major role has been reserved for the ECB as the lender of last resort for suffering states. Other building blocks for a more viable monetary union include the structural reforms to improve the foundations of growth, a permanent transfer union and, ultimately, a fiscal union. EMU members that form a currency area need to accept the costs in the name of a common destiny. This requires more solidity of fiscal policy, but also more solidarity or willingness to share each other's risks in order to make the EMU a more optimal currency region. This chapter presents a good example of where the markets are highly influenced by both institutional settings and behavioural aspects challenging the rational neo-classical theory.

In **Chapter 3**, Pierluigi Morelli, Giovanni B. Pittaluga and Elena Seghezza give us a new perspective on the international lender of last resort (ILOLR). New challenges give rise both to new instruments and institutional changes. The dollar shortage suffered by the European banking systems in 2007–2008 was overcome thanks to the swap lines operated by the US central bank and granted to the European banking systems in order to overcome the dollar shortage and reduce the risk of default. Emerging countries dealt with the dollar shortage by turning to the ample currency reserves they had at their disposal. What happened reopened the debate about the ILOLR. On the one hand, contrary to what has been shown by a vast amount of literature, the recent crisis has demonstrated that the IMF lacks a fundamental requisite for being an ILOLR – it does not have the capacity to create money. On the other hand, various emerging countries are unwilling to accept the drawbacks connected to the FED performing the function of an ILOLR. However, the authors argue that the FED plays the role of an ILOLR taking into consideration the protection of the interests of its country. Therefore, they recommend that other countries escape the state of dependency on the FED, and the uncertainty of its behaviour, by introducing new regulations to reduce the foreign currency liquidity risk.

Chapter 4 by Eleuterio Vallelado, Paolo Saona and Pablo San Martín, offers clear evidence on how the institutional setting of a country can play a role in forming different organizational outcomes. Ever since the LLSV (La Porta, Lopez-de-Silanes, Shleifer and Vishny, 1998) research was first submitted, our understanding of how different legal structures affect investor choice has increased. The LLSV approach fits well into the FSF paradigm as it shows how legal protection (i.e. different transaction costs for different types of financing), will affect capital structure decisions at a firm level. The goal of this chapter is to describe how decisions on the maturity of bank borrowing are conditioned by firm-based variables and the characteristics of the regulatory and the institutional setting within which the firms operate. The sample includes observations from Australia, Belgium, Canada, Denmark, France, Germany, Italy, Spain, the United Kingdom, and the United States over the period from 1996 to 2008. As a result, the authors observe that the funding of investments depends on the extent to which the financial system is either market-oriented or banking-oriented. Furthermore, the new regulation on transparency has modified the role of bank debt maturity in common-law countries as a disciplining device and reinforced its corporate governance role in civil-law countries. The relationship between the external funds needed and the ownership structure, and bank debt maturity is affected by corporate governance regulation and by a country's legal tradition.

In **Chapter 5** by Elisabetta Gualandri and Valeria Venturelli, the aim is to analyse how the credit crunch has modified the traditional bank–firm relationship, with particular attention to the Italian situation. Their analysis reinforces the finding that in Italy, the credit available to the real economy is insufficient not only in terms of quantity but also in terms of quality. The next step is to identify and discuss possible exit strategies for eliminating the effects of the credit crunch and then to overcome serious intrinsic shortcomings in terms of alternative instruments, markets and intermediaries. On one hand, the crisis has revealed the underdevelopment of the Italian financial market, the insufficient role of institutional investors, the embryonic state of the corporate bond markets and the virtual non-existence of commercial paper markets. On the other hand, this could finally provide the opportunity for the development of these channels. The changing role of banks in the new scenario is also analysed as well as the characteristics that firms will require in order to benefit from it.

Even if there is more than one way of best providing financial functions, which is the central lesson of the FSF paradigm put forward by Merton and Bodie, the Italian case shows that in times after crises, inefficiencies are revealed and institutional change is a natural outcome. Together with the other, richly described examples in this book, this chapter teaches us that the irrelevance proposition of financing decisions, as put forward in the neo-classical theory, does not hold.

In **Chapter 6**, Elisa Giaretta and Giusy Chesini provide us with further insight into the Italian financial markets. They investigate the Italian private equity industry and ask if a team manager does 'earn more than his coached players', offering an analysis of the earnings of Italian asset management companies and their portfolio companies in the field of private equity. Asset management companies (AMCs) collect investors' pooled savings into funds and manage these funds to match their declared financial objectives. There are some AMCs that specialize in private equity investments and use funds only to buy unlisted companies. These companies earn profits by charging their clients carried interest on the capital gain obtained by the sales of the portfolio companies and a percentage of the funds managed. This chapter analyses and measures the earnings of Italian AMCs ('the team manager') that invest in private equity with a comparison between their portfolio companies ('the coached players'). They find that Italian AMCs investing in private equity earn more than their portfolio companies – the team managers earn more than the trained players. This study also explores the characteristics of the portfolio companies that help to provide higher earnings for Italian AMCs. The results show that the AMCs that invest more per portfolio-company exhibit a better performance than others.

Chapter 7 presents a good example of a synthesis of public and private investments creating different potential solutions to existing needs. In this chapter, Andrea Paltrinieri, Flavio Pichler and Stefano Miani examine the Korea Investment Corporation's (KIC) investment strategies over the years 2005–2012, in order to evaluate whether the corporation shows a 'political bias'. The FSF paradigm put forward by Merton and Bodie has no ideological bias in suggesting which type of institutions should perform financial functions. They use the retirement system as an example of where the same financial engineering can be used, regardless of ownership. Merton and Bodie also emphasize both the role institutional settings, demographics and social structure have in producing the best organizational outcome and the fact that that this can lead to different efficient systems between countries.

The results of the case study presented in **Chapter 7** suggest that the KIC aims to maximize the portfolio risk/return relationship, while it manages foreign excess reserves. The authors argue that a form of 'internal political bias' affects the investment process, as most of the financial resources are managed in-house. Overall, the authors lend support to the hypothesis that KIC's investment strategies reflect both financial and political objectives. This chapter also exemplifies the importance of studying cases as a methodology for reaching a deeper understanding of real-world phenomena. The motivation of doing a case study on KIC in South Korea is that it is one of the most important economies among the so called 'emerging markets'. *The Economist* magazine (2011) stated that South Korea is an even better model of growth than China, Taiwan, Singapore or Hong Kong. KIC was also among the first SWFs to re-entrust financial resources to external managers, with important implications in terms of corporate governance and geographical asset allocation. The study makes an important contribution to the emerging body of literature dealing with case studies, by examining the KIC's investment process, asset allocation and portfolios. The study is also useful to policymakers, as it offers a definition of a regulatory framework that can regulate SWFs in a similar way to other institutional investors or, alternatively, introduce tighter regulation.

The FSF paradigm takes the neo-classical theorem as point of departure where rational agents operate opportunistically on a frictionless market. If the existing prices and allocation of resources is not in conformity with the neo-classical theory, the most plausible explanations, according to Merton and Bodie, are: 1) institutional rigidity 2) technological inadequacies 3) dysfunctional behaviour which cannot be offset by institutional changes.

In **Chapter 8**, Giusy Chesini and Elisa Giaretta examine high-frequency trading (HFT) in European, U.S. and Australian equity markets with a particular focus on the technological inadequacies of new computerized products, which, they argue, increase market efficiency. Merton and Bodie use the term 'the financial innovation spiral', in which the competition between intermediaries on the market is sometimes irrupted by new complements or products. However, the innovation described by the authors of this chapter is perhaps one of the largest technological shifts that the financial markets are facing. The detailed discussion in this chapter also includes issues, which, viewed from a FSF paradigm, relate to institutional rigidity. HFT, which involves the use of computer-driven techniques to trade on exchanges and other trading venues in fractions of a second, has become one of the financial industry's greatest concerns, mainly because it supposedly allows for profits to be made at the expense of traditional investors and causes outages and glitches on trading platforms. In contrast, some studies have found that HFT did level-out price differences between trading venues and provides valuable liquidity to markets; moreover, the activities of HFT firms have been credited with reduced bid-ask spreads, thereby making markets more efficient for all involved. Despite all the academic research, HFT seems to have an ambiguous impact on market integrity because of the increasing number of trading flash-crashes and outages. As a result, the impact of HFT on market integrity is now an issue of specific interest to market participants, scholars and regulators. Regarding the latter, even though there has been considerable progress made in the defining of HFT and there are moves towards standardization of definitions, there are still many approaches to regulation across different markets and regions.

The final chapter of the book is another good example showing that despite new financial products, improved computer design and advances in the globalization of the financial markets, we can still discern differences in the design of financial systems due to their institutional settings. In Chapter 9, Josanco Floreani, Andrea Paltrinieri, Maurizio Polato and Flavio Pichler compare financial performance across 31 conventional and Islamic exchanges during the time period: 2007 to 2011. The authors' focus is on the relationship between financial and industry-specific variables. Their results suggest that there are no significant differences in terms of performances although the two clusters operate with different business models. However, they do find that Islamic exchanges are less efficient than conventional ones. Furthermore, Shariah-compliant investments are not so relevant for Islamic stock exchanges in revenue generation. Finally, they find that the performances of conventional and Islamic exchanges are sensitive to different value drivers. The authors conclude that the main driver for demutualizing and increased divergence between stock exchanges around the world seems to be competition, which follows from the falling of national boundaries, which stimulates mobility on the listing side. The reduced barriers to entry encourage direct competition between electronic communication networks (ECNs) and stock exchanges.

References

Keynes, J. M. (1936) reprinted in 1967. *The General Theory of Employment, Interest, and Money*, London: Palgrave Macmillan.

DiMaggio, P. and W. Powell (1983) 'The iron cage revisited: Institutional isomorphism and collective rationality in organizational fields', *American Sociological Review*, 48, 147–160.

La Porta, R., F. Lopez-de-Silanes, A. Shleifer and R. Vishny (1998) 'Law and finance', *The Journal of Political Economy*, 106(6), 1113–1155.

Merton, R.C. and Z. Bodie, (2005) 'Design of financial systems: Towards a synthesis of function and structure', *Journal of Investment Management*, 3(1), 1–23.

2

The Road to a Viable Euro Zone and the Preconditions for Becoming a More Optimal Currency Region

René W. H. van der Linden

2.1 Introduction

Since the early 1950s European integration has been shaped by political, economic and monetary forces. Although political integration provided the initial impulse for a European community, since the Treaty of Rome in 1957 the authorities have chosen instead a process of functional integration (i.e. pursuing economic and financial integration in various incremental and feasible steps). As a result of the Treaty of Maastricht (1992) the creation of the EU as a single market with 'four freedoms', and ultimately the formation of the EMU, are the final stages in this integration process, backed by coordination of national economic policies and harmonization of relevant domestic laws to avoid protectionism. However, the start of the euro sovereign debt crisis, hereinafter referred to as the euro crisis, has raised the question of whether the EMU is an optimal currency area (OCA), whereby the optimal size of the currency area is one that maximizes the benefits from having a single currency relative its costs. Since the start of the EMU there has been an economic consensus that the EMU was not actually an OCA, even though the euro may foster some incentives for bringing its members closer together. Nevertheless, the EMU is likely to move towards becoming an OCA over time because the convergence of the individual economies within the euro area is likely to increase as common laws and policies are adopted, the single market deepens and and any remaining trade barriers gradually disappear. However, the costs of asymmetric shocks and hence the costs of the EMU will be greater, the weaker the practice of the 'four freedoms', the less there will be price and wage flexibility, and, as a result, there will be fewer alternative policies to turn to. Although the single currency has boosted deeper economic and financial integration, for many years the members have built up imbalances and they differ so much structurally that the EMU is still a great distance away from being an OCA. Not all the benefits of the single market proved to be sustainable as they were predicated on cheap and abundant short-term funding channelled mostly by the banking system. The global financial crisis from 2007 to 2009, hereinafter referred to as the credit crisis, undermined European money markets and the evaporation of cheap liquidity greatly contributed to the lack of confidence in the soundness of the financial system. When the credit crisis spread to the euro area government debt market in late 2009, the belief that the EMU would act as a shield against exchange rate volatility and credit risks disappeared and the euro was gradually perceived as an economic trap. Several criteria for an OCA have been advanced, but since none of these criteria is likely to be fully satisfied, no currency area is ever optimum. When the common monetary policy gives rise to a conflict of national interests, the EMU members need to accept the costs for the sake of a common destiny. The 'impossible trinity principle' theory states that it is impossible to reach the three aims of independent monetary policy (i.e. national supervision), fixed exchange rates (i.e. financial stability) and free capital mobility (i.e. integrated banking markets) simultaneously. Just like the 'golden standard' around a century ago this means that the EMU cannot be maintained in its current form and must therefore be abolished or modified.

One of the key sources of stress within the EMU is its competitiveness problem and external imbalances. Between 2000 and 2007 there was a boom in lending, particularly in the PIIGS countries,[1] which was encouraged by capital inflows and falling capital market rates in the build-up to the EMU. The growth in lending was a significant driver of economic growth in these peripheral EMU countries and also contributed to rising house prices, a growing current account deficit and a reduction in competitiveness. These developments did not occur in the core EMU countries to the same extent, making it difficult to use common monetary policy to combat them. However, following the start of the credit crisis, the transfer of capital from the core to the periphery came to a sudden stop, leaving the periphery with prices and wage costs that were well out of line with those of the core EMU members. Concerns about the solidity of banks and governments in the periphery led to a substantial cut in credit ratings and higher funding costs. The flaws of the EMU design emerged and it became more apparent that the monetary union was lacking a common crisis management and resolution framework, which included a deficiency in fiscal and monetary backstops for sovereigns and banks. A 'red line', measured in terms of the Maastricht Treaty '3/60' convergence criteria, has descended across the EMU, marking the segmentation of financial markets into a safe core and a potentially unstable periphery. In order to get out of the euro crisis, the periphery needed to depreciate in real terms, (i.e. reduce prices and wages relative to their trading partners), a difficult process that required painful adjustment programmes which caused social and political tensions within several EMU members. First Greece, and then, in 2011, Ireland and Portugal had to be granted emergency loans by the 'troika' of the EU, the ECB and the IMF to enable them to service their rising debts. In return and monitored by the IMF, they agreed to implement harsh austerity measures in the form of tight fiscal policy and structural reforms. From October 2012 the European Stability Mechanism (ESM) was implemented and was designed to support this bailout process by providing loans to struggling EMU countries. The recent political agreement reached on bank recovery via 'bail-in' measures, to shift the cost of bank losses towards private creditors, represents a major step forwards in limiting the interconnectedness between bank failures and government support.

The holistic approach of this conceptual chapter is an inductive qualitative research method wherein use is made of available relevant collected data from secondary sources mentioned in the bibliography. The aim of this chapter is to compare and contrast the benefits and costs of the EMU from the perspectives of its proponents and opponents, and to investigate the preconditions of being an OCA. It summarizes several lessons that could be learned from the credit and euro crisis and offers policy suggestions that could better facilitate the financial and economic stability of the euro area. These lessons could potentially serve as a reminder to policy makers of the side effects of some previous policies, while the policy suggestions could be referred to in order to improve the status quo.

The first part of the chapter consists of four sections about the desirability of the EMU from the perspective of Europhiles and Eurosceptics, the preconditions required to fulfil a monetary union and to become an OCA, the design failures of the euro zone and misdiagnosis of the euro crisis. Then, the second part explores five pillars for a viable monetary union in the EMU consisting of: structural reforms to improve the foundations of growth; deeper fiscal integration, eventually leading to a fiscal union; a permanent crisis resolution mechanism; a banking union; and acceptance, by the ECB, of its role as lender of last resort. This chapter abstracts from legal and institutional issues and does not address further steps to ensure a more democratic legitimacy of the euro area. Finally, this chapter closes with some concluding remarks and recommendations. The following research questions will be dealt with:

- To what extent is the EMU an optimum currency area?
- What is the rationale behind the EMU from the perspective of its sceptics and advocates?
- Which flaws in the EMU design should be adjusted to make it a more viable monetary union?
- Which policy measures will contribute towards making the EMU a more optimal currency region?

2.2 The rationale of the euro area from different perspectives

Starting from the early 1950s there were different views on the sequence and degree of economic and political European integration which ultimately resulted in a pragmatic approach to functional integration. In times of economic prosperity, the proponents of the EMU project encountered little contradiction, however, that changed completely when the survival of EMU and thus its pros and cons became increasingly challenged during the euro crisis. Ironically, both Europhiles and Eurosceptics were able to use the euro crisis as further evidence for their distinctive positions. An essential difference of opinion between them is the refusal of the Europhiles to contemplate the possibility of economic integration without political integration (Mongelli, 2013). Alongside this fundamental dispute the Europhiles stressed the following major advantages of the EMU: first, the elimination of the costs of converting currencies; second, increased competition and efficiency of production, which brings more transparency in pricing and puts greater downward pressure on prices in high-cost firms and countries; third, elimination of exchange rate uncertainty between members which reduces destabilizing speculation and encourages trade and investment between the EMU countries; fourth, increased inward investment from the rest of the world plus lower levels and a convergence of inflation and interest rates. This would convince financial investors that the euro will be relatively strong in comparison to other currencies and result in lower long-term interest rates, which would further encourage investments in the EMU countries. However, after 2007 the EMU faced major adjustment problems, with a collapse in real GDP growth as a consequence, and the resulting recession created a disaffection in several EMU members, which enhanced the different opinions between the proponents and opponents of the EMU project.

Many Eurosceptics consider the EMU as a surrender of national political and economic sovereignty and not an OCA at all. The lack of independent monetary and exchange rate policy on a national level is considered to be a serious shortcoming of the EMU. When certain members are faced with inflationary cost-push pressures (e.g. due to strong trade unions), they will have more difficulties in making their goods competitive with the rest of the world. This will lead to more divergence in welfare between different EMU members and will require more significant regional policies. Europhiles, however, argue that it is better to tackle the problem of high inflation in depressed regions of Europe through more competition, rather than merely feeding that inflation by keeping separate currencies and allowing repeated devaluations, with all the uncertainty that they bring. With free movement of labour and capital, resources are likely to be attracted to those countries or sectors with the highest value-added or competitive-cost advantage. The critics of the EMU counter this by arguing that labour is relatively immobile, given the different EU labour market regulations and cultural and language barriers.

Another serious criticism of the opponents of the EMU is the 'one size fits all' problem which refers to the single interest rate that the ECB imposes on all EMU members and the view that it is too low for booming countries and too high for the countries in recession. This turns out to be 'one size fits none' since the aims to curb inflation and strengthen the currency on the one hand and lower unemployment rates on the other hand are quite often in conflict with each other. If growth rates between the EMU members diverge strongly, an effective monetary policy for the average the economic situation in the EMU will lead to the ECB's interest rate policy becoming too restrictive for some countries and at the same time too expansionary for others, yet not optimal for anybody (Vetter, 2013). A counter-argument is that the ECB, which is accountable for stable prices in the EMU, is fully independent from national governments but responsible for the employment rates in their member countries. In this situation the Stability and Growth Pact (SGP) or at least a more disciplined fiscal policy should be used to prevent overly large differences between EMU members in government spending financed on the capital market.

Along with the 'one size fits all' problem, another difficulty for EMU members occurs in adjusting to 'asymmetric shocks', when these shocks affect members to different degrees. Different members may experience different-sized shocks to their economies, whether from inside or outside the euro area. When an adverse shock occurs in the EMU, the policy response is difficult, because there is little scope for independent monetary or exchange rate management. The OCA theory emphasizes the role of an asymmetric shock and proposes criteria by which to judge the costs and the desirability of sharing the same currency. The occurrence of asymmetric shocks is a concern in the EMU and can be dealt with through coordinated fiscal and monetary policies (Somers et al., 2010).

2.3 Preconditions for fulfilling the role of a monetary union

The EMU was designed within the context of the Maastricht Treaty and consists of a single market, a single currency, an independent central bank and a single monetary policy, whereby each member state does not lose its ability to set its own fiscal policy. It is therefore important that, as a monetary union, the EMU is backed by fiscal rules; consequently, the EMU members have to meet five 'convergence criteria', of which the 'fiscal criterion' has been most in the spotlight and consists of a budget deficit and a government debt target of no more than 3 per cent and 60 per cent of GDP respectively (the so-called 3/60 criteria or red line in Figure 2.1). Although the EMU members unambiguously met the interest, exchange rate and inflation criteria, many Eurosceptics have their doubts as to whether they have all genuinely met the other fiscal criteria. However, the Maastricht Treaty allows countries to exceed the red line as long as the debt is 'sufficiently diminishing and approaching the reference value at a satisfactory pace'. Critics argued that this phrase was interpreted too loosely and could now be considered as one of the flaws in the design of the EMU. Some countries only managed to achieve a deficit of 3 per cent or below by taking one-off measures, such as a special tax in Italy and allowing for privatization receipts in Germany. The concern was that countries that only just met this criterion at the time of entry would find it difficult to keep on track in times of a recession. This proved to be the case with France and Germany from 2002 to 2005, in which fiscal criteria were substantially above the convergence criteria in order to lower their high unemployment rates and push up their growth rates.

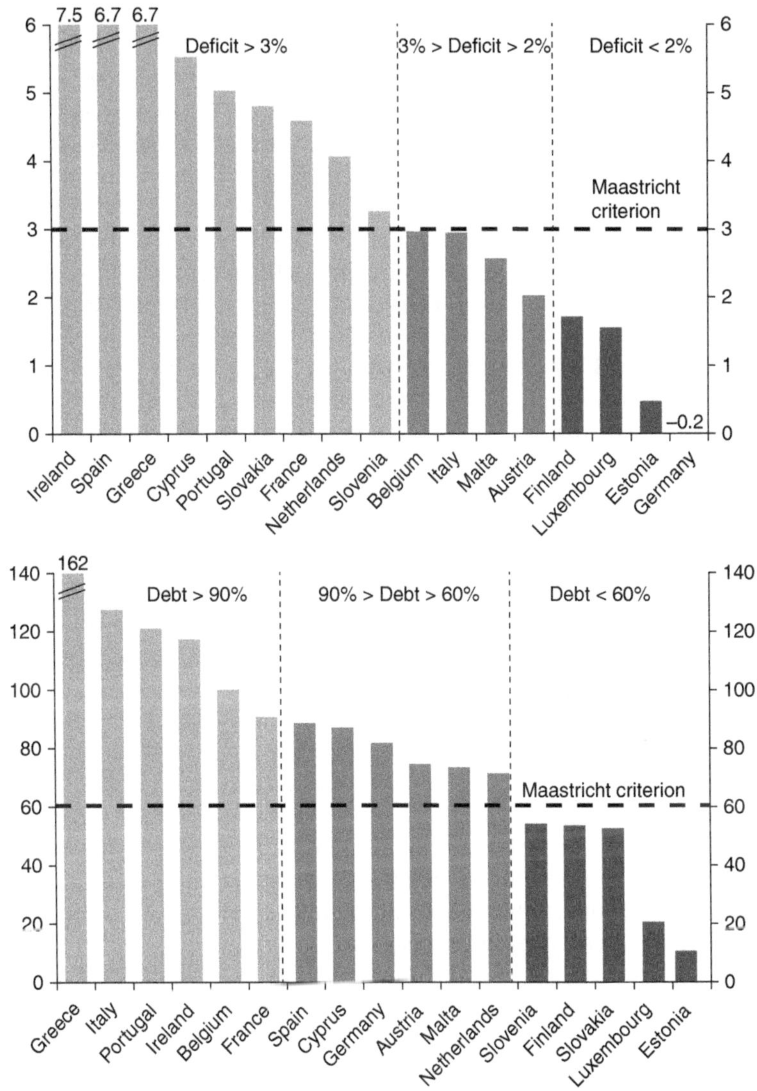

Figure 2.1 Government deficits and general government debt of EMU members in 2012 (% of GDP)

Note: Budget balance is corrected for capital injections into banks.

Source: ECB (2013:6) (based on European Commission's winter 2013 economic forecast and ESCB).

In June 1997 the EU countries agreed upon the SGP – significantly modified in 2005 – in which EMU governments should seek to balance their budgets, averaged over the course of the business cycle. The budget deficits should not exceed 3 per cent of GDP in any one year, otherwise the countries concerned are required to make deposits of money with the ECB which then become fines if the excessive budget deficit is not eliminated within two years. In 2005, Portugal, Germany and France had all exceeded this amount, but the Council of Ministers did not vote to fine those states. Subsequently, reforms were adopted to provide more flexibility and ensure that the '3/60 criteria' took into account the economic conditions of the member states. The main criticism of targeting a zero budget deficit over the business cycle has been that this would mean further fiscal tightening which might be inappropriate at a time when there were fears of a recession (Sloman, Wride and Garratt, 2012). Around a decade ago Germany faced a much bigger unemployment rate than now, so the fear about tight fiscal policy at that time was comprehensible. However, since the euro crisis the core EMU members backed by the troika have pushed for the implementation of austerity measures for highly indebted peripheral countries. Figure 2.1 shows that in 2012 most EMU members still do not fulfil the fiscal 3/60 criteria (i.e. countries above the shaded red line face increasing sovereign yields).

During the early 2000s, the 10-year government bond yields of EMU countries not only dropped but also converged to each other, until the collapse of Lehman Brothers in 2008. Since 2009, the private sector, including the peripheral banks, have been starved of credit and are only able to borrow at the very high interest rates caused by the loss of investor confidence in the peripheral governments. This credibility gap has two causes: first, doubts about the ability of countries to adjust their internal and external deficits; and second, doubts about the effectiveness of the crisis management mechanism that has been built over the last few years of the euro crisis. The historical low levels of German government bond yields, despite a fairly robust economy, point to investors' deep lack of confidence in the long-term survival of the euro (Mayer and Moebert 2012). However, at the start of 2012, the ECB's long-term refinancing operations provided the European banking sector with long-term liquidity on a large scale.

Furthermore, the ECB introduced its unconventional 'outright monetary transactions' (OMT) programme in July 2012, whereby it makes a pledge to do whatever it takes to stabilize the EMU, which includes an offer to buy the bonds of countries who sign up for a reform programme.

This reduced investors' fears for the disorderly failure of an EMU member and the break-up of the euro area. This OMT programme has opened the way for the support-buying of certain government bonds by the ECB, on the strict condition that countries receiving support adhere to a macroeconomic adjustment programme. Since then, interest rates on government bonds issued by peripheral EMU countries have fallen sharply and the capital transfer from peripheral to core EMU countries has been reversed to some extent (DNB, 2013).

The current big dilemma within the EMU is a conflict of interest between Germany and the peripheral countries with 3/60 criteria above the red line including France in 2012 (see Figure 2.1). Therefore, it is not surprising that Germany also differs in its approach to solving the euro crisis since the German post-war economy was built on a hard currency, prudent finances and strong exports: and from this perspective the euro crisis was caused by the lack of solidity or fiscal responsibility of individual EMU members. Consequently the German authorities favour tighter budgetary discipline, whereby institutions like the ECB and the IMF are essential to gain for more credibility. On the other hand, from a French perspective the euro crisis was caused by unregulated globalization of trade and finance, so their authorities place emphasis on solidarity (e.g. the use of joint euro bonds) and reregulation (e.g. introducing a financial transaction tax) and they urge the ECB to act on expansionary policy. However, if the PIIGS countries default on their debts, both German and French lenders would be the biggest losers. While if they leave the euro, it would lead to a legal and financial disaster for all concerned. This explains why the surplus countries are urging deficit countries to implement austerity measures while the former including France are increasingly in favour of more growth of investments rather than fiscal tightening. Austerity measures are hugely unpopular with the public, as they typically result in cuts to public services, higher retirement ages and reduced public sector wages and pensions. This, in turn, would deepen the recession with more strikes, unemployment and protests, but it pushes wages down to more competitive levels. Meanwhile, implementing austerity measures alone risks them becoming self-defeating, as domestic demand falls into line with consumers' rising concerns about job security and disposable incomes, eroding national tax revenues. However, by not implementing tight fiscal policy measures there is a risk of a financial collapse reflected in an increasing spread of government bond yields within the EMU (BBC News Business, 2012). Figure 2.2 shows the fiscal progress between 2009 and 2012, during which time it seems that the

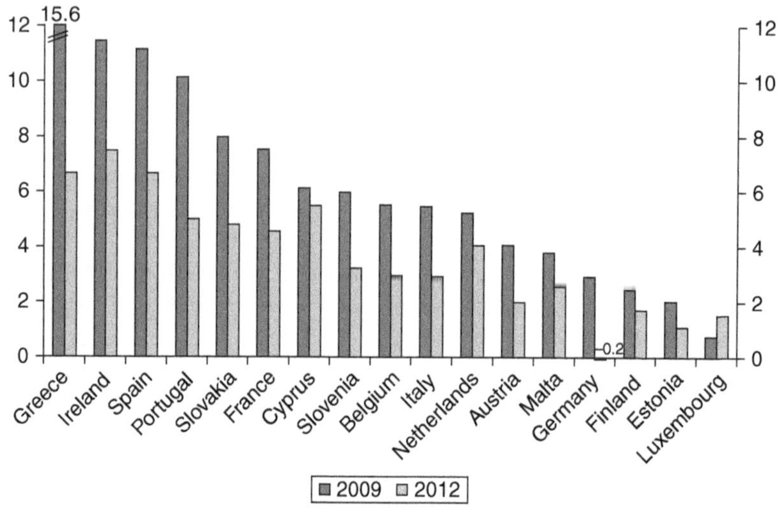

Figure 2.2 Government deficits of EMU members in 2009 and 2012 (% of GDP)
Note: Budget balance is corrected for capital injections into banks.
Source: ECB (2013), p.14 (based on European Commission's winter 2013 economic forecast and ESCB).

imposed austerity measures gradually started to reap in terms of diminishing government deficits.

The policy response to this dilemma can take several forms. The first approach is through bridging the red line by offering official troika rescue programs and EU banking regulation from the ECB or another financial supervisor as lender of last resort. Second, through breaking the red line by making the fundamental economic reforms required to establish the credibility of the peripheral countries. The European authorities' new policy initiatives have elements of both responses. The ECB's new sovereign debt purchase scheme offers a bridging device intended to maintain the flow of finance to the periphery, while the associated ESM conditionality is designed to support the reforms aimed at breaking the red line. In countries where some market access has been retained and problems are largely of a liquidity nature (e.g. Italy) this may prove sufficient. But where the fundamental challenges are greater (e.g. Spain), more aggressive bridging measures such as further credit-easing measures from the ECB would be beneficial and are likely at some stage so as to maintain the economic and political feasibility of the necessary but painful fundamental adjustments (Goldman Sachs, 2012).

2.4 Preconditions for becoming an optimum currency area

It is important to understand why a monetary union such as the EMU is desirable and what criteria are required to fulfil the role of an OCA. Three classic economic criteria are the 'labour mobility criterion' (proposed by Robert Mundell (1961)), the 'openness criterion' (proposed by Ronald McKinnon (1963)) and the 'production diversification criterion' (proposed by Peter Kenen (1969)). Robert Mundell (1961) argued that a single currency is more likely to be workable if the regions sharing that currency are characterized by high mutual factor mobility and flexibility in terms of domestic prices and costs of production. The idea is that the cost of sharing the same currency would eliminate unemployment if the factors of production were fully mobile across borders. Since it is conventionally assumed that financial capital is mobile the real obstacle comes from the lack of labour mobility, which is caused by several factors. First: not only do cultural and linguistic differences restrain migration across borders, but institutional barriers further discourage labour mobility (e.g. labour market regulations and traditions, differences in welfare system and the ability to strike agreements between firms, trade unions and governments). Structural reforms, for instance through changes in legislation, may make cross-border labour mobility easier and enlarge the size of an OCA. Second, the goods produced in one country may differ from those produced in another country (e.g. the cheese produced in Italy is different from that produced in the Netherlands), as a result, it may take some time to retrain workers. Thirdly, labour needs equipment to be productive. Although financial capital can move freely and quickly within the single market of the EU, installed physical capital (means of production such as plants and equipment) is not mobile. It takes time to build plants and shift the location of economic activities. The Mundell criterion thus focuses on the labour market's willingness to move in response to asymmetric shocks. Labour mobility and wage flexibility is not a panacea, but just one of the many factors that mitigate the costs of an asymmetric shock in a currency area (Baldwin and Wyplosz, 2012). More labour mobility within an OCA can also have adverse effects when it causes a region with low productivity to experience a rapid rise in wages because unemployment has caused the skilled workers to leave. Since the German reunification in 1990 the movement of workers from eastern to western Germany is a case in point. The EU enlargement in 2004 is another example of an event which caused many eastern workers to search for better job opportunities in western Europe.

Labour mobility is not always an appropriate solution for temporary disturbances in the demand for labour because the costs of moving are considerable and this might threaten the 'catching up' process of economically weaker EMU members. In the PIIGS countries the wage rates are relatively inflexible and real wage costs do not always reflect differences in productivity growth. Structural reforms could then be implemented in order to let the differences in unemployment be reflected more through corresponding differences in real wages. This means that asymmetric shocks, when they occur, are likely to be met by unemployment in countries facing a loss of competitiveness. Figure 2.3 shows the divergence of competitiveness and external imbalances in terms of an opposite development of wages as compensation per employee and productivity as real GDP per employee in both current account deficit and surplus countries during the period 1999–2012. From 1999 onwards there was a massive movement of capital from the EMU's surplus to deficit countries, leading to an economic boom in the latter and resulting in significantly higher inflation and wage rates in deficit countries (ECB, 2013).

The OCA theory, as developed by Robert McKinnon (1963), was based on an examination of the openness of the economy as a share of tradable and non-tradable goods. In a small open economy the domestic prices for goods are independent of the exchange rate and monetary policy cannot affect the competitiveness of the country. In that situation, giving up the exchange rate as a tool to adjust the competitiveness does not entail a serious loss of policy independence. As most economies of the EU are open and are therefore good candidates for the EMU, they could form an OCA with relative ease.

Peter Kenen (1969) extended the OCA theory by looking at the degree of diversification of production in the economy. He argues that countries most likely to be affected by severe adverse shocks are those that have specialized in a narrow range of goods, but those with sufficiently diversified production will not significantly be affected by exchange rate fluctuations. Although there some products made in the EMU are country-specific, most commodities are produced in several member states and exchange rate changes do not necessarily increase the degree of diversification of an economy. The more integrated and industrially similar the member states become, the less useful appropriate exchange rate adjustments to increase production will become. This explains why Kenen suggests that countries whose production and exports are widely diversified and of a similar structure could form an OCA.

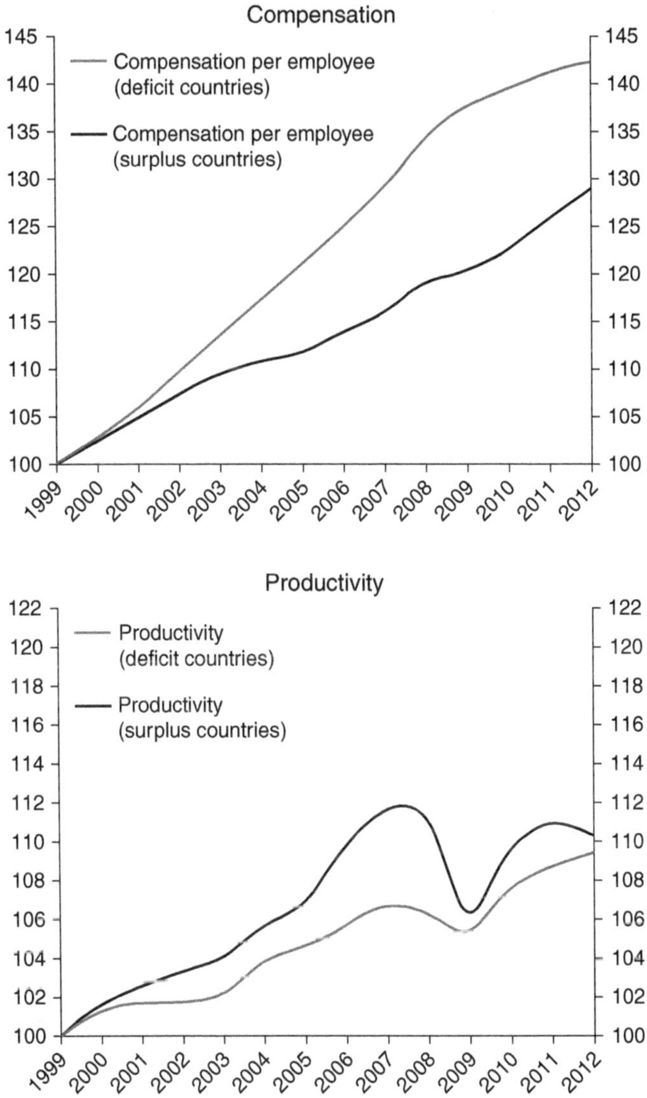

Figure 2.3 Wage and productivity developments in the EMU between 1999–2012

Note: 1999 = 100. Total economy. Productivity is defined as real GDP per employee. GDP-weighted average by country group.

Source: ECB (2013), p.9 (based on AMECO).

Alongside the 'old' classic economic criteria, there has recently been more attention focused on the 'new' socio-political criteria for fulfilling the role of an OCA, such as the homogeneity of 'policy preferences', 'fiscal transfer' and 'solidarity criterion'. The first criterion addresses the fact that an OCA requires symmetric economic shocks. However, the problem is that the bigger the OCA gets, the more likely the conditions are to diverge in the different parts of the area. Some parts of the OCA may have higher unemployment and require expansionary policies, while other parts may have low unemployment and suffer from inflationary pressures which may require tighter policies. In order to overcome the 'one size fits all' problem, EMU members must share a wide consensus on the way to deal with shocks (Baldwin and Wyplosz, 2012).

If fiscal transfer countries agree to compensate each other for adverse shocks and to deal with temporary imbalances in the form of direct payments, it will be more likely that these countries form an OCA. Germany and Switzerland used to operate explicit transfer systems to alleviate business tax competition, while an example of an implicit transfer is the convergence of interest rates between countries of the EMU during the first ten years of its existence. The ESM as a permanent rescue mechanism for distressed EMU members could be considered as a forerunner to a 'transfer union' between EMU countries (Heinen, 2011).

Since none of the previous criteria is likely to be fully satisfied, no currency area is ever optimum. When separate countries contemplate the formation of a currency area, they need to realize that there will be times when there will be disagreements which may follow national lines. When the common monetary policy gives rise to a conflict of national interests, the countries that form a currency area need to accept the costs in the name of a common destiny (solidarity criterion). It is hard to measure numerically whether the eurozone is an OCA or not, and equally difficult to measure are the OCA criteria, which may only be partially fulfilled; however, by combining theory with information about the actual economic performance of the EMU countries it will become more obvious whether the EMU is already an OCA, or whether it is gradually moving in that direction (Baldwin and Wyplosz, 2012).

2.5 Flaws of the EMU design and misdiagnosis of the euro crisis

Although the creation of the EMU has seen considerable trade creation effects, it seems unlikely that the combination of the creation of both a single market and single currency has yet turned the euro zone into a sustainable monetary union. Based on the criteria for an OCA, the current EMU cannot be considered as an OCA and during the euro crisis it is a matter of muddling along with a more or less failed EMU. Since the start of the credit crisis it has become more evident that external imbalances and having enough flexibility to handle shocks without recourse to the exchange rate do matter. Many EMU members are suffering from large government debts, sometimes combined with a large private debt and collapsing housing markets as well. Before the credit crisis the EMU worked almost too well. During the run-up to EMU, individual members undertook reforms to achieve the convergence criteria required to join the EMU. With the advent of the EMU both the elimination of exchange rate risk and the economic reforms have led to a decline in the cost of borrowing; helping all EMU members to achieve fiscal sustainability. The buoyant growth prospects in the periphery attracted abundant capital during a period of macroeconomic stability and high growth. However, when the economy of the periphery started to boom, inflation also picked up and as a result, the single nominal interest rate led to a low real interest rate, thereby aggravating the boom in the periphery. Some of the PIIGS countries started living beyond their means by accumulating debt, owed mainly to Germany as the safe haven. This would have been fine if they had used the borrowed resources to build up production capacity, including within the export sector, but much of the money went into real estate investment, other non-tradable sectors, and household and government consumption (especially in Greece and Italy). The resulting boost in domestic demand triggered higher wages and prices, which decreased competitiveness in relation to the rest of the world. With the exception of Greece, the origins of the euro crisis lay less with government profligacy and more with excessive private borrowing which allowed booms and bubbles to develop. When these became unsustainable and crashed, a large number of banks, firms and households, found themselves unable to repay their debts. As a result, they were forced to reduce their debt levels by selling assets and pushing down their prices. In the end a huge part of the private sector was forced to deleverage and their solvency continued to deteriorate, which pushed the economy into a deflationary spiral. The only way out is for governments to increase their own debts to make it possible for the private sector to deleverage without bringing the economy into a recession. For instance the rising private debt accumulation in Ireland, Spain and Portugal before the crisis caused severe government debt problems in these countries after the onset of the crisis (De Grauwe, 2013).

In contrast to the mortgage write-downs in the US, most EMU countries have achieved far less private sector deleveraging because the fiscal austerity imposed on peripheral economies deepened their recessions, which made it harder to reduce private debts. Moreover, weak banks have been reluctant to recognize, and hence make provisions for, non-performing loans and European bankruptcy law tends to be less disposed towards restructuring debt than the equivalent law in the US. Since the EMU's private, rather than government, debt has become a bigger drag on the slow pace of economic recovery within the eurozone, less stringent austerity measures combined with more prudent asset-quality supervision need to be given priority in the future, which will make it easier to create a banking union (*The Economist*, 2013d).

Other EMU design failures have to do with the wide range of different monetary transmission channels in several EMU countries, in relation to members and non-members. For instance, the degree of interest rate responsiveness to both the investments and the supply of money is different between the EMU countries. In addition, the exports to countries outside the EMU account for different proportions of the members' GDP, and thus their economies are affected differently by a change in the euro exchange rate. The ECB's monetary policy stance is not appropriate for all EMU members since the existence of the monetary union can exacerbate booms and busts at the national level (the 'one size fits all' problem).

National policies and institutions, financial markets and a lack of proper EMU policy coordination have all contributed to widening imbalances. First, policymakers adopted a very short-term perspective. Some governments increased their expenditures (e.g. Greece and to a lesser extent Portugal), aggravating the boost in domestic demand from the flow of credit. In other cases, governments tried (but failed) to successfully dampen booming private demand through an anti-cyclical fiscal policy, by building up sufficient fiscal buffers for periods of economic slowdown. Temporary increases in GDP caused by an oversized real estate sector and booming tax revenues were mistaken for permanent improvements in the budget position and were used to fund tax cuts and expenditure increases that proved unsustainable when the credit crisis hit.

Second, the structure of product and labour markets often contributed to excessive wage and price increases. Limited competition in the service sector, especially in the periphery, enabled firms to charge high mark-ups and grant large wage increases because these costs could be passed on to customers via higher prices. Wage bargaining between social partners at industry or regional levels often failed to adequately account for the impact of wage demands on the overall levels of employment and competitiveness. Widespread indexation of wages to inflation also contributed to the persistence of high inflation in some countries.

Third, financial markets failed to impose market discipline. Despite the increasingly unsustainable growth pattern and growing foreign debt of PIIGS countries, financial markets as well as regulators showed little concern until mid-2007. This may be attributable in part to a global decline in risk aversion during the pre-crisis period. Also, with the launch of euro, there was a belief that external imbalances would not matter and that the SGP would be enough to prevent crises. However, under the SGP the scope of using discretionary fiscal policy was curtailed which made it harder to influence the actual GDP growth and implement counter-cyclical fiscal policy effectively enough to strengthen a stagnating economy through an adjustment of taxes, government spending and transfer payments.

Fourth, the emergence of imbalances resulted from a failure to properly coordinate policy at an EMU level. The SGP was inconsistently applied and ignored, even by Germany and France. The EMU's inability to monitor and enforce the SGP contributed to the euro crisis (Jaumotte, 2011).

2.6 Five pillars for a viable monetary union in the euro area

The future scenarios for the euro area are largely dependent on the desire of EMU countries to opt for further economic convergence versus divergence between its members, and to choose either fiscal and political integration or fiscal fragmentation for European integration. It is obvious that more economic divergence will either break up the EMU, when it is combined with fiscal fragmentation, or will lead to large fiscal transfers from the core to the periphery. If EMU members only choose to take more economic convergence policy measures, without deeper fiscal, banking and/or political integration, it means the EMU will stumble but not fall. Assuming that the euro crisis has forced the EMU to change in the direction of more economic convergence, it is more likely that the EMU will implement new building blocks for a viable monetary union (Morgan Stanley, 2013). The debate over what it takes to achieve a well-functioning monetary union has been addressed by the OCA theory. Price and wage flexibility enables a country to adjust to asymmetric shocks and restore competitiveness by reducing wages

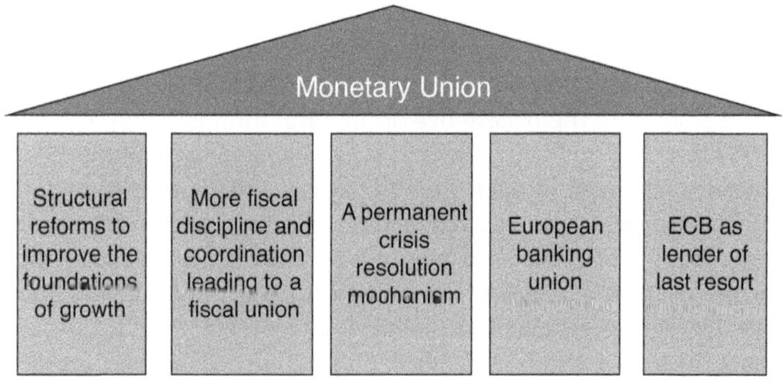

Figure 2.4 Five pillars for a viable monetary union
Source: Partly based on Morgan Stanley (2013), p.16.

and prices relative to other countries. Labour mobility allows people to move to faster growing regions, and well-designed fiscal transfers from stronger countries or regions to weaker ones can help to smooth these adjustments. The years prior to the credit crisis highlighted how to prevent domestic demand bubbles in the euro area. Such bubbles have undesirable lasting consequences since the accompanying wage and price increases are hard to reverse in a currency union, and debt-financed bubbles expose a country to refinancing risk once confidence decreases. This raises yet another challenge specific to the EMU, namely how to reduce speculative attacks on individual countries without an exchange rate buffer or a national lender of last resort (Jaumotte, 2011). In light of these challenges to adjusting the design of the EMU, the future framework will consist of the following five pillars for a viable monetary union: structural reforms to improve the foundations of growth; more fiscal discipline and coordination ultimately leading to a fiscal union; a permanent crisis resolution mechanism, a European banking union and a ECB as lender of last resort (see Figure 2.4).

2.7 Structural reforms and the controversy between growth and austerity

In the current debate about the economic recovery of the eurozone the policy measures of growth and austerity policy are often seen as competing trade-offs, but can also be regarded as complementary. Each EMU member needs a different mix of structural reforms, which tends to be difficult in the short term because the benefits do not come through immediately. Examples of this include flexible and productive labour and product markets; a more efficient public administration, tax and social security system; and adjustments in the conditions of pensions, health care and the real estate market. Moreover, institutional change will be necessary, including the use of a common framework to put into place adjustment mechanisms, in order to rebalance differences in regional performance as they occur (McKinsey, 2012). Austerity can be implemented through structural reforms or tight fiscal policy measures which will reduce growth and cause unemployment to rise. Proponents of austerity measures point out that government deficits cause government debt to increase, which in turn will lead to higher borrowing costs. Consequently, they conclude that their deficits should hardly be used to stimulate growth since that will push up the interest rate and possibly lead to a financial crowding-out effect when higher interest rates discourage the private sector from borrowing money and hence reduce their investments. On the other hand, expansionary fiscal policy will stimulate spending, increase economic growth, reduce unemployment and increase the government deficit. The foundations for growth come from the strengthening of global demand supported by monetary policy anchoring price stability and restoring confidence, credit lending and competition. The root of the recession in the EMU is a lack of confidence in the ability of individual countries to achieve the economic flexibility required for the EMU, given the area's divergent economic developments, so restoring confidence is crucial to rebuilding the euro area's recovery. The question therefore is not whether to give priority to fiscal austerity or economic growth but to find the optimal degree of fiscal austerity and structural reform in order to restore confidence. In this context prices and wages must be set with a view to preserving or regaining competitiveness. From 2012 onwards the recessionary impact of fiscal austerity measures was more severe than expected, that is why the tolerance against the implementation of austerity is gradually intensifying, bringing with it the danger that countries will give up on the painful structural reforms they need. A possible reconsideration is to go more slowly on fiscal austerity and faster on structural reforms, especially when political and social support is limited (*The Economist*, 2013a). During the second quarter of 2013, it has been possible to observe some GDP growth in the euro area, but in the third quarter EMU growth remains in first gear stalling, which begs the question of how far deficit-cutting should be slowed. The European Commission (EC) has become readier to allow countries to delay meeting fiscal targets in the face of recession. In March 2013 the EC presented a communication

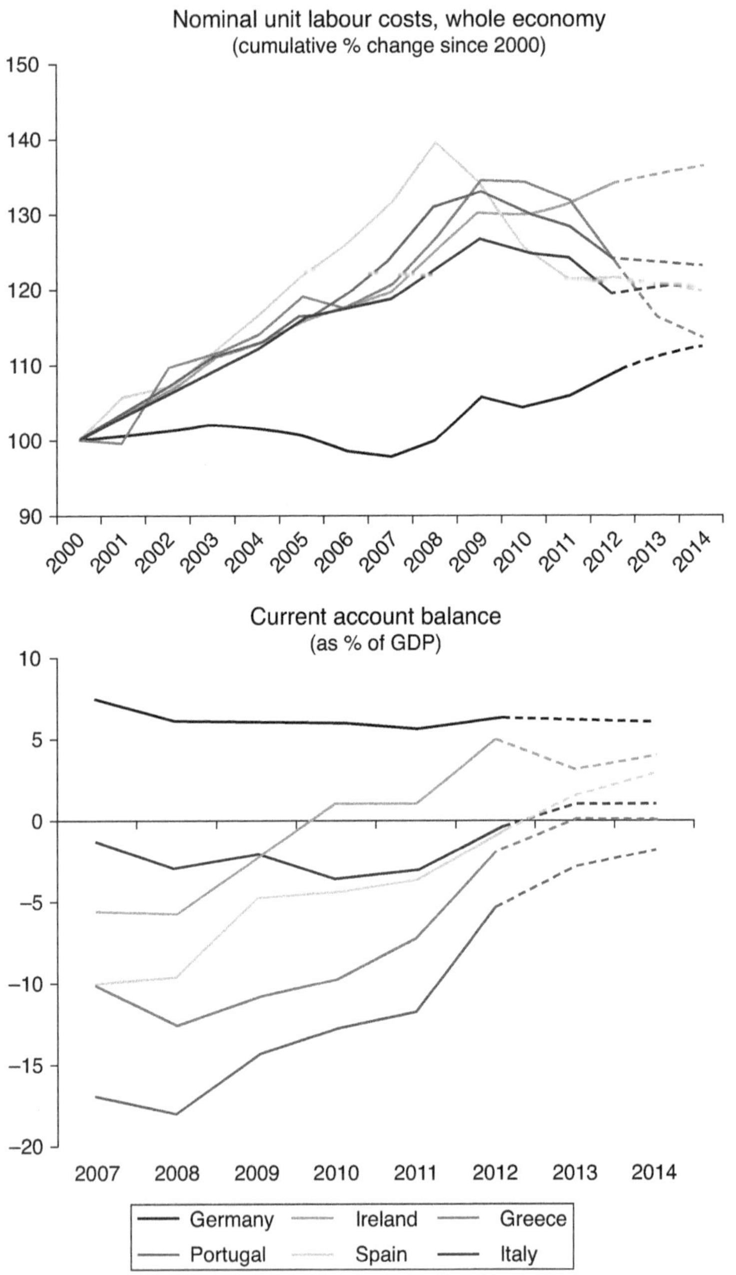

Figure 2.5 Nominal unit labour costs and the current account balance of Germany and the PIIGS countries between 2000 and 2014

Source: Eurostat, EC European Economic Forecast, Spring 2013.

about the coordination of plans for major economic policy reforms and a Convergence and Competitiveness Instrument (CCI) which could provide financial assistance for structural reforms in member states currently facing economic difficulties, in order for them to undertake reforms that are necessary for growth and competitiveness. For instance, if a member state wants to reform the functioning of the labour and product markets, then the CCI could support various relevant measures such as the modernization of vocational training systems (European Commission, 2013).

Although structural reforms are hard to measure, Figure 2.5 shows that divergences within the EMU are declining and competitiveness is improving in nearly all peripheral countries. Unit labour costs, which are a key factor for the competitiveness of a national economy, have fallen considerably in the crisis-hit countries. Greece is expected to see the strongest decline in nominal unit labour costs over the 2009–2013 period, with a drop of 14 per cent. In Ireland, these costs are expected to sink by 10 per cent. Over the same period, Spain and Portugal will be likely to see unit labour costs fall by 7 per cent and 4 per cent, respectively. The differences between current account balances have also decreased. Ireland has been running a surplus since 2010, while Portugal and Spain have significantly reduced their 2008 deficits of 12.6 per cent and 9.6 per cent of GDP respectively, and are expected to post surpluses in 2013. Greece has also radically reduced its 18 per cent current account deficit and it is only expected to be 2.8 per cent in 2013 (Federal Ministry of Finance, 2013).

2.8 From a fiscal compact to a fiscal union

The euro crisis has led to a debate on a new EMU architecture and whether reforms in the direction of a fiscal union are necessary. The fiscal part of the 'Treaty on Stability, Coordination and Governance', referred to as a 'fiscal compact', came into force on 1 January 2013 and builds on the budgetary rules outlined in the SGP, which are to be implemented by the end of 2013. This requires contracting members to ensure convergence towards the country-specific objectives as defined in the SGP, including the implementation of a correction mechanism (i.e. design measures to reduce the budget deficit with escape clauses for exceptional circumstances). Ultimately the fiscal compact could be the foundation for deeper fiscal integration and the path to a fiscal union which enables a federation of several countries to conduct a coordinated fiscal policy which includes greater powers for a European treasury.

The ultimate scope and shape of a fiscal union will remain a matter of social and political preferences, but to make a future crisis less severe, it needs to include several of the following components: structural fiscal targets with independent forecasts of the output gaps; a common set of fiscal rules, possibly embedding structural budget-balancing rules into the constitutional law of the country concerned; mechanisms for crisis intervention; fiscal equalization and transfer mechanisms between countries; and increased fiscal transparency and accountability backed by a common EMU budget (IMF, 2013b). The first two components have already seen relatively widespread implementation in the EMU. Reforms must enhance fiscal discipline at a national level and promote more active anti-cyclical fiscal policy. A common set of fiscal rules exists, consisting of the SGP and the supplementary legislation in the EU's economic governance package. This limits expenditure growth, enables the activation of excessive deficit procedures for countries with debt above the 60 per cent limit, and strengthens enforcement through quicker, semi-automatic sanctions. An even stronger measure would be to subject national budgets in violation of SGP limits to a veto from an EMU fiscal authority. All these components combined have the objective of making the EMU less vulnerable to financial and liquidity crises. However, the new measures fail to significantly alter the incentives for responsible fiscal policies. The EMU does not have jointly guaranteed debt instruments, fiscal equalization, or automatic EU-level fiscal transfer systems to offset temporary country-specific shocks. In addition, the EMU is lacking a common budget. These components are found solely at the national level and the extent to which these components should be integrated into the EMU architecture to ensure stronger fiscal discipline is still a matter of dispute. An EMU-wide system could make anti-cyclical fiscal policy more effective since countries save more in good times because part of the temporary surge in government revenues would be transferred to a central EMU budget instead of financing primary expenditures that are difficult to recoup. Countries would also have more room for fiscal expansion in downturns, without further increasing their debt, because they would benefit from fiscal transfers. A European banking union would significantly reduce the risk of contagion spreading from banks affected by the crisis, to whole countries: with the ESM as a crisis intervention mechanism, the need for deeper fiscal integration would be reduced. Even if the main focus of the current debate is on support in recession phases, effective counter-cyclical fiscal policy should also be able to rein in overheating economies, since during excessive boom phases inflation pressures in particular can develop, which may lead to the formation of price bubbles and further amplify subsequent recessions (Vetter, 2013).

2.9 A permanent rescue fund as a fiscal backstop

After three years of experience with temporary bailout mechanisms, which expired on 1 July 2013, it was decided in October 2012 to establish the ESM which is based in Luxembourg and has an initial maximum lending capacity of €500 billion.[2] ESM's mission is to safeguard financial stability within the euro area through securing liquidity for countries that can no longer obtain funding in the capital market by issuing debt instruments in order to finance loans and other forms of financial assistance to EMU members. The benefit of creating this permanent rescue or contingency fund is debatable, because the creditor EMU members are indirectly supporting the debtor nations of the EMU. That is why many of the means that the ESM can use to help member governments in trouble are subject to appropriate conditionality. For those EMU governments that are cut off from the markets, ESM can extend loans and for those that have some access, it can buy up to half the value of bonds they are issuing in the primary market. The ESM can also provide precautionary financial assistance in the form of credit lines and finance recapitalizations of financial institutions through loans to its members' governments. When applying for ESM support, the country concerned will be analysed and evaluated by the troika on all relevant financial stability matters in order to decide if support should be offered.

During the euro crisis governments were forced to support ailing banks, adding to their sovereign debt, and many banks continued to hold a sizeable share of the debt issued by their governments. This vicious circle between fiscal and financial instability, whereby banks raise doubts about sovereign creditworthiness and sovereign stress aggravates the pressure on the banks' balance sheets, has been widely regarded as a crucial destabilizing factor for the EMU, which it is imperative to break. The ESM can recapitalize banks indirectly by providing loans to EMU governments, but there is a risk that markets will start to doubt whether the country in question will be able to reimburse its debt. The ECB is better placed than the ESM to intimidate investors because it can print money to buy bonds. The rescue fund could still play a crucial role in the ECB's putative bond-buying, because it will be conducted only for countries that are getting help from the ESM and so are subject to conditions. Instead of lending indirectly to governments to pass on to banks, the ESM can also provide a bridge to permanent fiscal backstops through direct bank recapitalization, as was the case with the financial support to the Spanish banking sector. However, the amount of money that can be used for this purpose has been limited to €60 billion (*The Economist*, 2013c). In order to prevent severe adverse feedback loops between banks and their sovereigns, the European Council agreed on the creation of a banking union which would allow banks to strengthen their capital position without placing a large burden on the country in which the bank is incorporated.

2.10 The European banking union

The single monetary policy and the disappearance of exchange rate risk provided a substantial boost for financial integration within the EMU. However, the national governments continued to act as the safety net for their own banking sectors and banking supervision of the more global banks continued to be structured at a national level. As a consequence, losses at banks damaged the solidity of the government, while growing concerns about government finances also contaminated banks. The credit crisis showed that national supervision has not always been effective in spotting problems at banks. Also it showed how quickly problems in the financial sector of one country can spread to another. Therefore, the EU authorities have committed to a move towards a banking union, in which a single financial supervisory regulatory framework, deposit guarantees or safety net, and the handling of troubled banks through a resolution mechanism will be implemented for at least all of the EMU members, and possibly for some other EU members as well. This is the result of the idea that integrated banking systems require integrated prudential oversight (IMF, 2013a). The credit crisis has underlined that the 'impossible trinity principle' of simultaneously having integrated banking markets, national supervision and financial stability can only be achieved if either the aim of the financial integration or the aim of the national supervision is adjusted. In order to break the pernicious link between weak banks and enfeebled sovereigns, banks need to reduce their exposure to sovereign debt issued by their home state. In addition, the costs of cleaning up failed 'systemically important banks' should not only be borne by national governments, but could be shifted to shareholders and creditors, through 'bail-in' measures, as well (Speyer, 2013).

The banking union covered the following five interconnected stages: first, the European Banking Authority (EBA) was authorized to create a single supervisory rule book which would apply across the EU and which the ECB would be required to follow as the ultimate supervisory authority; second, a single supervisory mechanism (SSM), which is to be launched in November 2014, executed by the ECB and which implies common regulation and supervision of the European banking system with common rules, will be enforced uniformly; third, a single resolution mechanism (SRM) for troubled banks, likely to be launched in January 2016, will be carried out by a pan-European 'resolution authority' with the ECB as lender of last resort; fourth, a joint deposit guarantee fund in which the costs of making insured depositors whole are shared among EMU members; fifth, the possibility for the ESM, as a fiscal backstop, to directly recapitalize struggling banks (Schoenmaker and Gros, 2012). These five stages from rule-making to fiscal backstop are divided into preventative and remedial sections. The first two stages (preventative section) cover the mechanisms designed to reduce the fragmentation of financial markets, stem deposit flight and weaken the vicious loop of rising sovereign and bank borrowing costs, while the last three stages (remedial section) encompass the mechanisms designed to protect national public finances from the consequences of a bank failure by creating deposit guarantee schemes. The remedial section implies greater European solidarity, something which will only be politically acceptable if it is considered credible (Quignon, 2013).

In the short run, this will help solve the euro crisis by weakening or breaking the sovereign-bank nexus, where each side has added to the distress of the other. In the long run, it will make the single market in European banking and financial services substantially more effective. It is debatable whether it is wise to start with the preventative section first, because it will be easier to find political agreement, without knowing if resolution and guarantees will work. A half-hearted banking union raises more risks than it solves (*The Economist*, 2013b). With the lessons learned from the flaws of the Maastricht Treaty it will be more effective when the five stages of the banking union are designed transparently and implemented simultaneously. For the EBA and SSM this means applying the same rules to banks in different countries and supervising compliance with these rules in a common manner, overseen by a single ultimate authority. The ECB will have direct oversight of EMU systemically important banks, although in a differentiated way and in close cooperation with national supervisory authorities, which will retain substantial powers. In contrast to the EBA, the ECB would be able to impose its will on the national banking regulators. The common approach may be limited to the dominant banks, with smaller banks remaining subject solely to national authority, at least in the ordinary course of activity. The ECB would have the power to directly supervise any bank and to direct the national supervisors in their own activities. Within the EMU there is a difference of opinion about which banks should be included in the banking union and to what extent other financial institutions should be covered as well. German officials have urged that many smaller 'Sparkassen' or the regional 'Landesbanken' be left out of the banking union's supervision entirely because they have safer business models and their small size means they are not of systemic importance. However, there are many dangers in excluding any set of institutions, particularly ones that have strong local political ties and others that could develop serious systemic risks over time (Elliott, 2012).

When a bank is in danger of insolvency, the problem may be resolved through a restructuring process that includes liquidity assistance, capital injections, or other forms of aid. The restructuring of a 'bad bank' into a 'good bank' will often be part of the solution. In the event of actual insolvency, decisions need to be made about how any losses are divided between investors, creditors, trading counter-parties, taxpayers, deposit guarantee funds and other parties. The foregoing is focused on the losses that taxpayers end up bearing. One of the keys to an effective resolution regime is moving the trend from 'bailout' to 'bail-in' in order to maximize the extent to which losses are borne by creditors and shareholders. This excludes innocent depositors, who should be protected both for their own sake and to avoid damaging bank runs (*The Economist*, 2013e). For instance, the 'bail-in' measures of Cypriot banks in early 2013 hit the savings of uninsured depositors in order to recapitalize lenders with the risk of deposit flight from peripheral banks and a sharp increase in banks' funding costs. In such a situation, in a banking union, there would need to be a common process, whereby all EMU banks would be required to contribute annually to national resolution funds that could be used to absorb the cost of a bailout, and therefore reduce the cost to taxpayers. Just as the resolution process is essentially at national level, with some cross-border cooperation for international banks, deposit guarantee funds are purely national. In addition, the rules about how protection is provided, to whom, and at what levels differ considerably across countries. It is obvious that all observers believe that a banking union would be incomplete without a common guarantee fund, so that depositors would no longer need to be concerned about whether their national guarantee systems would remain solvent. On the other hand, an EMU-wide deposit guarantee fund could also be controversial for political and legal reasons. Creditor countries such as Germany are understandably reluctant to have their taxpayers cough up for the mistakes of bank supervisors abroad. There is a general desire among

EU politicians to avoid having to change European treaties, since this is usually cumbersome and time-consuming, and would further delay the whole banking union project. However, since each EMU member has its own way of dealing with this issue, in the long run a treaty change governing the EU would probably be needed to give a new financial supervisory body the power to seize bank assets and impose losses on creditors (*The Economist*, 2013b).

2.11 The ECB as a lender of last resort

The ECB is put into the position to force EMU members to deal decisively with the weaknesses of their banking systems and to influence the design of the banking union, whereby an effective pan-European supervision requires the existence of an effective resolution mechanism. The ECB can take measures to overcome problems in the monetary transmission channels through a potentially unlimited bond-buying programme to lower the struggling EMU countries' borrowing costs. If European banks are perceived as safer due to the existence of a banking union, then they will be more prepared to redeploy the reserves they hold at the central bank by lending them out. Thus, the monetary transmission channels will be released and monetary policy can work more effectively. However, a key problem with monetary transmission channels within the EMU is that the integrated European money markets have temporarily disintegrated into a series of national markets. Banks, in particular, are often unwilling to lend to banks in other countries. This contrasts with the pre-crisis period when there was a very active cross-border market. The re-emergence of national money markets presents a serious challenge for the ECB, since its traditional instruments only allow it to influence the price and availability of money in circulation in the EMU as a whole. In the current situation, a change in the official interest rates by the ECB has different effects in different countries, which makes it very difficult to fine-tune monetary policy. The disintegration in the European banking market also destroys many of the advantages envisioned when the EU moved to create a unified financial market. It is nearly impossible to have an integrated market under conditions where interest rates and credit availability vary so much between different countries (Elliott, 2012). However, the advent of the banking union is an opportunity to stimulate financial integration in the European banking sector and to make the monetary transmission channels, and hence monetary policy, more effective.

The aim of the unconventional outright monetary transactions, OMTs, is to repair monetary transmission channels which are hampered and to recreate a single monetary policy framework. OMTs could bring the bond yields down to levels that lower borrowing costs for countries that face problems selling debt, and provide investors with enough confidence in the euro for them to buy up bonds in a normal market. The activation of this OMT programme is in the hands of governments themselves since its use will be considered by the ECB once an EMU government asks for financial assistance. From the ESM and through OMTs, the ECB can, henceforth, buy government-issued bonds that mature in 1 to 3 years, subject to certain conditions (i.e. provided the bond issuing countries agree to certain domestic economic measures). The Spanish government has shown some reluctance to request a financial assistance programme on the basis that this could trigger a downgrade by rating agencies, or that primary market interventions by the ESM would not be effective, or that the prospective ECB programme is too vague. However, this hesitation is due to fear that the troika might eventually come up with very strict conditionality regarding the financing of the regions, which could create a sensitive controversy within Spain (Callow, Gudin de Vallerin and Fransolet, 2012).

Currently the OMT program raises a number of questions. First, it remains to be seen how credible the ECB can be in the long run if it is consistently opposed by the German Bundesbank. Second, the key question remains: to what extent Spain and Italy are willing to ask for help under the condition of austerity programmes? If the ECB's promise drives down yields in the short term, then the governments will be less inclined to ask for help. This might sound ideal, unless the ECB promise means the governments will simply postpone structural reforms. Assuming that governments do impose austerity measures, on the basis of the Greek experience, that will mean prolonged recessions and a weak eurozone economy. In turn, that will lead to resentment against the ECB. Third, it is likely that banks will have an unlimited appetite for holding money at the ECB and this means that banks will be huge lenders to the ECB, which, in turn, is a big buyer of government debt and will, therefore, become the backstop for the banks. Fourth, the ECB will buy debt of short-term maturity: 3 years or less. The temptation will be for governments to issue debt in that range, since it will be cheaper. So the debt of those governments will gradually become more short term. Last but not least, there is the moral hazard problem. In theory, the ECB will stop its bond-buying if governments cannot adhere to the agreed program, but it remains to be seen to what extent such a monetary policy will prove to be credible (*The Economist*, 2012).

2.12 Concluding remarks and recommendations

The euro area was created as a monetary union without effective fiscal discipline and coordination. The Maastricht Treaty and the SGP were established to act as a fiscal union, but failed in the face of the euro crisis. Although the monetary policy of the EMU is executed in a supranational way, this is certainly not the case when it comes to other types of supervision of the financial sector. To avoid encouraging public debt and to ensure the central bank's autonomy, the ECB must be prevented from rescuing governments, except when the existence of the eurozone is at stake. The EMU is lacking genuine fiscal federalism and as long as government finance is the direct cause of troubles in the banking system, monetary policy cannot be truly autonomous. In the unfolding of the euro crisis, at times asymmetric shocks arose from the impact of banking crises on public finances (e.g. Ireland) and at other times they arose from the impact of public finances on the banking system (e.g. Greece). As a result, the troubles of both the banking and public sector were linked with each other, while responsibility for financial stability was still, in the main, nationally oriented. This vicious loop between sovereign and bank costs shows that the ECB has to broaden its mandate with a preventative mission as lender of last resort and without interfering withits monetary policy aims.

Since the advent of the euro crisis the single currency has become an economic trap and the resulting recession has created a disaffection in several EMU members, which only enhanced the disagreement between Europhiles and Eurosceptics about the design of the EMU. This issue resurfaced and gained credence during the euro crisis, as it became more apparent that the euro had both intended and unintended effects. Although the single currency has expanded intra-euro area trade, credit flows and cross-border investments and was also aimed at increasing the convergence of economic differences between member states, not all these benefits proved to be sustainable as they were predicated on cheap and abundant short-term funding channelled mostly by the banking system. During the euro crisis the creditor EMU countries indirectly financed the peripheral debtor countries through their banking systems, rather than through fiscal transfers. Furthermore, many EMU members have not consistently complied with the Maastricht convergence criteria for various reasons. Subsequently, reforms within the SGP were adopted to provide more flexibility and ensure that the 3/60 criteria took into account the economic conditions of the member states. At the root of the current recession in the euro area is a lack of confidence in the ability of individual countries to achieve the necessary economic flexibility required for a monetary union of regions with divergent economic developments. The restoration of confidence is essential to end the recession and return to economic growth. The question therefore is not whether to give priority to fiscal austerity or economic growth, but to find the optimal degree of austerity and structural reforms in order to restore confidence. Currently most EMU members still do not fulfil the fiscal 3/60 criteria (i.e. countries above the shaded 'red-line' face increasing sovereign yields). The lack of guarantee provided by EMU governments could trigger a self-fulfilling liquidity crisis that would degenerate into solvency problems. When investors lost confidence in the governments of the peripheral countries, they sold massive amounts of the government bonds of these countries, pushing interest rates to unsustainable high levels. An announcement in July 2012 by the ECB president Mario Draghi to do 'whatever it takes' to preserve the single currency turned out to be necessary in order to break the rising government bond yields of the periphery, but just a little bit of socio-political uncertainty could easily add 'fuel to the fire'.

Several fundamental flaws in the EMU design were brought into the spotlight during the euro crisis and it became more obvious that ambitious integration projects should be put in place in a coordinated manner. With no ability to compensate for differences in country-specific price and cost developments through exchange rate adjustments, the EMU needs to rely on other forms of adjustment known in the OCA theory. Based on the criteria for an OCA, the current EMU cannot be considered as an OCA. First, although the EMU has led to a high degree of capital mobility and deep integration of capital markets, the geographical and occupational cross-border mobility of labour has improved but is still rather low, partly due to cultural differences including language, nationalism and government regulations. On the other hand, the flexibility in terms of prices and costs of production and the mobility and adaptability of labour and capital is enhanced by a higher level of education, labour market participation and improved labour matching. In order to move towards an OCA, the current EMU differences in unemployment and productivity levels should be reflected more in real wages. Second, the openness within the EMU reduces the likelihood of asymmetric shocks and hence the usefulness of national exchange rates; it also spurs competition and improves the allocation of resources. However, there are structural differences between the core and peripheral EMU members in terms of capital and skilled labour availability which could be reduced by the accomplishment of a single market. Third, in the long run, there is a need for self-correction promoted by low and similar inflation rates, similar production and trade patterns, and broadly similar or homogenous policy preferences, in order to reduce the possible impact of country-specific shocks. This means that the EMU members need to be agreed on economic policy as a whole, such as whether to target inflation or unemployment, or whether to favour exporters or importers.

The architects of the EMU undoubtedly hoped that the emergence of a single currency would create the conditions for an OCA by encouraging labour mobility and by reducing the specialization of national economies. In the absence of perfect economic and financial integration, a monetary union creates externalities that require fiscal transfers between member countries to compensate for not being able to adjust the exchange rate automatically, to offset regional divergences and to deal with temporary imbalances. However, as the EMU currently stands, fiscal transfers from the EU budget are too small to work as an adjustment mechanism so there is a need for a significantly larger EMU budget to reduce cyclical differentials. The euro crisis has two dimensions, one being flaws in the governance of the EMU, and the other being an erosion of trust in the viability of the euro area itself. The first dimension could be addressed through more effective implementation of the classic economic criteria for an OCA combined with an effective anti-cyclical fiscal policy. It is preferable for functional economic integration to be accompanied by structural reforms in order to reassure the investors and to improve the foundations of growth. As far as financial integration is concerned it is important to take into account the differences between bank-based (e.g. Italy) and more market-oriented (e.g. Ireland) financial systems. In addition, the differences between more segmented (e.g. Germany) and consolidated (e.g. the Netherlands) banking industries will have to be aligned to a greater degree within the EMU, since an OCA requires similar monetary transmission channels. This could be supported by common European banking regulation and supervision ultimately leading to a banking union that represents a response which offers a balance between financial integration and fiscal federalism. A banking union is obviously not a panacea, but it can be pivotal in fighting the euro crisis by breaking the sovereign-bank nexus and by fixing the broken monetary transmission mechanism from ECB policy rates to final borrowing and lending rates across the full span of the euro area. Together with the introduction of the ECB as the single supervisor of EMU banks, in 2014, this has also redeployed the trend 'from bailout to bail-in'. Instead of taxpayers routinely having to bailout banks, creditors to the banks will be bailed in on a large scale. Although the theory of OCA does not explicitly refer to a banking union, it is obvious that a major role has been reserved for the ECB as the lender of last resort for ailing states. This revision in the eurozone could also address its 'trilemma' of not being able to reach the aims of integrated banking markets, national supervision and financial stability, simultaneously. It is a matter of give and take, if EMU members do not want to completely forego the benefits of the single market and the single currency, they have to truly transfer power over their national financial system to a supranational European body. The second dimension applies to fundamental changes in the EMU framework including a fiscal union, a permanent transfer union, crisis management and adjustment funding with the ECB as a monetary backstop and the ESM as a fiscal backstop. Last but not least, the EMU members that form a currency area need to accept the costs for the sake of a common destiny. This requires more solidarity or willingness to share each other's risks, along with a similar mission and vision to make the EMU a more optimal currency region.

In retrospect the euro crisis can be regarded as an important wake-up call or asymmetric shock in itself, but also as a catalyst for change. The eurozone can become more workable in the future which could help rebalance the views of both its advocates and critics: but there are still many bridges to overcome. The emerging banking union must credibly spread financial sector risk, labour and product markets have to be liberalized and the single market needs to be deepened, particularly in terms of services. The future scenarios for the euro area are largely dependent on the desire of EMU countries to opt for further economic convergence and to take further steps towards a fiscal union. If EMU members only choose to take more economic convergence measures without the necessary initiatives to move towards a fiscal and banking union, it implies muddling along with a more or less failed EMU. It is more likely that the EMU will implement new building blocks for a viable monetary union and that an improved institutional architecture will turn the EMU into a stability union. Since there is some overlap between components of the banking and fiscal union, and there are moral hazard issues that arise if the banking union is more complete than the fiscal union, it is important that the development of both unions is well coordinated. Since the summer of 2013, the average labour costs in most peripheral countries have been falling and their huge current account deficits are gradually disappearing. In contrast to 2012, there is now little positive economic growth in the euro area along with unemployment that is still very high. So there is some light at the end of the tunnel, and hope for a European 'renaissance', which will gradually reduce the controversy between EMU proponents and opponents.

Notes

1. The highly leveraged peripheral EMU members are sometimes abbreviated to 'PIIGS countries' referring to Portugal, Italy, Ireland, Greece and Spain.
2. This is achieved with subscribed capital of €700 billion (backed by €80 billion paid-in capital, the rest callable).

References

Baldwin, R. and C. Wyplosz (2012) *The Economics of European Integration*, McGraw-Hill Companies, 408–427.
BBC News Business (2012) 'Eurozone crisis explained', last updated on 19 June 2012.
Callow, J., P. Gudin de Vallerin and L. Fransolet (2012) 'Saving the euro', Barclays, ECB watching, 6 September, 2–4.
De Grauwe, P. (2013) 'Design failures in the Eurozone: Can they be fixed?', London School of Economics and Political Science, LEQS Paper No.57.
DNB (2013) 'Overview Financial Stability, Autumn 2013', De Nederlandsche Bank Eurosystem, October.
ECB (2013) 'Euro area economic situation and the foundations for growth', Brussels, 14 March.
Elliott, D.J. (2012) 'Key issues on European banking union: Trade-offs and some recommendations', Global Economy and Development at Brookings, Working Paper 52, November.
European Commission (2013) 'Towards a deep and genuine economic and monetary union. The introduction of a convergence and competitiveness instrument', Brussels, COM, 165, 20 March.
Federal Ministry of Finance (2013) 'Moving towards a stability union. The state of the eurozone', 6 September.
Goldman Sachs (2012) 'Europe's red line', Economics Research, *European Economist Analyst*, 12(20), 6 September, 1.
Heinen, N.(2011) 'A European transfer union: How large, how powerful, how expensive?', Deutsche Bank Research, Reports on European integration, EU Monitor 81, 2 August.
IMF Staff Discussion Note (2013a) 'A Banking Union for the Euro Area', SDN/13/01, 13 February.
IMF Staff Discussion Note (2013b) 'Toward a Fiscal Union for the Euro Area', SDN/13/09, September.
Jaumotte, F. (2011) 'Imbalances in the Euro Area: How to prevent their recurrence, finance and Development', Fixing the Flaws in EMU, IMF Staff Discussion Note, December, 48(4).
Kenen, P. (1969) 'The theory of optimum currency areas: an eclectic view' in R. Mundell and A.Swoboda (eds), *Monetary Problems of the International Economy*, University of Chicago Press, 41–60.

McKinnon, R. (1963) 'Optimum currency areas', American Economic Review, 53, 717–725.
McKinsey (2012) 'The future of the euro: An economic perspective on the euro zone crisis', Germany, January.
Mayer, T. and J. Moebert (2012) 'Growth versus austerity in euroland', Deutsche Bank Research, Research Briefing European integration, 4 May.
Mongelli, F. P. (2013) 'The mutating euro area crisis: Is the balance between "sceptics" and "advocates" shifting?', ECB, Occasional Paper Series No. 144, February.
Morgan Stanley Research (2013) 'Macro Ideas & Insights Forum', 2 May.
Mundell, R.A. (1961) 'The theory of optimum currency areas', *The American Economic Review*, 51(4), 657–665.
Quignon. L. (2013) 'The challenges of banking union', BNP Paribas Economic research, February, 20–37.
Schoenmaker, D. and D. Gros (2012) 'A European Deposit Insurance and Resolution Fund', An Update of an earlier paper published by the Duisenberg school of finance and the Centre for European Policy Studies, DSF Policy Paper Series, No.26, September.
Sloman, J., A. Wride and D. Garratt (2012) *Economics*, 8th edition, Pearson, 792–796.
Somers, F., S.A. Van Hall, C. Van Leeuwen, E.E. Lengton and R.W.H. Van der Linden (2010) *European Business Environment: Doing business in the EU*, 1st edition, Noordhoff Publishers, Groningen, 56–58.
Speyer, B. (2013) 'EU banking union: right idea, poor execution', Deutsche Bank Research, 4 September.
The Economist (2012) 'The eurozone crisis: The ECB and OMT: OTT, OMG or WTF?', 7 September.
The Economist (2013a) 'After austerity, what? The backlash against Europe's austerity is intensifying', 4 May.
The Economist (2013b) 'Europe's banking union, till default do us part: A half-hearted banking union raises more risks than it solves', 8 June.
The Economist (2013c) 'The European stability mechanism: Gearing up for business, Europe's new rescue fund will have plenty to keep it busy', 12 October.
The Economist (2013d) 'Europe's other debt crisis', 26 October.
The Economist (2013e) 'European banks, from bail-out to bail-in', 14 December.
Vetter, S. (2013) 'Do all roads lead to fiscal union? Options for deeper fiscal integration in the eurozone', Deutsche Bank Research, EU Monitor European integration, 11 April.
Wyplosz, C. (2013) 'Europe's quest for fiscal discipline', European Commission, European Economy, Economic Papers 498, April.

3

Gross Imbalances, Liquidity Shortage and the Role of the Federal Reserve

Pierluigi Morelli, Giovanni B. Pittaluga and Elena Seghezza

3.1 Introduction

There has been much debate about the link between global imbalances and the financial crisis of 2007–2008. The most recent contributions show that the recent global financial crisis was preceded not so much by a widening of current account imbalances as by a pronounced increase in gross capital flows between countries. In particular, between 2002 and 2007 several banks from major European countries dramatically increased their long-term assets in dollars, in particular as asset-backed securities (ABS), by stocking up on short-term funding on the interbank market or the money market.

When the financial crisis occurred and rarefied the supply of dollars on the money market and interbank markets these banks experienced increasing difficulties in rolling over their short-term liabilities in US dollars. As shown in Section 3.2, European banks were led to apply for short-term US dollar refinancing.

This demand was met by the provision of swap lines to European central banks by the Fed. The effects of these refinancing operations are illustrated by the use of econometric tests in Section 3.3. The results of these tests confirm that the provision of swap lines from the Fed reduced the illiquidity and credit risk of banking systems with serious US dollar shortages.

By giving support to the central banks of advanced countries, the Fed operated as an international lender of last resort (ILOLR). The exercise of this function by a national central bank has several drawbacks that have emerged from the case of the granting of swap lines by the Fed. These problems, illustrated in Section 3.4, tend to favour the emergence of net imbalances. The latter can be countered through tighter regulation of liquidity management by commercial banks.

3.2 Demand for US dollar swap lines

As shown by several scholars[1] the increase in gross capital flows to the United States in the early part of the last decade was linked less to the performance of the current account balance of the United States, and more to the increasing financial integration of economies.

In 2007, 54.7 per cent of capital inflows to the US came from advanced countries, while only about 25 per cent came from the countries of South-East Asia and the major oil-producing countries: that is, from countries with a huge current account surplus. Moreover – and in contrast to emerging countries – for Europe and Canada the amount of inflows and outflows from the US is largely equivalent.

It is also to be noted that in the period between 2003 and 2007, unlike the countries in surplus, whose purchases of US assets consisted mainly of Treasuries and Agencies, European countries acquired corporate debt securities: they bought about two-thirds of the foreign purchases of corporate debt and about half of foreign purchases of ABS (Bernanke et al., 2011; Bertaut et al., 2011).

To finance their investments in US dollar assets, European countries relied heavily on wholesale funding (Johnson, 2009).[2] As opposed to what happened in the surplus countries, in the pre-crisis period the European financial systems engaged in the risky activity of maturity transformation, exposing them to a high risk of illiquidity. In mid-2007 the US dollar funding gap of the European banking systems reached 1 to 1.3 trillion dollars. About half of this gap was covered by European banks through FX swaps and the remainder by resorting to money market funds, by using the interbank market and by borrowing from central banks (McGuire and Von Peter, 2009).

It is already well known that in the summer of 2007 the US money market started to deteriorate severely. Things became worse after the collapse of Lehman Brothers in September 2008 and the spread of insolvency in the subprime mortgage sector (Bank of International Settlements, 2008). Consequently, for banks with high maturity mismatching there emerged serious rollover problems. These problems were particularly marked for the European banking systems, given both their extensive short-term liabilities in US dollars and the large foreign currency liquidity risk to which they were exposed. For these banking systems, the liquidity crisis threatened to turn into insolvency (Brumnermeier, 2009).

A banking system can face a high maturity mismatching between assets and liabilities in US dollars in the following ways:

1. By resorting to forms of refinancing in US dollars through national central banks. This course of action was possible only if the country had sufficient currency reserves. On the other hand, given the low yield of the assets in which they are held, having currency reserves brings with it inevitable costs for the economy.
2. By refinancing in national currency through the country's central bank and selling local currency to purchase US dollars on the open market. This course of action would inevitably bring with it a lowering of the exchange rate. This would lead to a currency and financial crisis, as happened in the Asian crisis of 1997–1998.
3. By selling off long-term assets in dollars. In this case, the banks would incur heavy losses since these assets are likely to be sold at fire sale prices. Such serious losses could compromise the stability of the banking system and could have a contagious effect at an international level.
4. By obtaining from the US central bank credit lines in dollars. This course of action would lead to close cooperation between central banks and, in particular, the decision by the Fed to meet demand for short-term loans in US dollars from other central banks and to assume the risk that the financed states might default.

The alternative set out in point *iv* was the one adopted by the advanced economies, as shown in Table 3.1. The ECB, the Bank of Japan and the Bank of England were the central banks that made the largest withdrawals on the reciprocal currency arrangements. The ECB and the Bank of Japan reached a peak of use of $291 billion and $122 billion, respectively, in December 2008, while the Bank of England hit a peak of $74 billion in October 2008.

With the gradual return of the US money market to normal conditions and the decrease in the dollar shortage, the number of FX swap lines granted by the Fed declined rapidly in the first half of 2009, and reached zero in early February of 2010 (Table 3.1).[3]

In order to ascertain the variables that affected the demand for swap lines with the Fed we have performed a cross-section OLS regression on the data of 21 countries[4] that have made use of the Fed swap lines: in the model we have regressed the percentage amount of these transactions on the foreign reserve assets of each country (SWAP / RES)[5] on the following variables: the share of the foreign interbank system on GDP (FOR/GDP) or on reserves (FOR/RES), the share of the banks' official reserve on total banking assets (RES/ASS) and of the latter on GDP (ASS/GDP). Since the Fed took action only after the consequences of the dollar shortage had manifested themselves, while the number of SWAP transactions refers to the average of 2008, all other variables refer to averages of the pre-crisis periods.[6] In Table 3.2 we report the main statistics of the variables used in the regression.

The results of the estimates show that, despite their different specifications (Table 3.3):

Table 3.1 Drawing of swap lines by the Fed (millions $)

End of quarters	2007–2004	2008–2001	2008–2002	2008–2003	2008–2004	2009–2001	2009–2002	2009–2003
ECB	20,000	15,000	50,000	174,472	291,352	165,717	58,899	13,662
Switzerland	4,000	6,000	12,000	28,900	25,175	7,318	369	–
Japan	–	–	–	29,622	122,716	61,025	17,923	1,530
UK				39,999	33,080	14,963	2,503	13
Denmark				5,000	15,000	5,270	3,903	580
Australia				10,000	22,830	9,575	240	–
Sweden					25,000	23,000	11,500	2,700
Norway					8,225	7,050	5,000	1,000
Korea					10,350	16,000	10,000	4,050
Mexico							3,221	3,221
Total	24,000	21,000	62,000	288,263	533,728	309,918	144,585	56,576

Source: Federal Reserve Bank of New York.

Table 3.2 Descriptive statistics

	Swap/Res	For/GDP	Res/Ass	Ass/GDP	For/Res
Mean	0.21	0.24	0.08	2.67	5.64
Median	0.17	0.20	0.02	2.35	4.16
Max	0.72	0.88	0.54	7.28	21.97
Min	–	0.02	0.00	0.44	0.12
St.Dev.	0.24	0.20	0.13	1.70	5.97
N.Obs.	21	21	21	21	21

Table 3.3 OLS estimate of the demand for swap lines

Variable	Specification 1	Specification 2	Specification 3
C	0.053	0.044	–0.001
	(0.049)	(0.051)	(0.041)
FOR/GDP	0.799**	0.647**	
	(0.140)	(0.143)	
RES/ASS	–0.449**	–0.366**	
	(0.133)	(0.122)	
ASS/GDP			0.051**
			(0.010)
FOR/RES			0.002**
			(0.000)
DUATBE		0.403**	0.530**
		(0.045)	(0.017)
R2	0.58	0.84	0.87
S.E.	0.153	0.095	0.085
N. Obs	21	21	21

Legend: *significance at 95%; ** significance at 99%.

a. the greater exposure of banks on the foreign exchange interbank market is associated with a greater demand for U.S. dollar swaps with the Fed. The size of this causal factor is significant in that a standard variation of the indicator of liquidity tension determines a variation of demand between 35 and 70 per cent of the average of the dependent variable. What is just set out is confirmed by the fact that the OECD countries with the greatest exposure in the short term in US dollars are those that used more swap lines: This is clearly evident from a comparison of Tables 3.1 and 3.4.
b. as expected, high amounts of reserves reduce the need to resort to swaps;
c. the size of banking systems relative to the size of the relevant country's economy favours greater demand for dollar liquidity.† The demand of swap lines has been particularly high in the advanced economies and in countries with a highly developed financial market.

† The analysis of residuals show two outliers, the Austrian and Belgian banking systems. Austria was affected by considerable exposure to eastern European countries, Belgium by the liquidity crisis of the country's largest banking group. For this reason the introduction of a joint dummy for these countries (DUATBE) results in a significant improvement of in the fit of the regression.

Table 3.4 Short-term claims of US banks on OECD economies ($ US millions)

Destination of funds	2007Q4	2008Q1	2008Q2	2008Q3	2008Q4
Austria	4,179	4,207	4,841	3,537	2,256
Belgium	8,742	13,911	17,453	15,630	15,567
Czech Republic	527	716	798	894	518
Finland	,3191	2,837	2,386	3,024	2,928
France	57,952	69,098	41,790	43,719	55,287
Germany	56,910	65,933	48,407	40,111	39,266
Greece	3,947	4,857	3,005	2,164	2,428
Hungary	894	1,003	900	1,113	491
Ireland	28,317	27,471	28,082	27,357	23,550
Italy	25,180	25,521	26,215	17,012	17,243
Korea	26,254	27,435	28,027	29,873	21,518
Luxembourg	26,050	24,730	22,826	21,398	11,943
Mexico	6,492	7,752	7,497	6,574	7,734
Netherlands	43,132	46,995	52,071	45,699	37,230
Poland	2,356	2,254	2,279	2,308	2,521
Portugal	2,861	2,331	2,054	1,549	1,226
Spain	2,8267	28,367	25,370	15,853	18,420
Turkey	7,320	6,916	7,014	6,009	5,107

Source: BIS International banking system.

3.3 The supply of swap lines from the Fed

The situation of a dollar shortage that plagued other banking systems, particularly those of the eurozone, was significantly alleviated by the swap lines provided by the Federal Reserve to other central banks from the end of 2007 onwards. Between December 2007 and mid-September 2008, the swap lines granted by the US Federal Reserve were essentially an extension of the TAF (Fleming and Klagge, 2010). After the failure of Lehman Brothers, the Fed increased both the number and total of FX swap lines. Before 15 September the Fed granted FX swaps lines to a total of \$ 67 billion. This went up to \$ 247 billion on September 18 and reached \$ 620 billion on September 29 (Table 3.5). In mid-October 2008, the Fed removed all limits on swap lines to the ECB, the Bank of England, the Swiss National Bank and the Bank of Japan.

The granting of swap lines by the Fed and the effective cooperation between central banks reduced the banks' funding rollover risk. This helped to reduce pressures on the funding market in US dollars and the risk of insolvency for some large banks, especially the major European banks. Confirmation of this comes from different empirical papers. In Taylor and Williams (2009) and McAndrews, Sarkar and Wang (2008), the effects of the dollar swaps are considered alongside those of the TAF. However, while the former conclude that the TAF auctions had no effect on the LIBOR-OIS spread, the latter show that both the TAF auctions and the swap lines led to a significant reduction of this spread. When considering the FX swap market, Baba and Packer (2009) reach the conclusion that the swap lines granted by the Fed and the dollar term-funding auctions held by the ECB, the BoE and the SNB contributed significantly to a reduction in the FX swap deviations.[7]

It is, therefore, likely that the Fed's swap line operations contributed to reducing the rollover risk of banking systems heavily indebted in US dollars. Furthermore, as shown by Acharya, Gromb and Yorulmazer (2012), high rollover risk translates into high default risk. Hence the need to consider the effects of the swap lines on the prices of five-year bank credit default swap (CDS) in relation to the countries that benefit from this form of support.

An empirical check was carried out on a sample of 42 banks in countries that made use of the Fed's swap lines. Table 3.6 shows, for each extension of swap lines from the Fed, the analysis of the variation in CDS spreads between the average spread five days prior to the date of the transaction and the average spread after the operation: in particular the first five days following the operation, the next five and a further

Table 3.3 Timeline of dollar swap announcements

Date	Event	New participants	Total authorization (US bn)
12 December 2007	Establish dollar swap with ECB ($20 bn) and SNB ($4 bn); 28-day auctions; agreement for 6-months		24
11 March 2008	Expand lines with ECB ($30 bn) and SNB ($6 bn)		36
2 May 2008	Expand lines with ECB ($50 bn) and SNB ($12 bn)		62
30 July 2008	Expand lines with ECB ($55 bn)		67
18 September 2008	Expand lines with ECB ($110 bn) and SNB ($27 bn)	Establish facilities with BoJ ($60 bn), BoE ($40 bn), BoC ($10 bn)	247
24 September 2008		Establish swap with RBA ($10 bn), Danmarks Nationalbank ($5 bn), Sweden Riksbank ($10 bn), Norges Bank ($5 bn)l	277
26 September 2008	Expand lines to ECB (($120 bn) and SNB ($30 bn)		290
29 September 2008	Expand ECB ($240 bn), SNB ($60 bn), BoC ($30 bn), BoE ($80 bn), BoJ ($120 bn), Danmarks Nationalbank ($15 bn), Norges Bank ($15 bn), RBA ($30 bn), Riksbank $30 bn)		620
13 October 2008	Expand ECB, SNB, and BoE: no pre-specified limit		
14 October 2008	Expand BoJ: no pre-specified limit		
28 October 2008		Extend $15 bn swap line to RBNZ: no pre-specified limit	
29 October 2008		Extend $30 bn swap line to Brazil, Mexico, Korea, Singapore: no pre-specified limit	
3 February 2009		Extend swap agreements until 30 October 2009	
25 June 2009		Extend swap agreements until 1 February 2010	
1 February 2010	Swap agreements expire		

Source: Goldberg, Kennedy and Miu, (2011).

five. We take into consideration both the variation in bank CDS and the difference between these and the corresponding sovereign CDS. We show both the measure of absolute change and its significance level[8] and the percentage of banks that have registered, in the space of time considered, a negative variation of spread on CDS.

In general, there is confirmation of the fact that swap transactions have made it possible to contain the growth of the risk perceived by the market in terms of the strength of banking systems considered. The analysis shows that this containing effect was particularly significant in the first operation (carried out at the end of December 2007). This effectiveness decreased in the following operations and then increased again in mid-October 2008 when the Fed decided to provide US dollar liquidity without any quantitative limit (Table 3.6).

Table 3.6 CDS prices and swaps operations (sample of 42 banks)

				Bank CDS			Bank-sovereign CDS		
				Var 5 day pre and Day after			Var 5 day pre and Day after		
Date	Level of Cds spread	No. of banks		5 day	10 day	15 day	5 day	10 day	15 day
12/12/2007	36.2	26	Level	–7.3	–5.1	–4.4	–8.9	–7.4	–6.3
			Sign	*	*	*	*	*	*
			% reduction	100.00%	92.30%	88.50%	100.00%	100.00%	95.80%
11/3/2008	125.8	31	Level	28.3	3.8	–14.5	26.2	3.3	–12.8
			Sign	*		*	*		*
			% reduction	0.00%	48.40%	87.10%	0.00%	44.80%	82.80%
2/5/2008	60.7	27	Level	–4.1	–3.3	–2.7	–2.4	–2.7	–1.9
			Sign	*	*	*	*	*	
			% reduction	96.30%	81.50%	70.40%	84.00%	68.00%	60.00%
30/07/2008	82.5	36	Level	3.1	3.7	6.5	2.7	3	5.7
			Sign	*	*	*	*	*	*
			% reduction	19.40%	22.20%	8.30%	23.50%	26.50%	14.70%
18/09/2008	159.9	35	Level	4.5	23.1	6	5	15.4	–13.9
			Sign		*				
			% reduction	60.00%	25.70%	45.70%	60.60%	36.40%	57.65%
13/10/2008	114.5	32	Level	–29.7	–9.4	–12.9	–28.6	–27.7	–33.1
			Sign	*			*	*	*
			% reduction	81.30%	56.30%	62.50%	83.30%	90.00%	90.05%

Legend: * indicates 99 per cent significance.

These results are confirmed when, instead of the level of bank CDS, we consider the differential between the prices of bank CDS and those of CDS on sovereign debt. Even the provision of swap lines in October 2008 led to a reduction in the differential between the prices of bank CDS and the CDS on sovereign debt over time, rather than this being limited to a short period, as happened in the case of the level of bank CD prices.

Further confirmation of the conclusions outlined above comes from an econometric estimate of the level of the spread between the prices of bank CDS and sovereign debt prices (BAEUR-STEUR) for the eurozone. In our model specification the dependent variable is explained through the spread between the interbank rate of the eurozone and the OIS rate (EURIBOR-OIS) as an indicator of liquidity tensions, the quantities of US dollars providing operations by the European Central Bank[9] (ECB US $) and two dummy variables that relate to the post-Lehman period (LEHMAN) and the period after the Federal Reserve's commitment to provide unlimited dollar swap lines to the European central banks on 13 October 2008 (DUSWAPUNL).[10] As in Baba and Packer (2009) we thought it useful to assess an exponential model GARCH (1.1) (EGARCH (1,1)) in the version proposed by Nelson (1991), because this model allows us to evaluate the effect of swaps both on the level of risk differential for banks and on its variability. Moreover, it recognized that GARCH models are particularly used in the analysis of financial time series and for the analysis of the effects of monetary policy announcements on asset prices (Beine, Janssen and Lecourt, 2009; Ehrmann and Fratzscher, 2008).

Within the family of GARCH models we use the EGARCH model, because it specifies the conditional variance in the log-form and thus we do not need to impose any non-negativity constraints on the variance equation. Consequently the mean equation includes the previous variables, while the variance equation can be written as:

$$\ln(\sigma^2) = \alpha + \beta|\varepsilon_{t-1}/\sigma_{t-1}| + \mu\ln(\sigma^2_{t-1}) + \Upsilon(\varepsilon_{t-1}/\sigma_{t-1}) + \pi\ln(\text{US\$BCE}) \qquad (3.1)$$

where the first term on the right-hand side of the equation is the ARCH component, the second the GARCH component, while the third enables us to evaluate the asymmetry of the impacts of the shocks on volatility, that is: if the bad news has an effect on volatility greater than, less than, or equal to the good news: in our case, since the dependent variable is the spread between bank and sovereign CDS, the bad news is defined by $\varepsilon_{t-1}>0$, and vice versa for the good news.[11]

The inclusion of provisions of dollars from the central bank in the equation of the variance permits us to assess whether the effect of these transactions, rather than only acting on the mean value of the CD prices of European banks, also had an impact on their volatility. The estimate was carried out on daily data from the beginning of December 2007 to the end of January 2009: a sample of 305 days.

The results are given in Table 3.7. The results of the estimate confirm the indications found in Table 3.6. The ECB's provision of liquidity in dollars significantly reduced the prices of bank CDS, compared to those of similar sovereign bonds, both in relation to their size and in relation to the effect of the Fed's announcement, in the middle of October 2008, of its intention to supply US dollars to major international central banks, including the ECB, without any limit. In particular, the latter effect can be evaluated in the order of one percentage point. The amounts refunded in dollars appear to have reduced the volatility of the quotations relative to bank CDS, although the estimate of the relative coefficient in the variance equation is not sufficiently precise.[12]

The empirical evidence set forth above shows that the interventions by the Fed, in the form of swap lines, were successful. What prompted the Fed to grant such large a number of swap lines, in other words, to act as a quasi-ILOLR?

A possible explanation for this behaviour is that the American central bank was driven by the concern that the banking systems of the countries

Table 3.7 EGARCH estimate of the spread between bank CDS and sovereign CDS (eurozone)

Variable	Coefficient	Z-stat	Prob
Mean equation			
C	0.760	61.15	0.00
EURIBOR-OIS	0.077	3.19	0.00
LEHMAN	0.695	66.89	0.00
ln(US$BCE)	–0.021	–7.27	0.00
DUSWAPUNL	–0.957	–65.89	0.00
Variance equation			
C	–2.584	–7.29	0.00
ARCH	1.652	7.55	0.00
GARCH	0.726	12.78	0.00
ASSIMMETRY	–0.022	–0.18	0.85
ln(US$BCE)	–0.065	–1.69	0.09

Legend: Dependent variable: BAEUR – STEUR. EGARCH(1,1) Model: method ML ARCH (Marquardt) – Generalized error distribution. Sample 12/03/2007–01/30/2009. Bollerslev–Wooldridge robust standard errors and covariance. Log likelihood: 259.59.

afflicted by a dollar shortage would sell off their long-term assets in US dollars.

This would have inevitably had negative repercussions on the market price of these assets. The consequent losses could have led to numerous banks defaulting, making them unable to repay short-term debts to American financial institutions. This would have had a contagious effect on the American banking system.

However, as we have seen, these interventions were limited to banking systems characterized by a high degree of interconnection with the US banking system. This has meant that the dichotomy between economies highly integrated with the US financial system and the peripheral economies has grown steadily wider. The latter, as they were unable to count on measures of support from the Fed in a crisis, were forced to preempt phases of financial instability by holding large amounts of foreign exchange reserves and introducing restrictions on banking activities. This negatively affected their competitiveness and hindered their integration into international financial markets. The gap between the financially developed and the less developed systems has the tendency to widen.

3.4 A discussion of the results

In the previous section we saw how, during the recent financial crisis, the Fed acted as ILOLR by allowing swap lines to central banks of advanced countries. Undoubtedly, this episode, on the one hand, shows that an ILOLR must have the capacity to create money:[13] the amount of liquidity pumped into the international economy by the Fed was impressive. At its peak, the total amount of swap lines granted by the Fed reached $533bn. On the other hand, the case of the swap lines granted by the Fed in the recent financial crisis was a case of successful cooperation between central banks (Allen and Moessner, 2010). The analysis of the context and the way in which this cooperation was achieved also allows us to highlight the limitations of an international financial architecture in which the functions of ILOLR are carried out not by an aseptic international organization, but by a national central bank, albeit the central bank of the country issuing the international currency (McDowell, 2011).

The empirical analysis conducted in Section 3.2 shows how the demand for swap lines has been particularly high from developed countries and from those countries with high financial interdependence with the United States. This leads us to believe that the primary reason for the intervention of the Fed has been to avoid a deepening of the crisis in its financial system. In fact, banks in advanced economies with liquidity problems (namely, problems with rollover of their short-term debts, denominated in US dollars) could be induced to sell their assets in US currency.

Given the large scale of these operations, the price of these assets would be further decreased. It could cause further injury to the stability of the US banking system. Awareness of this possibility, and the need for the Fed to prevent such sales through interventions as ILOLR, may have favoured the emergence of moral hazard behaviour. In particular, the advanced economies, characterized by high financial interdependence with the United States, may have been induced to hold a volume of foreign exchange reserves lower than predicted (Obstfeld, Shambaugh and Taylor, 2010). It is a fact that 'for every advanced country except Japan the size of the swap exceeded 50 per cent of actual reserves held and in the case of the UK, Australia and the ECB, the swap was larger than existing reserves... In contrast, the swaps to emerging countries are never larger than 50 per cent of their actual reserves'.[14] When Korea received $30bn from the Fed, it held $260 billion of official reserves. These values were, respectively, $30 billion versus $162 billion for Singapore, $30billion versus $180billion for Brazil.

It follows that if the ILOLR functions are carried out by a national central bank the problems of moral hazard are inevitably higher than would be the case if these functions were carried out by an aseptic international organization. In a nutshell, an organization of this kind could mitigate moral hazard problems by maintaining a policy of constructive ambiguity.[15] However, as pointed out by various scholars (see, among others, Giannini, 2002), the creation of an institution of this type is problematic for several reasons. It is not surprising that, at present, the functions of ILOLR are superseded by the Fed, that is: by the central bank of the country issuing the international currency.[16] However, this central bank cannot stick to a policy of constructive ambiguity. Its interventions as ILOLR in fact, are aimed primarily at the safeguards of its national financial stability.

The fact that the Fed acts as ILOLR only to protect its own national interests means, as we have seen above, that countries whose banking systems have a low level of interdependence with the US system hold a large amount of foreign exchange reserves: higher than optimal. By contrast, countries with banking systems characterized by a high degree of interdependence with American banks tend to hold low levels of official reserves.

This situation favours the persistence of net imbalances between countries. On one hand, the advanced economies are not stimulated to save more and, therefore, to reduce their current account imbalances with the rest of the world. On the other hand, the peripheral economies bear the costs of holding high foreign reserves. This fact tends to favour the persistence of net imbalances in two ways. First, the peripheral economies are encouraged to achieve current account surpluses, that is: to pursue forms of monetary mercantilism. Second, the need for the peripheral economies to hold, for precautionary reasons, a high volume of official reserves affects their competitiveness[17] and reduces the ability of these economies to integrate into the international financial system, which slows down the development of their domestic financial system. This contributes to the persistence of international asymmetries in the supply of and/or demand for financial assets. In particular, savers in emerging countries, given the low level of development of their financial systems, are encouraged to maintain high levels of savings (Carroll and Jeanne, 2009) and to demand assets from countries with more advanced financial markets (Mendoza, Quadrini and Rios-Rull, 2009). Also, as shown by Caballero, Farhi and Gourinchas (2008a, 2008b), this has fostered the emergence of large net imbalances between countries.

It can be concluded that '…actions which enhance the apparent financial resilience of the individual country may well, at the same time, undermine that of the international financial system as a whole' (Obstfeld, 2011:10).

If it is true that, at least in the present circumstances, it is difficult to create an international organization with the functions of ILOLR and it is likely that these functions will be carried out by the Fed, then it is necessary to limit the drawbacks, especially the problems associated with moral hazard, which can emerge in a similar situation. To this end, regulatory measures that limit the currency maturity mismatching can be used. This can only happen with an international cooperation agreement, possibly in the context of the Basel accords.

3.5 Conclusions

One of the main causes of the financial crisis of 2007–2008 was the significant increase in gross capital flows between countries that occurred between 2002 and 2007. This increase resulted primarily in a close interdependence between the European and US financial systems. In particular, several European banks took out short-term dollar debts and bought long-term high-rated assets in US dollars.

At the onset of the crisis in September 2007, given the scarcity of liquidity on the US money market, some banking systems, particularly in Europe, encountered significant difficulties in rolling over their short-term liabilities in US dollars.

This led to a significant increase in the CDS prices of the banks concerned, in other words, in their risk of default. If this risk had materialized, this would inevitably have led to the contagion spreading to the US banking system. This possibility was warded off by the intervention of the Fed, which, by allowing a large number of swap lines to central banks, solved the problem of the dollar shortage that plagued banks with high maturity mismatches between assets and liabilities in US dollars. As a result of these measures the prices of CDS on banks with short-term debt in dollars fell immediately. However, the resolute intervention of the Fed was primarily motivated by the need to avoid the liquidity shortage of European banks leading to negative externalities on the US financial system. In short, the Fed exercised the functions of ILOLR, but primarily for its own national interests.

However, the experience described above allows us to point out some problems related to the exercise of the functions of ILOLR by a national central bank. The main problem is the emergence, in financially interdependent economies, of behaviours tainted by moral hazard. It is a fact that the European economies whose banking systems had the highest problems of rollover held a very low volume of official reserves before the crisis. They were presumably induced to behave in this way by the belief that the Fed would intervene to support them in the case of a lack of dollar liquidity. In a nutshell, a central bank acting as ILOLR cannot follow policies of constructive ambiguity. In this context, a deep dichotomy in the world financial system will emerge. On the one hand, there are the financial systems of advanced economies regarded as interconnected with the US financial system, which can count on intervention by the Fed in the guise of a quasi-ILOLR. These countries may hold a limited amount of reserves: they are not encouraged to achieve a high level of national saving. On the other hand, there are the peripheral economies, with a low degree of interconnection with the US financial system. These economies tend to protect themselves from the risk of currency and financial crises by holding large amounts of reserves and by imposing severe regulatory constraints on domestic banks. This limits the financial development of these countries and favours the emergence of international asymmetries in the supply of and/or demand for financial assets. The foregoing dichotomy favours the persistence of high current account imbalances between countries. It can be presumed, therefore, that to some extent these deficits arise from the fact that the functions of ILOLR are currently exercised by a national central bank, such as the Fed.

The moral hazard problems that arise from this situation, and their current account implications, can be limited through regulatory interventions on the liquidity management in the banking systems of advanced countries.

Notes

1. See among others Borio and Disyatat (2011).
2. Acharya and Schnabl (2010) provide a detailed description of how the European banking systems operated. Commercial banks were creating security investment vehicles (SIVs) to hold AAA-rated assets backed by subprime mortgages. In turn, the SIVs were financed largely by placing asset-backed commercial papers (ABCP) mainly in money market funds. In some cases, as with the German Landesbanken, the ABPCs were explicitly or implicitly guaranteed by the government. In addition to ABPCs, the European financial systems financed their assets in dollars using the interbank market and foreign exchange swaps.
3. Contrary to the provisions of Bagehot (1873), the conditions applied by the Fed to FX swap lines were not penalized in any way. On the one hand, they did not involve any exchange rate risk, since the exchange rate at which central banks would have to buy back currency from the Fed was the same as when they drew on its swap line. On the other hand, the interest rate applied to the FX swap lines was that applied to its domestic lending operations.
4. The sample consists of 11 countries of the euro area (Italy, France, Germany, Spain, Austria, Belgium, Holland, Ireland, Portugal, Greece and Finland) and of another five European countries (UK, Switzerland, Denmark, Sweden and Norway), Japan and the four emerging countries that used the swap lines of the Fed (Brazil, Mexico, Korea and Singapore).
5. The dollar swap operations with the Fed and the level of official reserves are taken from the BIS 'Data Template on International Reserves and Foreign Currency Liquidity'.
6. More precisely, the reserves are valued in the last quarter of 2007, while the assets and the foreign interbank market have as a reference the average of the period from the first quarter of 2005 to the second quarter of 2007.
7. Aizenman and Pasricha (2009) consider four emerging countries, two of which benefited from the Fed swap lines. The empirical analysis shows that in the short term the swap lines led to a rise in the exchange rate of the swap countries over the non-swap countries. However, the repercussions of the swap lines on the CDS of the first countries compared to the latter are negligible.
8. More precisely, if the change is significant to 99 per cent.

9. See Baba and Packer (2009).
10. Both this and the previous dummy are equal to 1 for the days following the event in question and 0 previous to the event.
11. So, if we believe that the bad news has a greater effect, Υ will be significantly positive.
12. However, the estimate of the relative coefficient in the variance equation is not sufficiently precise. The statistical significance of this coefficient would be higher if one assumed the errors to be normally distributed.
13. Several scholars, with reference to the 1990s financial crises in emerging countries, were convinced that the ILOLR could simply be a crisis manager, and as such, may also be exercised by an institution, like the IMF, with a low capacity of create money. See Fischer (1999) and Giannini (1999).
14. See Obstfeld et al. (2009: 484).
15. This helps to explain why, as shown by Aizenman, Jinjarak and Donghyun (2010), for some emerging countries high reserves and granting of swap lines by the Fed are complementary. For these countries, the official reserves are, in fact, a guarantee to the lender of funds. On this point see also Baba and Shim (2011).
16. During the international financial crises that preceded the one of 2008–2009, and that affected emerging countries, the IMF was a crisis manager rather than a crisis lender. Furthermore, the latter feature is essential for an ILOLR, See Keleher (1999).
17. This is because the holding of reserves is costly.

References

Acharya, V. and P. Schnabl (2010) 'Do global banks spread global imbalances? Asset-backed commercial paper during the financial crisis of 2007–2009', *IMF Economic Review*, 58, 37–73.

Acharya, V., D. Gromb and T. Yorulmazer (2012) 'Imperfect competition in the inter-bank market for liquidity as a rationale for central banking', *American Economic Journal: Macroeconomics*, 4, 184–217.

Aizenman, J. and G. Pasricha (2009) 'Selective swap arrangements and the global financial crisis: Analysis and interpretation', NBER Working Paper No. 14821.

Aizenman, J., Y. Jinjarak and Donghyun (2010) 'International reserves and swap lines: Substitutes or complements?', Santa Cruz Center for International Economics Working Paper No. 10–03.

Allen, W. and R. Moessner (2010) 'Central bank cooperation and international liquidity in the financial crisis of 2008–09', BIS Working Paper No. 310.

Baba, N. and F. Packer (2009) 'From turmoil to crisis: Dislocations in the FX swap market before and after the failure of Lehman Brothers', Bank of International Settlements, Working Paper No. 285.

Baba, N. and I. Shim (2011) 'Dislocations in the won-dollar swap markets during the crisis of 2007.09', BIS Working Paper, No. 344.

Bagehot, W. (1873) *Lombard Street*, London: William Clowes and Sons.

Bank of International Settlements (2008) '78th Annual Report', Basel, June.

Beine, M., G. Janssen and C. Lecourt (2009) 'Should central bankers talk to the foreign exchange markets?', *Journal of International Money and Finance*, 28, 776–804.

Bernanke, B.S., C. Bertaut, L. Pounder DeMarco and S. Kamin (2011) 'International capital flows and the returns to safe assets in the United States, 2003–2007', International Finance Discussion Papers No. 1014, Board of Governors of the Federal Reserve System.

Bertaut, C., L. Pounder De Marco, S. Kamin and R. Tryon (2011) 'ABS inflows to the United States and the global financial crisis', Board of Governors of the Federal Reserve System, International Finance Discussion Paper, No. 1028.

Borio, C. and P. Disyatat (2011) Global imbalances and the financial crisis: link or no link? BIS Working Paper No. 346.

Brumnermeier, M. (2009) 'Deciphering the liquidity and credit crunch 2007–2008', *Journal of Economic Perspectives*, 23, 77–100.

Caballero, R., E. Farhi and P. Gourinchas (2008a) 'An equilibrium model of global imbalances and low interests', *The American Economic Review*, 98, 358–393.

Caballero, R., E. Farhi and P. Gourinchas (2008b) 'Financial crash, commodity prices and global imbalances', CEPR Discussion Paper No. 7064.

Carroll, C. and O. Jeanne (2009) 'A tractable model of precautionary reserves, net foreign assets, or sovereign wealth funds', NBER Working Paper No. 15228.

Ehrmann, M. and M. Fratzscher (2008) 'Communication by central bank committee members: Difference strategies, same effectiveness?', *Journal of Money, Credit and Banking*, 39, 509–541.

Engel, C. (2009) 'Exchange rate policies', Federal Reserve Bank of Dallas Staff Papers No. 8.

Fischer, S. (1999) 'On the need for the international lender of last resort', *Journal of Economic Perspectives*, 13, 85–104.

Fleming, M. and N. Klagge (2010) 'The Federal Reserve's foreign exchange swap lines', *Federal Reserve of New York 'Current Issues'*, 16(4), 1–7.

Giannini, C. (1999) 'Enemy of none but a common friend of all? An international perspective on the lender of last resort function', IMF Working Paper No. 99/10.

Giannini, C. (2002) 'Pitfalls in international crisis lending' in Goodhart C. and G. Illing (eds) *Financial Crises, Contagion, and the Lender of Last Resort. A Book of Readings*, Oxford: Oxford University Press, 511–546.

Goldberg, L., C. Kennedy and J. Miu (2011) 'Central bank dollar swap lines and overseas dollar funding costs', *Federal Reserve Bank of New York, 'Economic Policy Review'*, May, 3–20.

Johnson, K. (2009) 'Gross or net international financial flows: Understanding the financial crisis', Council on Foreign Relations, Working Paper, July.

Keleher, R. (1999) 'An international lender of last resort', the IMF and the Federal Reserve, Joint Economic Committee United States Congress.

McAndrews, J., A. Sarkar and Z. Wang (2008) 'The effects of the Term Auction Facility on the London interbank offered rate', Federal Reserve Bank of New York, Staff Report No. 335.

McDowell, D. (2011) 'The US as "sovereign international last resort lender": The Fed's currency swap programme during the great panic of 2007–09', *New Political Economy*, 17, 157–178.

McGuire, P. and G. Von Peter (2009) 'The US dollar shortage in global banking and the international policy response', BIS Working Paper No. 291.

Mendoza, E.G., V. Quadrini and J. V. Rios-Rull (2009) 'Financial integration, financial development and global imbalances', *Journal of Political Economy*, 117, 371–416.

Nelson D. (1991) 'Conditional heteroskedasticity in asset returns: A new approach', *Econometrica*, 59, 347–370.

Obstfeld, M. (2011) 'International liquidity: The fiscal dimension', IMES Discussion Paper Series, No. 2011-E-22.

Obstfeld, M., J.C. Shambaugh and A.M. Taylor (2010) 'Financial stability, The trilemma, and international reserves', *American Economic Journal: Macroeconomics*, 2, 57–94.

Taylor J. and J. Williams (2009) 'A black swan in the money market', *American Economic Journal: Macroeconomics*, 1, 58–83.

4

Firm-based and Institutional-based Determinants of the Bank Debt Maturity: New Evidence for Developed Countries

Eleuterio Vallelado, Paolo Saona and Pablo San Martín

4.1 Introduction

The choice between various financial instruments under perfect capital markets is inconsequential to the value of the firm. This basic irrelevancy theorem, originally developed by Modigliani and Miller (1958), covers all types of complexities which commonly characterize financial liabilities. Contributions in the field of finance introduce market imperfections, such as the agency costs of equity and debt, to bridge the gap between theory and the observed reliance of corporations on complex financial instruments. Jensen and Meckling (1976) identify these agency costs as bankruptcy costs associated with managerial consumption of perks, and costs associated with managerial incentive to undertake suboptimal risky projects (Dang, 2011), which transfer wealth from bondholders to shareholders, such as asset substitution problems (Douglas, 2009; Myers, 1977). On the other hand, contributions from the field of law and finance indicate the relevance of institutional setting in the financial decisions of corporations.

The literature on corporate finance shows that the optimal choice of securities and their maturities depends on both the information available to investors and their ability to monitor compliance by reducing agency conflicts as corporate governance mechanisms improve. Since the amount of information available to investors, and their ability to protect their interests, depend on financial and legal institutions, the firms' financial structures – their maturity and source – should be systematically defined by each country's circumstances (Alcock, Finn, and Tan, 2012; Demirgüç-Kunt and Maksimovic, 1999; Saona and Vallelado, 2010).

Therefore, the goal of this chapter is to examine how companies' characteristics, the institutional setting where they operate, and the introduction of additional regulations on corporate governance impact the firms' bank debt maturity choice. Our empirical analysis includes ten countries (Australia, Belgium, Canada, Denmark, France, Germany, Italy, Spain, the United Kingdom, and the United States) that belong to different institutional settings and have introduced, during the period of study, additional regulations on corporate governance. Four of them have their institutional and legal settings based on common law (Australia, Canada, the United Kingdom and the United States) and the other six countries belong to the civil-law tradition of continental Europe (Belgium, Denmark, France, Germany, Italy, and Spain). The common element is that the ten countries are developed countries belonging to the OECD group, which allows us to consider similarities in the economic framework of this set of countries. It is important to bear in mind that keeping certain economic standards is a requirement for being part of the OECD group, for instance, inflation levels, competitiveness, and income per capita, among others.[1]

Our main contribution is to show how the introduction of new regulation on corporate governance modifies bank debt maturity decisions in corporations located either in civil-law countries or common-law countries. The main findings indicate that the institutional context and the regulations on corporate governance are drivers of the bank debt maturity adopted by listed firms. Thus, the higher transparency associates with additional regulations on corporate governance increases the use of short-term bank debt by corporations. In our opinion, the introduction of new corporate governance regulation has had a substitution effect on ownership structure and short-term bank debt as corporate governance mechanisms. In addition, we observe that funding investments with bank debts of different maturities depends on the extent to which the financial system is either market oriented or banking oriented. The relationship between the external funds needed, the ownership structure, and the bank debt maturity seems to be conditioned by institutional settings. For instance, firms from common-law countries have less concentrated ownership, use lower proportions of short-term bank debt and have a larger need for external funds than firms from civil-law countries.

The chapter is organized in five sections. After the introduction, a second section presents our arguments about the determinants of the maturity of bank borrowing. The third describes the sample used for the empirical analysis. Section 4.4 presents the main results. The final section of the chapter summarizes the main conclusions.

4.2 Determinants of the maturity of bank borrowing

The maturity of bank borrowing can be examined in the context of agency theory, contracting costs, signalling hypothesis, and the law and finance proposals. From these approaches, we analyse how company characteristics, civil-law/common-law origin and corporate governance regulation influence non-financial firms' bank debt maturity.

The use of short-term bank borrowing might mitigate underinvestment/debt overhang and asset substitution problems more efficiently than public debt (Dewatripont and Tirole, 1994; Galai and Masulis, 1976; Jensen, 1986; Jensen and Meckling, 1976; Myers, 1977). Thus, these problems can be addressed through the choice of lender. In comparison with public debt, banks are in a better position than arm's-length lenders to reduce managerial discretion because of the debt-ownership concentration (Blackwell and Kidwell, 1988; Denis and Mihov, 2003; Fama, 1985; James and Smith, 2000). In the same vein, Lin et al. (2012) find that firms able to choose public debt do so to avoid scrutiny and to insulate themselves from bank monitoring. Underinvestment and asset substitution problems are expected to be more severe for firms with more growth options, where managers have higher degrees of managerial discretion since they have more flexibility in the choice of future investments (Billett, King, and Mauer, 2007; Chen, Ho, and Yeo, 1999). Furthermore, short-term debt could help to alleviate debt overhang (Diamond and He, 2013).[2]

The relevance of bank financing and maturity choice will be the result of the relative incidence that financial markets and intermediaries have on the financial system (Bancel and Mittoo, 2004; Demirgüç-Kunt and Levine, 2001; Korajczyk and Levy, 2003). The law and finance approach is based on the legal tradition of each country (La Porta et al., 1998). According to this approach, the set of institutional factors will also play a relevant role in decisions about bank debt maturity. From this point of view, countries might be classified into two groups: the civil-law countries and the common-law countries. In the first one, bank debt is the most important source for financing firms' operations; while in the common-law countries, the public debt and capital markets play a determinant role in satisfying firms' financing needs.

Growth options involve agency problems between bondholders and shareholders (De Andrés, Azofra, and Rodríguez, 2000; González, 2012), asymmetries of information (Goyal, Lehn, and Racic, 2002; Myers and Majluf, 1984), and higher derived bankruptcy costs (Harris and Raviv, 1990; Shleifer and Vishny, 1992; Williamson, 1988). Bank borrowing, specifically that which matures sooner, reduces these problems (Flannery, 1986; Guedes and Opler, 1996). This argument can also be supported by the role played by financial intermediaries in each institutional framework. Whereas in the market-oriented financial systems – most of the common-law countries – corporate control is addressed by external mechanisms such as hostile takeovers, the discipline of public (negotiable) debt, and the enforcement of law; in banking-oriented countries – most of the civil-law countries – the corporate governance mechanisms are internal, such as ownership concentration, institutional investors, bank financing, and more specifically, the maturity of bank debt, which helps to match the interests of managers and shareholders (La Porta, Lopez-de-Silanes, and Shleifer, 1999, 2002; La Porta et al., 1997). Consequently, we should observe that the bank debt maturity of firms with growth opportunities is related to the institutional environment where they operate. In banking-oriented countries, the reduction of bank debt maturity helps to improve corporate governance, whereas in market-oriented countries, firms have alternative mechanisms of corporate governance to bank debt maturity.

The capacity of firms to internally generate cash flow affects agency and the asymmetries of information problems (Bessler, Drobetz, and Grüninger, 2011; De Jong, Verbeek, and Verwijmeren, 2010). Thus, the higher the deficit of funds internally generated, the higher the agency problems, regardless of the institutional setting. Denis and McKeon (2012) point out that the firms that generate a deficit of funds tend to cover such deficits with more debt. With regard to this, Modigliani and Perotti (2000) point out that in financial systems where banking is fairly developed financing through bank debt is pursued, and, more specifically, the issuance of short-term bank debt is used for financing investment with external funds. Hence, firms with insufficient internal funds should issue short-term bank debt to mitigate the moral hazard problems generated by the deficit. Firms with low cash inflows, and therefore higher needs of external funds, are more likely to suffer from an inefficient liquidation process (Houston and Venkataraman, 1994;

Shleifer and Vishny, 1992) and/or an inefficient debt pricing for longer maturities. In this scenario, managers of good firms are motivated to issue short-term bank debt. Thus, the moral hazard problems of firms with a deficit of internal funds to finance their investments can be solved using bank debt with short maturities. Then, the short-term bank debt becomes an efficient corporate governance mechanism that interacts with the regulatory and institutional setting.

The zero agency cost base case is, by definition, a firm owned solely by a single owner-manager (Jensen and Meckling, 1976). When management owns less than 100 per cent of the firm's equity, shareholders incur agency costs resulting from the management's shirking and perquisite consumption. Empirically, Ang, Cole and Lin (2000) have observed that agency costs are indeed higher among firms that are not entirely owned by their managers, and that these costs increase as the equity share of the owner-manager declines. Thus, when ownership is concentrated, managers have the incentive to choose the debt maturity that maximizes the firm's value as their first-best policy (Bharadwaj and Shivdasani, 2003; Denis and Mihov, 2003). In countries that offer weak protection of the shareholders' interests, the concentrated ownership structure becomes an efficient mechanism of corporate governance (López, López, and Santamaría, 2007). Thus, if concentrated ownership contributes towards reducing managerial incentives to overinvest it opens the door to external financing. External funds will come mainly from banks due to the civil-law institutional setting. Furthermore, banks that are not shareholders will prefer shorter maturities to cope with asymmetric information about growth opportunities.

Institutional investors serve as an alternative mechanism to control the overinvestment problem (Shleifer and Vishny, 1986) because of their greater experience in gathering information. Besides, the proportion of equity owned by an institutional investor in a particular firm increases its incentives to closely oversee managerial activities in comparison with the situation of a minority investor (Moon and Tandon, 2007). In the same vein, the convergence hypothesis states that firms with high managerial ownership have lower agency costs of debt, leading to higher levels of leverage (Kim and Sorensen, 1986). Therefore, a concentrated ownership structure along with a reduction in the debt maturity structure might be seen as complementary mechanisms of corporate governance to solve the conflicts of interest between shareholders, debt-holders, and managers (Yafeh and Yosha, 2003).[3] Correspondingly, the higher the ownership concentration in a firm, the more it uses bank debt with short maturity. This situation is particularly relevant in bank-based financial systems where concentrated ownership and bank debt maturity become complementary elements of optimal corporate governance.

The Sarbanes–Oxley Act[4] (Public Law 107–204, 116 Stat. 745) passed in the United States and the equivalent regulation in many other countries were the key to improving the protection of investors and introduced the most comprehensive changes in both corporate governance regulation and in financial practices of listed firms since the 1930s. Specifically, this new legislation promotes transparency by improving the accuracy and reliability of financial information.

The Sarbanes–Oxley law was originally applied to all American listed firms. However, this law has had implications beyond the American frontiers because foreign firms trading in the American stock markets are forced to draw up their financial statements according to the US GAAP, along with subsidiaries of American firms. Additionally, this law directly affected the international financial community, motivating the development of similar legislations in other countries, for instance, the CLERP in Australia; the Corporate Governance Act in Belgium (Lippens Code); Bill 198 in Canada; the Danish Companies Act in Denmark; the Financial Security Law in France; the German Corporate Governance Code (Cromme Code) in Germany; the L262–2005 in Italy; the Law 44/2002 in Spain; or the Companies Act in the United Kingdom. Table 4.1 provides a brief description of the extent of the corporate governance legislations passed across the counties included in our sample.

If civil-law countries are associated with lower protection of investors' rights in comparison to common-law countries, then additional regulation on corporate governance should have a greater impact on civil-law countries' usage of bank debt maturity. For instance, if new corporate governance regulation is effective, we should observe greater benefits of such regulation in civil-law countries than in common-law countries, improving market and legal systems efficiency, and an effect on the corporate governance role of bank debt maturity. Furthermore, one of the goals of corporate governance regulation is to improve transparency which should help to alleviate asymmetries of information. Thus, we should observe that, after the new regulation is passed in each country, shareholders are more worried about inefficient liquidation than about underinvestment when companies use bank debt maturity.

Table 4.1 Description of the corporate governance legislations across countries

Country	Name Act	Details	Characteristics
Australia	CLERP (Corporate Law Economic Reform Program Governance)	Passed on June 30, 2004.	Improvements in transparency, accountability and rights of shareholders.
Belgium	Corporate Governance Act	The Act was adopted on April 6, 2010 and published in the Belgian State Gazette on 23 April 2010	The Act, which applies to companies listed on a regulated market in Belgium (i.e., Euronext Brussels), amends the Belgian Company Code in four main areas: a) Creation of a remuneration committee; b) Approval of a corporate governance statement; c) Approval of a remuneration report; and d) Specific rules on executive remuneration and severance packages.
Canada	Bill 198	Passed on 7 April 2003.	It provides the Ontario Securities Commission (OSC) with authority over corporate controls. Specifically, the OSC is given power to: Enact rules requiring audit committees; systems of internal controls; disclosure controls and procedures; request CEOs and CFOs to provide certifications related to internal controls and to disclosure controls and procedures. It also allows the OSC to define auditing standards for the reporting of internal controls.
Denmark	Danish Companies Act	Danish Executive Order No. 172 (22 February 2010).	The new act regulates public and private companies and modernizes and simplifies the overall regulation of both types of company.
France	Financial Security Law of France	Law 2003–706 (1 August 2003).	The Financial Security Law rests mainly on: An increased responsibility of leaders; a strengthening of internal control; and a reduction in the sources of conflicts of interest.
Germany	German Corporate Governance Code	Approved on 26 February 2002, the Code adopted various amendments on 26 May 2010.	The Code presents essential statutory regulations for the management and supervision of German listed companies and contains internationally and nationally recognized standards for good and responsible governance.
Italy	L262–2005 ('Disposizioni per la Tutela del Risparmio e la Disciplina dei Mercati Finanziari')	Passed on 28 December 2005.	The law was promulgated for the protection of savings and regulation of the financial markets. It is part of a broad set of measures aimed at guaranteeing the stability of the financial markets and protecting investors.

Continued

Table 4.1 Continued

Country	Name Act	Details	Characteristics
Spain	Law 44/2002 ('Financial System Refrom Measures')	Passed on 22 November 2002, and revised in its last version on 24 March 2013	The goals of this regulation are basically three: to increase efficiency and to enhance the competitiveness of the Spanish financial industry; to improve the protection of consumers of financial services; and to improve the financing conditions of small and medium enterprises (SMEs)
UK	Companies (Audit, Investigations and Community Enterprise) Act 2004	The key provisions of the Companies Act 2004 came into force on 6 April 2005.	It includes the strengthening of auditors' rights to information from directors and employees, the widened powers of the FRRP (Financial Reporting Review Panel) to obtain information from auditors, and the new regime for regulating auditors.
USA	Sarbanes–Oxley Act	Pub. L. No. 107–204, 116 Stat. 745 (30 July 2002).	Principal components of the SOX Act: Established independent oversight of public company audits. Strengthened audit committees and corporate governance. Enhanced transparency, executive accountability and investor protection. Enhanced auditor independence.
Europe	8th EU Directive	The former version was released on 10 April 1984.	The 8th EU Directive, also known as the audit directive or Euro SOX, regulates the auditing of financial statements in the European Union (EU). Its aim is to ensure that investors and other interested parties can rely fully on the accuracy of audited financial statements. EU member states were required to translate it into national law by 29 June 2008.

4.3 Data and variables

Our source of information is twofold: financial information and firms' market value was obtained from the Osiris database; whereas the information about the ownership structure has been gathered from Thomson ONE Banker. Our total sample includes 2,592 firms from Australia, Belgium, Canada, Denmark, France, Germany, Italy, Spain, the United Kingdom, and the United States, with a total of 12,184 firm-year observations. The period under study ranged from 1996 to 2008 to avoid biases in our findings due to the financial recession. These countries are part of different institutional settings: they either have a common-law background (Australia, Canada, the United Kingdom and the United States) or a civil-law tradition (Belgium, Denmark, France, Germany, Italy, and Spain). All the countries belong to the OECD group and, therefore, share similar economic characteristics which make them comparable.

We included all listed non-financial firms from ten OECD countries. The panel data is unbalanced because some firms disappear during the period of analysis and/or we discarded those observations for which we had incomplete data. Likewise, we exclude financial firms, since the very nature of their business would distort the results. We also excluded the years in which firms have no debt in their balance sheets, since this situation does not allow us to account for the problems of asymmetric information and agency costs related to debt. The sample was divided into two groups according to their legal tradition (Table 4.2). As an additional institutional factor, we compare the results for the pre- and post-periods of the introduction of corporate governance regulations in each country (hereafter CGR) in order to assess the structural change generated by the new regulations that increased monitoring of management's activities by independent directors, auditors, and regulators.

The maturity of bank borrowing is measured as the ratio of short-term bank debt to total bank debt (SBDBD).[5] Johnson (1997b) argues that there is no clear empirical distinction between short- and long-term debt. In spite of this, we have used bank debt with a maturity less than or equal to one year as short-term bank debt, and the rest as long-term bank debt. Unfortunately, the available data does not allow any other classification. Most other works also use this accounting classification to measure bank debt maturity (Demirgüç-Kunt and Maksimovic, 2002; Johnson, 1997b; Ozkan, 2002).

Following Johnson (1997a, 1997b), Cuñat (1999), Krishnaswami, Spindt and Subramaniam (1999), and Barclay, Max and Smith (2003b)

Table 4.2 Descriptive statistics and test of mean differences among the variables by legal system and application of corporate governance legislation (CGR)

	Mean				Mean Common-law			Mean Civil-law		
Variables	Total Sample	Common Law	Civil Law	Mean Diff Test P-Value	Before CGR	After CGR	Mean Diff Test P-Value	Before CGR	After CGR	Mean Diff Test P-Value
SBDB	0.2094	0.1900	0.3138	(0.0000)	0.1780	0.1989	(0.0000)	0.2857	0.3192	0.0755
Q	1.2347	1.2473	1.1672	(0.0013)	0.7150	1.6418	(0.0000)	0.9248	1.2133	0.0000
NEF	0.0782	0.0918	0.0053	(0.0000)	0.2311	−0.0114	(0.0000)	0.0695	−0.0069	0.0237
OWN	0.3126	0.2791	0.4925	(0.0000)	0.2806	0.2780	(0.5679)	0.5386	0.4838	0.0008
LNTAB	12.9170	12.8191	13.4425	(0.0000)	12.7751	12.8517	(0.0721)	14.1952	13.2993	0.0000
ROA	0.0220	0.0198	0.0338	(0.0000)	0.0239	0.0168	(0.0012)	0.0295	0.0346	0.2181
SGROWTH	0.1560	0.1577	0.1470	(0.6017)	0.2569	0.0841	(0.0000)	0.1589	0.1447	0.7065
Z	6.8351	6.5541	8.3433	(0.0000)	6.9522	6.2590	(0.0000)	7.5195	8.5000	0.0841
NDTS	0.0032	0.0005	0.0178	(0.0000)	0.0006	0.0004	(0.5128)	0.0285	0.0157	0.0504
CGR	0.6161	0.5743	0.8402	(0.0000)	0.0000	1.0000	(0.0000)	0.0000	1.0000	0.0000
Obs.	12184	9591	2593		4083	5508		414	2179	

Note: This table shows the descriptive statistics and the test of mean differences among the subsamples of common-law and civil-law countries and by the application of the new legislation on corporate governance measured by CGR variable. The null hypothesis is that equal means exist among the variables for each category. The statistical significance proves whether this hypothesis is accepted. The variables are: short-term bank debt to bank debt (SBDBD), growth opportunities (Q), the external funds needed for financing of the firm's portfolio of projects (NEF), the ownership in the hands of the main shareholder (blockholder) and in the hands of the executives (OWN), the company size (LNTAB), the return of assets (ROA), the sales growth (SGROWTH), default risk (Z), the non-debt tax shield (NDTS), and the dummy variable used to account for Sarbanes-Oxley Act in the case of the US and the legislation on corporate governance in the other countries included in the sample (CGR).

among others, we used as a proxy for growth opportunities the market to book value ratio (Q).

According to Hawawini and Viallet (2011) we computed the ratio of external funds need (NEF) as the difference between the growth rate in total assets and the ROE over 1-ROE.

As a measure of ownership concentration, we used the percentage of closely held stocks, which corresponds to the percentage of shares in the hands of the controller stockholder plus the ownership of the managers (OWN).

We also included in our analysis: the firm's size, return on assets, the growth of sales, the bankruptcy risk, and the non-debt tax shield. These variables appear in most empirical works on bank debt (Barclay, Max, and Smith, 2003a; Dang, 2010; Gottesman and Roberts, 2004; Ozkan, 2002; Rauh and Sufi, 2010; Saona and Vallelado, 2005, 2010). The logarithmic transformation of the book value of firm assets was our measure of firm size (LNTAB).[6] To measure the profitability of the firms' portfolio of projects, we used return on assets (ROA) measured as the earnings before taxes over total assets. Sales growth is the measure of the firm's activity (SGROWTH). We measured the bankruptcy risk (Z) as EBITDA plus equity over total assets and all this was divided by the standard deviation of return on equity. Annual depreciation over total assets is the measure for the non-debt tax shield (NDTS). To account for corporate governance regulation we built a dummy variable (CGR) that takes value 1 for all the years after the regulation was passed in each country and 0 otherwise.

We highlight the importance of the role played by the capital market financing in these countries in comparison with bank financing, and the different institutional environments in which the firms have to make their debt decisions. To do so, we built one sample for civil-law countries and another for common-law countries (Demirgüç-Kunt, Laeven, and Levine, 2004; Demirgüç-Kunt and Maksimovic, 1999, 2002).

In the same vein, the firm-year observations for the subsamples of civil-law companies and common-law companies are divided according to whether they are before or after the introduction of corporate governance regulation in each country.

The empirical analysis includes a descriptive analysis and a mean-difference analysis aimed at exploring the main differences between the variables included in this study for each institutional framework, comparing them before and after the introduction of corporate governance regulation.

4.4 Results

Table 4.2 shows that using short-term bank borrowing is clearly different in our two institutional/legal contexts. In the civil-law regime firms have in average a higher proportion of short-term bank debt (31.38 per cent), lower maturity, than in the common-law regime (19.0 per cent). On the other hand, the firm size for civil-law countries is larger than in the common-law countries, as well as the profitability which is about 3.38 per cent versus 1.98 per cent for firms in common-law countries.

Moreover, we can observe in Table 4.2 that after the introduction of additional corporate governance regulation (CGR variable), firms in both common- and civil-law countries have increased their use of short-term bank debt. Historically, firms in civil-law countries use bank debt with lower maturities than in common-law countries. This result confirms the dependence of civil-law companies on their banks. Banks become a supplier of funds and are delegated supervisors for non-financial firms. Even though the introduction of corporate governance regulation improves transparency it does not modify the controlling role of the banking system as a cornerstone in civil-law countries.

In both institutional environments the growth opportunities are higher than 1 on average, which means that the companies in the sample have growth options. Nevertheless, firms in common-law countries have statistically more growth opportunities than in civil-law countries. The operating activities of firms for the entire period of analysis (1996–2008) seem to grow at the same pace regardless of the institutional setting the firms are part of: there is no statistically significant difference in terms of how fast the sales grow in both contexts.

Our data shows that in common-law countries higher growth opportunities are related with a lower proportion of short-term bank debt and lower bank debt maturity. This means that firms in common-law countries do not solve the moral hazard problems of growth opportunities with short-term bank debt. Once the corporate governance regulation is considered the capital structure decisions change in common-law countries, as we observe lower maturities and higher growth opportunities. This result is in agreement with the findings of Custódio, Ferreira and Laureano (2013) that show a decrease in debt maturity of US firms which concentrates on those with higher information asymmetry.

In the same way, firms in civil-law countries reduce the maturity of bank debt and increase their growth opportunities after the introduction of corporate governance regulation. The reduction in bank debt maturity is not as significant as in common-law countries. The higher disciplining devices and tighter regulation push managers to use more short-term bank debt for financing the firms' growth options. This governance mechanism involves higher supervision by banks and short-term outflows of money, which reduce the discretional behaviour of managers in using the available cash flow in suboptimal investment decisions.

A higher need for external funds is observed for firms operating in common-law countries. Furthermore, we observe higher bankruptcy risk (lower values of Z) and a lower non-debt tax shield than in civil-law countries. As expected, the ownership structure is more concentrated for firms operating in the civil-law regime. The higher concentration observed in this context is considered the answer to weak protection of the interests of investors.

Firms in common-law countries combine higher needs for external funds (NEF) and a lower proportion of short-term bank debt. The opposite finding is observed in companies operating in the civil-law countries. Thus, the use of bank debt maturity to deal with moral hazard problems is conditioned by the environment where the firm operates. However, it is not only the institutional setting that seems to play an important role in both financing and governing firms, but also corporate governance regulation. Before the introduction of CGR, firms in common-law countries show a higher need for external funds and lower proportions of short-term bank debt. However, once the corporate governance regulation is adopted in the common-law countries of our sample, we observe no need for external funds, on average, and a higher proportion of short-term bank debt. The situation looks quite similar for firms in civil-law countries. Thus, these results confirm the interaction between bank debt maturity and regulatory and institutional settings as an explanation for how companies finance their investment projects.

The ownership structure (OWN) is an important corporate governance mechanism particularly in civil-law countries, where the protection of investors' rights is much weaker than in common-law countries. We observe a substitution effect between the ownership structure and the short-term bank debt, with both operating as corporate governance mechanisms. Thus, after the introduction of additional corporate governance regulation our data shows a significant reduction in ownership concentration and an increase in the proportion of short-term bank debt. In civil-law countries particularly, ownership concentration plays a major role in explaining bank debt maturity. Before corporate governance regulation (CGR) the ownership structure and bank debt maturity were complementary mechanisms of governance, but such complementarities moved towards substitutive after the CGR.

The passing of the new regulations has increased transparency regardless of the institutional setting, improving the internal governance mechanisms of firms in both institutional environments and favouring some convergence in the role played by ownership structure and debt maturity to cope with moral hazard problems.

Profitability (ROA) is higher in civil-law countries than in common-law countries. The introduction of corporate governance regulation influences profitability in a different way in civil and common-law countries. In civil-law countries profitability is higher before than after CGR whereas we observe the opposite for common-law countries.

The firm's activity, measured by the growth rate of annual sales (SGROWTH), presents similar results for civil-law and common-law countries, before as well as after corporate governance regulation (CGR). Concerning bankruptcy risk (Z) we can see that firms in civil-law countries have lower insolvency risk than companies in common-law countries. Additionally, common-law firms increase their insolvency risk after the introduction of corporate governance regulation whereas civil-law companies reduce it.

Non-debt tax shields (NDTS) are higher in companies operating under civil-law. The introduction of corporate governance regulation produces significant changes in civil-law countries. In this case, firms in this institutional setting before the CGR have a higher proportions of tax shields. Thus these firms will be the ones able to take advantage of longer maturities in order to benefit from higher tax shields. The opposite is observed after the CGR.

4.5 Conclusions

The way capital structure, and specifically the source of debt and its maturity, helps stockholders to control their managers is, on the one hand, by reducing the free cash flow, and with it the likelihood of undertaking unprofitable investment projects (overinvestment problem); and on the other hand, by avoiding both the underinvestment problem and the asset substitution problem. Thus, our research documents that there are interactions between regulatory and institutional setting and the source of debt and its maturity to reduce firms' agency problems between stockholders, debt-holders, and managers.

Our aim is to relate the decisions of bank debt maturity to firm-based, institutional settings, and regulatory changes in corporate governance, as drivers of this decision. Specifically, we use growth opportunities, the external funds needed, the ownership structure, the size of the company, profitability, the growth of sales, bankruptcy risk, and non-debt tax shields as firm-based determinants of bank debt maturity. As institutional-based determinants we have considered the legal origin and the banking/capital market-orientation of the different countries included in this study as institutional-based determinants. Finally, the regulatory changes have been included by considering the introduction of corporate governance regulation (CGR) during the period of analysis in each country of the sample.

Thus, we observe that the relationship between the external funds needed, the ownership structure, and the bank debt maturity seem to be conditioned by institutional setting. For instance, firms from common-law countries have less concentrated ownership, use lower proportions of short-term bank debt and have a larger need for external funds than firms from civil-law countries.

Our data does reveal the differential effect of the institutional contexts and regulatory changes in corporate governance on the bank debt maturity adopted by listed firms. For instance, we find that the asymmetries of information related to investment are better solved by shortening the bank debt maturity in the common-law context after the introduction of new rules on firms' transparency (CGR). In the civil-law countries the short-term bank debt is systematically used to finance companies' investments, which means bank debt maturity is a disciplining device over the entire period analysed. In this legal setting, the introduction of corporate governance regulation to increase transparency helps to reinforce the role of bank debt maturity as a disciplining device. Thus we observe a decrease in ownership concentration and a higher proportion of short-term bank debt in the period where the new regulation on corporate governance has been implemented. Furthermore, the introduction of similar regulation in countries with different legal traditions produces some degree of convergence in the use of bank debt maturity as a disciplining device.

Notes

The authors are grateful to two anonymous referees for their detailed comments and suggestions. Eleuterio Vallelado acknowledges financial support from the Spanish Ministry of Education (ECO2011–29144-C03–01). Any errors are the responsibility of the authors.

1. For instance, the OECD obligates the members to improve their individual standards in the institutional, legal, and budgetary areas.
2. Diamond and He (2012) argue that short-term debt could increase debt overhang problems if volatility of the firm value is high, market leverage increases due to bearish stock markets or the firm is close to default.
3. These arguments are supported by Dewatripont and Tirole (1994) who hold that firms with highly concentrated ownership structures will issue bank debt because bank debt and the concentrated ownership structure are complementary elements in the design of an optimal corporate governance system.
4. Senator Paul Sarbanes and Representative Michael Oxley are the main creators of the proposal.
5. We have to recognize that the limited available information about bank debt, in general, and bank-debt maturity in particular, has significantly reduced the number of observations in some countries considered in this study. Nevertheless, the size of the firms' sample per country is representative of each country in terms of total assets and market capitalization.
6. This is the usual solution to working with variables that have non-negative and high-variance values.

References

Alcock, J., F. Finn and and K. J. K. Tan (2012) 'The determinants of debt maturity in Australian firms', *Accounting and Finance*, 52(2), 313–341.

Ang, J. S., R. A. Cole and J. W. Lin (2000) 'Agency costs and ownership structure', *The Journal of Finance*, 55(1), 81–106.

Bancel, F. and U. Mittoo (2004) 'Cross-country determinants of capital structure choice: A survey of European firms', *Financial Management*, 33(4), 103–132.

Barclay, M., L. Max and C. Smith (2003a) 'The joint determination of leverage and maturity', *Journal of Corporate Finance*, 9, 149–167.

Barclay, M., L. Max and C. Smith (2003b) 'The joint determination of leverage and maturity' *Journal of Corporate Finance*, 9(2), 149–167.

Bessler, W., W. Drobetz and M. Grüninger (2011) 'Information asymmetry and financing decisions', *International Review of Finance*, 11(1), 123–154.

Bharadwaj, A. and A. Shivdasani (2003) 'Valuation effects of bank financing in acquisitions', *Journal of Financial Economics*, 67, 113–148.

Billett, M., T. King and D. Mauer (2007) 'Growth opportunities and the choice of leverage, debt maturity, and covenants', *The Journal of Finance*, 62(2), 697–730.

Blackwell, D. and D. Kidwell (1988) 'An investigation of cost differences between public sales and private placement of debt', *Journal of Financial Economics*, 22, 253–278.

Chen, S., K. Ho and G. Yeo (1999) 'The determinants of debt maturity: The case of bank financing in Singapore', *Review of Quantitative Finance and Accounting*, 12, 341–350.

Cuñat, V. (1999) 'Determinantes del plazo de endeudamiento de las empresas españolas', *Investigaciones Económicas*, 23(3), 351–392.

Custódio, C., M. A. Ferreira and L. Laureano (2013) 'Why are US firms using more short-term debt?', *Journal of Financial Economics*, 108 (1), 182–212.

Dang, V. A. (2010) 'Leverage, debt maturity and firm investment: An empirical analysis', *Journal of Business Finance and Accounting*, 1–34.

Dang, V. A. (2011) 'Leverage, debt maturity and firm investment: An empirical analysis', *Journal of Business Finance and Accounting*, 38(1/2), 225–258.

De Andrés, P., V. Azofra and J. Rodríguez (2000) 'Endeudamiento, oportunidades de crecimiento y estructura contractual: un contraste empírico para el caso español', *Investigaciones Económicas*, 24(3), 641–679.

De Jong, A., M. Verbeek and P. Verwijmeren (2010) 'The impact of financing surpluses and large financing deficits on tests of the pecking order theory', *Financial Management (Blackwell Publishing Limited)*, 39(2), 733–756.

Demirgüç-Kunt, A. and V. Maksimovic (1999) 'Institutions, financial markets and firm's choice of debt maturity', *Journal of Financial Economics*, 54, 295–336.

Demirgüç-Kunt, A. and R. Levine (2001) 'Financial structure and economic growth: a cross-country comparison of banks, markets, and development', Massachusetts: Massachusetts Institute of Technology.

Demirgüç-Kunt, A. and V. Maksimovic (2002) 'Funding growth in bank-based and market-based financial systems: evidence from firm–level data', *Journal of Financial Economics*, 65, 337–363.

Demirgüç-Kunt, A., L. Laeven and R. Levine (2004) 'Regulations, market structure, institutions, and the cost of financial intermediation', *Journal of Money, Credit and Banking*, 36(3), 593–622.

Denis, D. and S. McKeon (2012) 'Debt financing and financial flexibility evidence from proactive leverage increases', *Review of Financial Studies*, 25(6), 1897–1929.

Denis, D. and V. Mihov (2003) 'The choice among bank debt, non-bank private debt and public debt: Evidence from new corporate borrowings', *Journal of Financial Economics*, 70, 3–28.

Dewatripont, M. and J. Tirole (1994) 'A theory of debt and equity: Diversity of securities and management–shareholders congruence', *Quarterly Journal of Economics*, 109(4), 1027–1054.

Diamond, D. W. and Z. He (2013) 'A theory of debt maturity: The long and short of debt overhang', *The Journal of Finance*, (forthcoming).

Douglas, A. (2009) 'Interactions between corporate agency conflicts', *The Financial Review*, 44(2), 151–178.

Fama, E. (1985) 'What's different about banks?', *Journal of Monetary Economics*, 15, 29–39.

Flannery, M. (1986) 'Asymmetric information and risky debt maturity choice', *Journal of Finance*, 41, 19–38.

Galai, D. and R. Masulis (1976) 'The option pricing model and the risk factor of stock', *Journal of Financial Economics*, 3, 53–81.

González, V. M. (2012) 'Determinants of debt maturity structure across firm size', Unpublished manuscript.

Gottesman, A. and G. Roberts (2004) 'Maturity and corporate loan pricing', *Financial Review*, 39(1), 55–77.

Goyal, V., K. Lehn and S. Racic (2002) 'Growth opportunities and corporate debt policy: the case of US defence industry', *Journal of Financial Economics*, 64, 35–59.

Guedes, J., and T. Opler (1996) 'The determinants of the maturity of corporate debt issues', *Journal of Finance*, 51, 1809–1833.

Harris, M. and A. Raviv (1990) 'Capital structure and the informational role of debt', *The Journal of Finance*, 45, 321–349.

Hawawini, G. and C. Viallet (2011) *Finance for executives: Managing for value creation*, (4th edition) Mason, OH: South-Western Cengage Learning.

Houston, J. F. and S. Venkataraman (1994) 'Optimal maturity structure with multiple debt claims', *The Journal of Financial and Quantitative Analysis*, 29(2), 179–197.

James, C. and D. Smith (2000) 'Are banks still special? New evidence on their role in the corporate capital-raising process', *Journal of Applied Corporate Finance*, 13(1), 52–63.

Jensen, M. (1986) 'Agency cost of free cash flow, corporate finance, and takeovers', *American Economic Review*, 72(6), 323–329.

Jensen, M. and W. Meckling (1976) 'Theory of the firm: managerial behaviour, agency cost and ownership structure', *Journal of Financial Economics*, 3(4), 305–360.

Johnson, S. (1997a) 'The effect of bank debt on optimal capital structure', *Financial Management*, 26(4), 47–56.

Johnson, S. (1997b) 'An empirical analysis of the determinants of corporate debt ownership structure', *The Journal of Financial and Quantitative Analysis*, 32(1), 47–69.

Kim, W. S. and E. H. Sorensen (1986) 'Evidence on the impact of the agency costs of debt on corporate debt policy', *The Journal of Financial and Quantitative Analysis*, 21(2), 131–144.

Korajczyk, R. and A. Levy (2003) 'Capital structure choice: Macroeconomic conditions and financial constraints', *Journal of Financial Economics*, 68, 75–109.

Krishnaswami, S., P. Spindt and V. Subramaniam (1999) 'Information asymmetry, monitoring, and the placement structure of corporate debt', *Journal of Financial Economics*, 51, 407–434.

La Porta, R., F. Lopez-de-Silanes, A. Shleifer and R. Vishny (1997) 'Legal determinants of external finance', *The Journal of Finance*, 52, 1131–1150.

La Porta, R., F. Lopez-de-Silanes, A. Shleifer and R. Vishny (1998) 'Law and finance', *The Journal of Political Economy*, 106(6), 1113–1155.

La Porta, R., F. Lopez-de-Silanes and A. Shleifer (1999) 'Corporate ownership around the world', *The Journal of Finance*, 54(2), 471–517.

La Porta, R., F. Lopez-de-Silanes and A. Shleifer (2002) 'Government Ownership of Banks', *The Journal of Finance*, 57(1), 265–301.

Lin, C., Y. Ma, P. Malatesta and Y. Xuan (2012) 'Corporate ownership structure and the choice between bank debt and public debt', Unpublished manuscript.

López, Ó., F. López and M. Santamaría (2007) 'Ownership structure, sharing of control and legal framework: International evidence', *Corporate Governance*, 15(16), 1130–1143.

Modigliani, F. and M. Miller (1958) 'The cost of capital, corporation finance and the theory of investment', *The American Economic Review*, 48(3), 261–297.

Modigliani, F. and E. Perotti (2000) 'Security markets versus bank finance: legal enforcement and investor protection', *International Review of Finance*, 1, 81–96.

Moon, D. and K. Tandon (2007) 'The influence of growth opportunities on the relationship between equity ownership and leverage', *Review of Quantitative Finance and Accounting*, 29, 339–351.

Myers, S. (1977) 'Determinants of corporate borrowing. *Journal of Financial Economics*, 5, 147–175.

Myers, S. and N. Majluf (1984) 'Corporate financing and investment decisions when firms have information that investors do not have', *Journal of Financial Economics*, 13, 187–221.

Ozkan, A. (2002) 'The determinants of corporate debt maturity: evidence from UK firms', *Applied Financial Economics*, 12(19–24).

Rauh, J. D. and A. Sufi (2010) 'Capital Structure and Debt Structure', *The Review of Financial Studies*, 23(12), 4242–4280.

Saona, P. and E. Vallelado (2005) 'Ownership structure and growth opportunities as determinants of bank debt: Evidence from Chilean companies', *Management Research*, 3(2), 119–134.

Saona, P. and E. Vallelado (2010) 'Is the use of bank debt as a governance mechanism conditioned by the financial system? The cases of Chile and Spain', *Applied Economics*, 42(13), 1709–1726.

Shleifer, A. and R. Vishny (1986) 'Large shareholders and corporate control', *The Journal of Political Economy*, 94(3, Part 1), 461–488.

Shleifer, A. and R. Vishny (1992) 'Liquidation values and debt capacity: A market equilibrium approach', *The Journal of Finance*, 47(4), 1343–1366.

Williamson, O. (1988) 'Corporate finance and corporate governance', *The Journal of Finance*, 43, 567–591.

Yafeh, Y. and O. Yosha (2003) 'Large shareholders and banks: Who monitors and how?', *Economic Journal*, 113, 128–146.

5
The Financing of Italian Firms and the Credit Crunch: Findings and Exit Strategies

Elisabetta Gualandri and Valeria Venturelli

5.1 Introduction

The second wave of the financial crisis – the sovereign debt crisis – which started in 2010, hit Italian banks hard, and since 2011 it has been causing a severe credit crunch for households and non-financial corporations.

The aim of the chapter is to analyse the way in which the credit crunch is leading to what has now become structural disintermediation within the banking channel, and has also modified the traditional bank–firm relationship. As a consequence of these factors, changes to the entire structure of the Italian financial system are required, in order to overcome serious intrinsic shortcomings in terms of instruments, markets and intermediaries.

This topic is important given the ongoing debate concerning the presence and nature of the credit crunch in Italy, since the availability of credit in Italy has decreased compared to similar European countries and credit has also become more expensive. This chapter is one of the first attempts to provide a clear measure of the credit crunch in Italy, as well as giving an overview of the potential tools that could facilitate access to finance for Italian SMEs.

To discuss these points, the chapter is organised as follows. The first part will analyse the characteristics of and current trends within Europe's main financial systems: those of Italy, France, Germany, the United Kingdom and Spain. The aim is to assess the extent to which the banking system is central to companies' financial strategies, with a focus on the different size categories. We then move on to briefly describe the impact of the crisis on the euro area credit markets, the process of fragmentation of the single financial market along national lines and the actions taken by the European Central Bank to combat this trend. The next step is to consider the trend in bank lending to non-financial corporations during the last few years for each of the main European countries, in order to assess the significance of financial constraints and the severity of any credit crunches. The findings reveal that in Italy, above all, there are clear signs of a credit crunch, affecting SMEs in particular.

The final step is to identify and discuss possible exit strategies for eliminating the credit crunch in Italy: one possible way of overcoming financial constraints is for firms to turn to the bond and equity markets, which would require the involvement of old and new categories of financial intermediaries (institutional investors, equity funds and venture capitalists); the emergence of new financial operators and vehicles (credit funds); private and public guarantees for the securitization of firms' loans; and new funding platforms (crowd funding). The changing role of banks in the new scenario is analysed as well as the characteristics that businesses will require to benefit from it.

The debate about possible exit strategies has been ongoing for some time in Italy. However, it is far from certain that they will be implemented, especially in the short term, due to delays in modernizing Italy's economic and financial system and in simplifying the complex bureaucratic machine. Other complicating factors include the excessively small size of Italian SMEs and their reluctance to open out to new venture capital investors.

5.2 The evolution of financial systems and the financial structure of non-financial companies in Europe

The last two decades have seen profound changes in the structures of the main financial systems, and in operators' financial behaviours. In financial literature (Thakor, 1996; Allen and Gale, 1999), the financial system of continental Europe has been described as a bank-based intermediation model, contrasting with the Anglo-Saxon model, in which flows of finance pass mainly through the financial markets. Theoretical and empirical literature is in no doubt about the implications of these two models, in terms of economic growth and the allocation and management of risks between operators. Bank-centred systems are considered to provide better inter-temporal distribution of risks (Allen and Gale, 1995) but are thought to be less effective in supporting new business ventures and technological innovations (Rajan and Zingales, 2003).

The development trends of the financial systems under consideration are analysed over the medium–long term, using the harmonized statistics produced by Eurostat financial accounts (1995–2011), with a focus on the structural changes reflected in the evolution of financial aggregates and balance-sheet structures for non-financial corporations in a number of key European countries: Italy, France, Germany, Spain and the United Kingdom.

Within the Italian financial system, the level of indebtedness for non-financial corporations continues to be lower than that of the other countries, with the sole exception of Germany. All countries show a slowdown in the indebtedness of non-financial corporations, with the financial intensity ratio, measured as the ratio of non-financial liabilities over GDP, falling from the peak recorded in 2007 (Table 5.1).

The financial surplus/deficit trend enables us to assess the extent of the imbalances arising from operators' real savings and investment decisions, and the effects of these imbalances on the creation of financial assets and investment trends. A net financial surplus or deficit indicates whether an institutional sector is tending to be a net lender or borrower, while an analysis of changes in the financial assets and liabilities structure enables us to assess to what extent financial investments and new loans originate from real imbalances or are merely reflecting the operator's tendency to focus on the financial dimensions of their balance sheets.

If we focus our attention on the trend in indebtedness of non-financial corporations, Italian firms consistently show a net financial deficit. In 2011 this deficit amounted to –2.1 per cent of GDP (Table 5.2).

An initial assessment of the way in which financial variables affect the operations of SMEs in the various countries surveyed can be made by examining firms' financial structures, considering both levels of debt (meaning their degree of dependence on external sources of finance) and the breakdown of borrowing from a technical view (including the type of intermediary involved). A greater or lesser degree of capitalization,

Table 5.1 Financial intensity ratio: non-financial corporations' financial liabilities/GDP (amount outstanding)

	1995	2000	2005	2007	2008	2009	2010	2011
Italy	1.55	2.13	2.19	2.32	2.34	2.30	2.28	2.18
France	1.90	3.60	3.34	3.95	3.14	3.59	3.66	3.43
Germany	1.36	1.90	1.77	1.92	1.72	1.87	1.89	1.81
Spain	1.63	2.70	3.31	3.81	3.31	3.37	3.34	3.12
United Kingdom	2.22	2.95	2.65	2.73	2.49	2.69	2.72	2.59

Source: Our processing of Eurostat financial accounts.

Table 5.2 Financial surplus/deficit of non-financial corporations (percentage of GDP)

	1995	2000	2005	2007	2008	2009	2010	2011
Italy	−3.8	−4.9	−3.6	−2.7	−4.9	−1.6	−2.1	−2.1
France	−1.9	−1.7	−1.9	−1.8	−2.9	−0.8	−0.9	−2.3
Germany	4.6	−5.0	1.4	10.8	−3.5	2.4	0.7	0.0
Spain	0.7	−4.3	−7.4	−11.5	−6.7	−0.4	1.6	1.1
United Kingdom	1.1	−1.0	2.3	2.1	2.8	3.3	4.7	4.1

Source: Our processing of Eurostat Financial Accounts.

varying levels of dependence on bank lending, and the prevalence of medium–long term loans, are all good indicators of SMEs' relationships with the financial system in the various countries, and these features also affect the economic soundness and growth prospects of firms.

During the period under consideration, the variation in the volumes of financial intermediation and the trend in net financial surpluses/deficits were accompanied by major changes in the composition of investors' financial portfolios. The breakdown of companies' sources of finance is illustrated with reference to total stocks of financial liabilities (Table 5.3).

If, within the institutional sectors, attention is focused on companies' financial structures, a number of important differences between the behaviour of Italian businesses and those of their European competitors emerge. European non-financial corporations show a clear preference for bank loans, especially in Spain and Italy, where on average loans account for more than 50 per cent of total financial liabilities. If we exclude unlisted shareholdings, the second largest item in terms of size is listed shares, the value of which reflects the trend on the stock market: in almost all countries except Germany, this item peaked in 2000 and fell drastically from 2008 onwards.

In Italy, specifically, bank lending is particularly important, accounting for almost 54 per cent of total financial liabilities at the end of the period; as a logical consequence, listed shares (11 per cent) and debt securities (4 per cent) are less significant for Italian firms. However, the increase in the proportion of debt securities recorded in all countries during 2008–2009, with the sole exception of Germany, should be underlined. Last but not least, the 'Other accounts payable/receivable' heading appears to account for a similar proportion of the financial liabilities of all non-financial corporations; in this case, it is in the United Kingdom that the item is least significant.

Table 5.3 Non-financial corporations: breakdown of liabilities^ (percentage composition)

		Debt Securities*	Loans	of which: short term loans/total loans	Listed shares	Insurance technical reserve	Other accounts (receivable/ payable)
Italy	1995	1.53	47.51	59.37	10.15	5.04	35.78
	2000	1.27	39.85	55.81	29.60	4.40	24.89
	2005	3.27	46.64	39.36	18.74	5.22	26.12
	2007	3.04	49.40	38.47	18.89	4.75	23.91
	2008	2.95	55.75	36.95	10.80	5.02	25.48
	2009	3.82	54.43	31.93	13.08	4.91	23.76
	2010	4.32	52.68	32.12	12.98	4.64	25.38
	2011	4.01	53.61	33.67	10.81	4.59	26.98
France	1995	8.82	42.71	21.10	18.79	0.00	29.68
	2000	7.91	30.62	27.65	40.56	0.00	20.91
	2005	8.99	35.76	29.90	33.29	0.00	21.96
	2007	6.63	36.15	28.80	36.09	0.00	21.14
	2008	7.96	43.75	28.15	23.96	0.00	24.33
	2009	9.28	39.99	26.83	27.49	0.00	23.24
	2010	9.73	38.87	26.75	27.86	0.00	23.53
	2011	10.43	40.24	26.74	24.19	0.00	25.14
Germany	1995	2.77	43.60	33.04	20.88	6.88	25.86
	2000	1.74	37.60	34.10	33.17	5.59	21.90
	2005	3.52	39.34	32.10	27.35	6.81	22.98
	2007	3.29	36.52	32.33	32.83	5.98	21.37
	2008	4.16	42.50	33.53	21.26	6.63	25.46
	2009	3.98	42.00	33.00	22.61	6.49	24.92
	2010	3.98	41.23	35.43	25.79	6.18	22.82
	2011	4.15	44.35	37.47	21.92	6.23	23.35
Spain	1995	n.d.	n.d.	n.d.	n.d.	n.d.	n.d.
	2000	1.43	41.49	24.33	25.33	0.51	31.24
	2005	0.58	49.27	20.11	20.52	0.10	29.53
	2007	0.48	51.94	17.61	21.57	0.00	26.00
	2008	0.56	59.61	16.69	14.45	0.00	25.39
	2009	0.61	61.14	13.34	15.51	0.00	22.74
	2010	0.56	61.57	12.49	14.55	0.00	23.32
	2011	0.64	62.80	11.70	12.77	0.00	23.79
UK	1997	7.33	24.71	62.15	59.62	0.00	8.34
	2000	9.78	23.85	53.47	60.18	0.00	6.19
	2005	12.47	35.11	53.22	46.42	0.00	6.00
	2007	12.03	37.15	59.40	45.40	0.00	5.41
	2008	13.02	47.85	59.03	33.26	0.00	5.87
	2009	14.06	39.97	56.40	40.59	0.00	5.38
	2010	11.67	39.19	54.92	43.94	0.00	5.20
	2011	n.d.	n.d.	n.d.	n.d.	n.d.	n.d.

^ Total liabilities are indicated net of: currency and deposits, derivatives, unlisted shares.

Source: Our processing of Eurostat financial accounts.

Further pointers can be derived from the prevalence, or otherwise, of medium–long term loans. There is a very high degree of variation in the duration of bank loans from country to country, reflecting the differences in the bank–firm relationships within the main systems examined. In Italy, where short-term indebtedness has always been the rule, during the last few years the balance of the financial structure has improved, with short-term borrowing accounting for little more than one third of total bank credit.

It is also worth assessing the differences in financial structure between the companies in different size categories. However, assessing European SMEs' forms of financing by size categories is highly problematical due to the differences in the ways financial statements are drafted in the various countries. Generally, the BACH harmonized database is the only reliable source for comparing the performance of European firms.[1] It provides the basis for an international comparison between companies in different size categories with the aid of information drawn above all from the national financial statement databases and surveys carried out by the main countries' central banks. When examining the main financial statement indicators of SMEs compared to companies in other size categories, it is important to remember that the BACH database's coverage of SMEs is much more limited than that of medium- and large-sized firms. In particular, within the small enterprises category it underestimates the number of extremely small businesses, which are also, generally, the most financially and economically fragile.

Table 5.A1 in the Appendix contains the main financial structure indicators for the various company size categories for 1999–2011, for the European countries under consideration.

For the period considered, except for the case of Germany, with regard to the capitalization indicator there are no substantial differences between the different size categories of company. It is interesting to note that small and medium Spanish enterprises have a higher degree of capitalization than the country's large companies. However, it should be remembered that the database used tends to underestimate the proportion of very small businesses, which normally have a much lower level of capitalization than other firms.

Bank indebtedness accounts for a significant proportion of small enterprises' financial liabilities, but this proportion decreases significantly as the firm's size increases. This is consistent with the tendency of large European corporations to make greater use of the bond market as an alternative to bank loans.

Last but not least, there is a very high degree of variation in the duration of bank loans from country to country, reflecting the differences in the bank–firm relationship in the main systems examined.

From this initial survey, it is quite clear that the structure of the financial system varies from country to country, with banks paying the central role in financing non-financial corporations, especially those of smaller size: this applies in particular to Italy, Spain and Germany. This makes it particularly important to investigate the way in which the crisis, and especially the sovereign debt crisis, has impacted on firms' ability to finance their operations, categorizing borrowers by company size, where possible.

5.3 The crisis and the credit market in the euro area

During the first few years of its existence, the euro area witnessed a growing convergence of the different member states' financial markets, in the progression towards a single financial market. However, since the beginning of the crisis, and especially the sovereign debt phase, the euro area has experienced the opposite trend, with severe fragmentation of the single financial market along national lines.

Since the onset of the sovereign debt crisis, in the peripheral states – Greece, Portugal and Ireland and then, since summer 2011, Spain and Italy – the credit markets have become strongly differentiated, with disparities from country to country in the growth of lending and the cost of credit.

Figure 5.1 describes the growth in lending since 2010 for non-financial corporations and households in selected euro area countries. For non-financial corporations the divergence of growth in lending has increased since 2012: the trend is a negative one for Greece, Ireland, Portugal and Italy, and is particularly severe for Spain; it is slightly positive for Germany and France; and it is positive for the Netherlands.

The cost of bank financing is different between the various countries, with an increasing level of divergence. An analysis of lending rates in the euro area (Neri, 2013) reveals that for non-financial corporations the standard deviation of interest rates on loans increased only slightly during the first phase of the crisis, from 0.6 percentage points (2003–summer 2007) to 0.7 (September 2007–April 2010), but rose to 1.4 percentage points during the sovereign debt crisis. In this phase the variation in the cost of new loans reflected a strong correlation between lending rates and sovereign spreads.

One clear indication of the fragmentation of the credit markets comes from the differentials in the cost of credit for corporations between

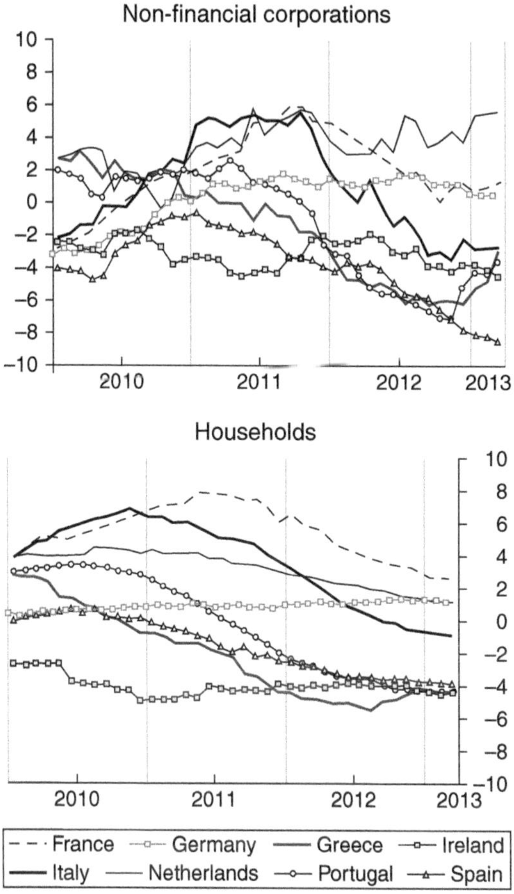

Figure 5.1 Lending[1] by borrower sector (12-month percentage change)

Note: Loans in euros and other currencies granted by monetary financial institutions, adjusted for the accounting effects of securitizations

Source: Banca d'Italia 2013, Annual Report 2012, Figure 7.6.

peripheral and core countries. Interest rates on loans to businesses, which until 2011 were more or less the same in Italy (about 5 per cent) and Germany (about 4.7 per cent) have since strongly diverged: in 2013, German corporations are financing their operations on average at a cost of 3 per cent, as are those in France, while both Italian and Spanish corporations are paying rates of more than 6 per cent.

The trend in the differentials in interest rates on bank loans to firms, between Italy and the euro area, is depicted in Figure 5.2.

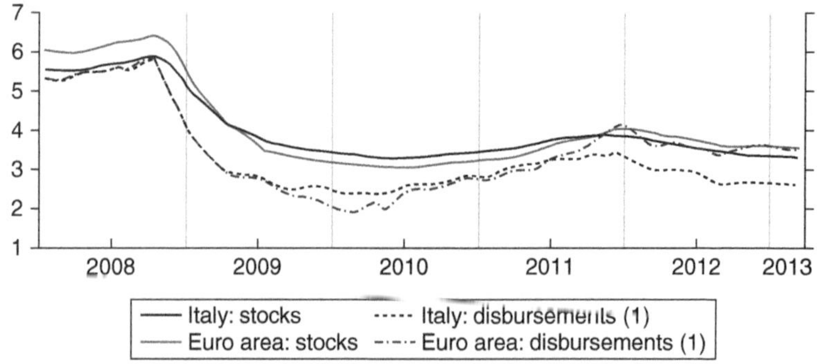

Figure 5.2 Interest rates on bank loans to firms (monthly data/per cent)

Source: Banca d'Italia 2013, Annual Report 2012, Figure 14.9 a.

(1) New transactions other than current accounts.

The negative effects of this financial fragmentation are particularly damaging for SMEs: the interest rate differential between new small and large (over one million euro) loans in 2012 averaged about 150 basis points, compared to about 80 during 2003–2009 (Banca d'Italia, 2013b: 78). In 2012–2013 the divergence in interest rate differentials between peripheral and core countries is particularly high: it is 2.3 percentage points in Spain but just one point in France (Draghi, 2013).

In a single currency area, domestic markets that are severely fragmented along national lines hamper the transmission of monetary policy and are an obstacle to the communication of uniform messages across the economies of the various states. The use of non-standard monetary policy instruments by the European Central Bank (ECB), which started in 2011 and 2012 – the securities market programme (SMP), the long-term refinancing operations (LTROs) and the announced introduction of outright monetary transactions (OMTs) – and the transfusion of large amounts of liquidity into the market, have all been intended to restore the proper transmission of monetary policy in the financial market (Draghi, 2012).

Italian banks have made ample use of the refinancing on offer from the ECB, especially the LTROs of December 2011 and February 2013, and have received about 25 per cent of all the funds granted. In spite of this, and notwithstanding official interest rates which have been gradually reduced to levels close to zero, Italian banks' lending volumes and the interest rates charged are being adversely affected by a number of key factors: initially, from 2011, these were the credit squeeze and the higher cost of borrowing on the markets due to the sovereign risk and the tightening of capital ratios (Cosma and Gualandri, 2012). Since 2012, other factors related to the increased risk level within the economy, due to the seriousness of the ongoing recession, have made their effects felt: in Italy, GDP fell by seven percentage points in real terms between 2007 and 2012, while industrial output slumped by 25 per cent. This triggered a considerable rise in the rate of non-performing loans (NPLs), especially of defaults, and a decrease in the coverage ratio (provisions for NPLs in relation to NPLs), leading to the need for additional large provisions to cover bad debts. The rate of NPLs rose from 4.5 per cent at the end of 2007 to 12.3 per cent in June 2012, while during the same period the coverage ratio fell from 49.4 per cent to 37.7 per cent (Banca d'Italia 2013a and 2013b). In 2102, the Bank of Italy (Banca d'Italia, 2013c) performed in-depth checks, with on-site supervision, on the country's 20 biggest banks (except for the two largest), which led to higher provisions for default and raised the coverage ratio, for the sample of positions analysed, from 31 per cent on 30 September 2012 to 43.5 per cent on 31 December 2012. These checks continued in 2013 and led to further provisions.[2]

In the meantime, the introduction of Basel III, and in particular the new rules regarding capital adequacy, liquidity and stable funding, have produced further pressures on Italian banks. Moreover, the higher risk associated with the present economic conditions, as described above, has created a bias towards investments in national government bonds, which is also due to their eligibility for ECB refinancing.

The final result of this situation is the emergence of a severe credit crunch. Banks have implemented strict creditworthiness assessment procedures, with strong rationing to low-rated firms, and an increase in the cost of lending to cover the increased risk pricing (Cosma and Gualandri, 2014), as we will see in the next section.

5.4 Italian firms: financial constraints and the credit crunch

In view of the banks' centrality in supporting the financial structures of companies, we now focus more closely on an analysis of bank lending flows (Figure 5.3), in particular from 2008 onwards, when the credit crunch became widespread.

In actual fact, the negative trend in credit flows is also linked to demand factors, as can be seen from the trend in investments (that in

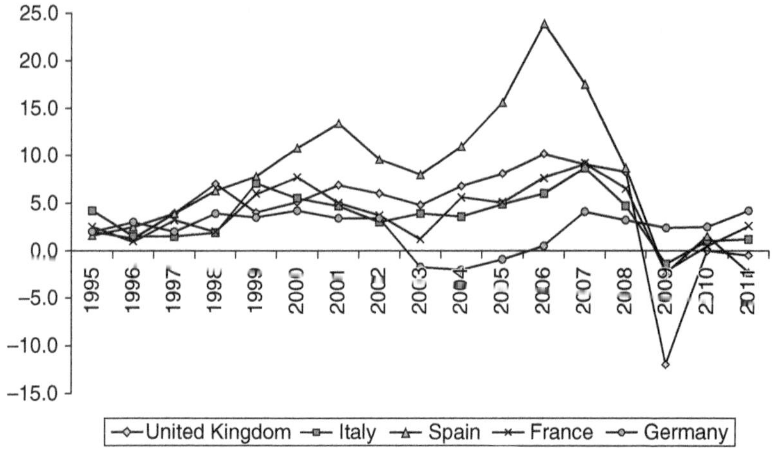

Figure 5.3 Bank lending flows/GDP

Source: Our processing of Eurostat – financial accounts.

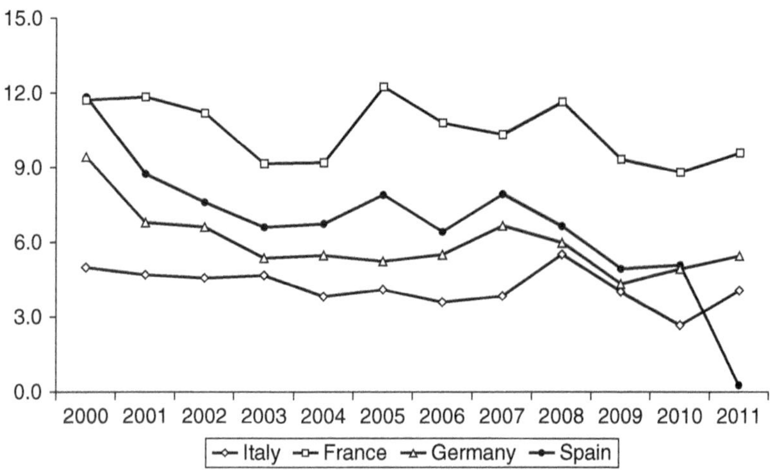

Figure 5.4 Corporate investment trends in Europe (as a percentage of total balance sheet)

Source: Our processing of BACH data set.

this case includes all investments in tangible and intangible fixed assets, in relation to the balance sheet total), which slowed dramatically from 2008 onwards and remained at very low levels, at least for the following two years, in all countries (Figure 5.4).

The extent of financial constraints for the various size categories of company and concerns about the difficulty in accessing finance can be analysed with the aid of the six-monthly 'Survey on the access to finance of SMEs in the euro area' (SAFE) conducted by the European Central Bank. The data presented in the report was collected through a survey of companies in the euro area. The companies in the sample were selected randomly from the Dun & Bradstreet database of firms. The sample was stratified by firm size, area of business and country. The total euro area sample size was 7,510 firms, of which 6,960 had fewer than 250 employees. Table 5.4 enables us to evaluate the importance of 'access to finance' as a key concern.

For the majority of countries, 'access to finance' as a concern peaked in 2009H2; after that it declined or remained stable for most euro area SMEs, except for Italy, where recently, in 2012H1 this concern peaked at a level even higher than in 2009H2. Moreover, for Italy the situation improved in the last period surveyed for all size classes except small firms, for which it peaked during that period. In absolute terms, access to finance is a matter that is of greatest concern to Spanish SMEs, closely followed by Italian SMEs.[3]

Financing constraints therefore appear to be particularly tight for Italian firms (De Mitri et al., 2013). Similar indications are obtained from an assessment of the net percentage of respondents reporting an increase (+) or decrease (–) in their need for bank loans over the preceding six months (Table 5.5).

Regarding needs for external financing in all the largest euro area countries, except for Germany, on balance, SMEs reported an increased need for bank loans, particularly during the second half of 2009. The net percentage of SMEs reporting an increased need was especially high in Spain and even more so in Italy, which may be linked to the high net percentage of SMEs in Italy reporting a steep decline in profitability.

On balance, SMEs in all the euro area countries show a (in some cases considerable) deterioration in the availability of bank loans (in the form of new loans or the renewal of existing ones). For all the periods (Table 5.6), Spanish SMEs report the lowest availability, with French SMEs experiencing fewest problems until 2010. From 2010H2 the net percentage of French SMEs reporting a deterioration in the availability of bank loans increased. In Italy the situation partially improved from 2010H1 until 2011H2 and then deteriorated drastically. The net percentage of German SMEs reporting a deterioration in the availability of bank loans significantly decreased from 2010H1 onwards.

Table 5.4 Percentage of firms reporting 'access to finance' as their principal concern

		2009H1	2009H2	2010H1	2010H2	2011H1	2011H2	2012H1	2012H2
Italy									
Large			18.2	14.4	15.5	17.1	27.5	19.9	15.0
SMEs		14.7	20.4	13.7	16.1	14.2	19.0	23.4	18.4
	Micro	19.8	19.6	12.7	14.7	13.2	17.2	24.6	16.6
	Small	9.6	22.4	17.7	19.7	16.9	21.7	20.5	22.4
	Medium	2.7	20.1	10.7	15.4	13.8	22.4	22.9	19.9
Total			20.0	13.8	15.9	14.8	20.8	22.7	17.7
France									
Large			5.1	10.7	4.2	11.4	18.4	11.1	9.6
SMEs		18.6	11.4	12.2	13.0	16.1	13.4	13.2	13.1
	Micro	19.3	16.5	15.5	18.1	22.7	15.2	13.8	14.5
	Small	15.3	7.0	12.5	13.3	13.5	13.0	14.0	11.8
	Medium	21.7	9.0	6.8	5.2	9.6	11.1	11.4	11.9
Total			8.8	11.6	9.5	14.3	15.4	12.4	11.8
Germany									
Large			13.9	7.1	8.5	6.3	2.8	11.3	8.4
SMEs		15.3	18.1	11.2	12.0	11.0	11.0	9.5	8.5
	Micro	11.5	22.6	13.1	12.5	9.6	13.8	12.0	10.7
	Small	18.9	15.5	13.9	14.0	14.1	10.2	10.1	7.4
	Medium	15.4	16.1	6.5	9.2	9.2	8.9	6.4	7.3
Total			16.5	9.7	10.6	9.2	8.0	10.2	8.4
Spain									
Large			24.7	21.6	19.3	15.3	25.6	25.8	21.1
SMEs		26.0	34.1	23.3	25.0	24.4	29.2	27.2	25.1
	Micro	22.1	30.6	23.8	22.9	25.0	30.5	26.5	23.9
	Small	28.2	39.7	23.5	27.6	21.8	27.0	29.1	27.1
	Medium	33.0	34.9	21.4	26.9	26.7	28.5	26.2	25.9
Total			31.7	22.8	23.5	22.1	28.3	26.8	24.0

Source: Our processing of microdata/dataset from the 'Survey on the access to finance of SMEs in the euro area' (SAFE).

Table 5.5 SMEs' need for bank loans: net percentage of respondents reporting an increase (+) or decrease (–) over the preceding 6 months

	2009 H1 (%)	2009 H2 (%)	2010 H1 (%)	2010 H2 (%)	2011 H1 (%)	2011 H2 (%)	2012 H1 (%)	2012 H2 (%)
Germany	9	13	0	0	–3	1	–6	–4
Spain	12	19	6	6	5	8	4	5
France	6	7	1	16	12	8	10	6
Italy	19	28	8	12	12	19	15	12

Source: Our processing of microdata/data set from the 'Survey on the access to finance of SMEs in the euro area' (SAFE).

Table 5.6 Availability of bank loans: net percentage of respondents reporting an increase (+) or decrease (–) over the preceding six months

	2009 H1 (%)	2009 H2 (%)	2010 H1 (%)	2010 H2 (%)	2011 H1 (%)	2011 H2 (%)	2012 H1 (%)	2012 H2 (%)
Germany	–24	–32	–8	–2	–6	–1	–1	7
Spain	–51	–48	–16	–20	–17	–26	–30	–17
France	–19	–14	–2	–13	–14	–19	–21	–18
Italy	–26	–29	–6	1	–9	–27	–27	–7

Source: Our processing of microdata/data set from the 'Survey on the access to finance of SMEs in the euro area' (SAFE).

Turning to the Italian situation, Figure 5.5 confirms the results of the survey.

During the period bank lending has been contracting at a similar pace among all sizes of firm. Access to credit continues to be tighter for smaller businesses, since their capacity to tap alternative sources of finance is lower; medium-sized and large firms deal with the credit squeeze by means of large bond issues. Signs of a credit crunch can be inferred from the high percentage of smaller firms declaring that they have not obtained the credit requested (Figure 5.6).

Figure 5.6 shows the percentage of manufacturing firms reporting that they have applied to a bank or financial company for credit within the last three months and have been refused. From the graph it is clear that access to credit continues to be tighter for smaller businesses. The percentage of the latter declaring that they had not obtained the credit requested was considerably higher than in the larger size classes.

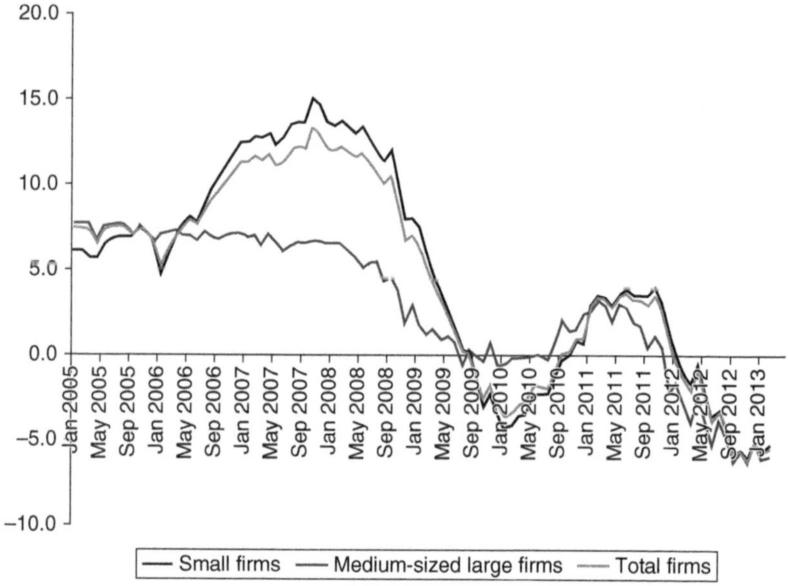

Figure 5.5 Access to credit of Italian firms in relation to firm size (3 month percentage variations)

Source: Banca d'Italia, Financial Stability Report No. 5, April 2013.

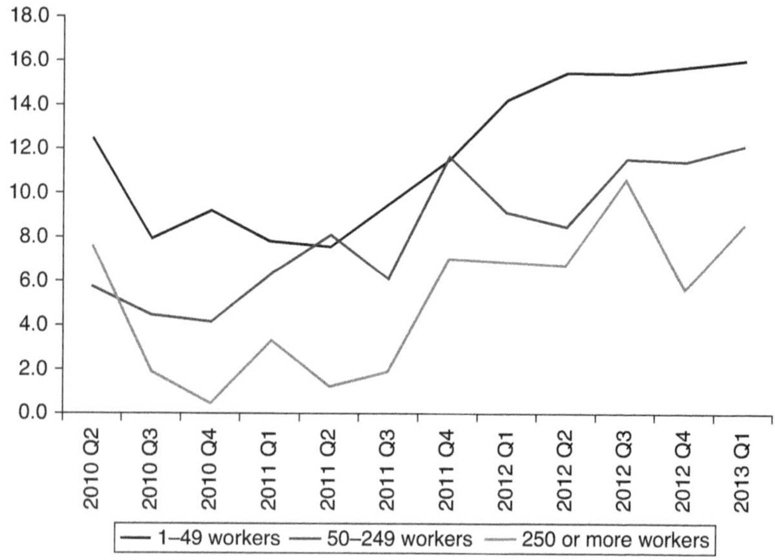

Figure 5.6 Proportion of credit-rationed firms (per cent)

Source: Banca d'Italia, Financial Stability Report no. 5, April 2013.

Another important point is the cost of funding for the different categories of firms. Figure 5.7 describes the trend in interest rates on banks' loans to firms in Italy by firm size and area of business. It clearly emerges that SMEs, especially those in manufacturing, are paying an increasingly higher cost than larger corporations.

In contrast with previous years, the reduction of bank credit has affected not only companies in fragile financial conditions, but also those with sounder balance sheets (Table 5.7); for the latter companies the reduction largely, but not entirely, reflects the replacement of credit with bond issues. Small firms felt the effects of credit restrictions the most.

The analysis therefore reveals signs of a credit crunch not only for SMEs but also for sound corporations, perhaps indicating a structural problem within the Italian banking system, where intermediaries may

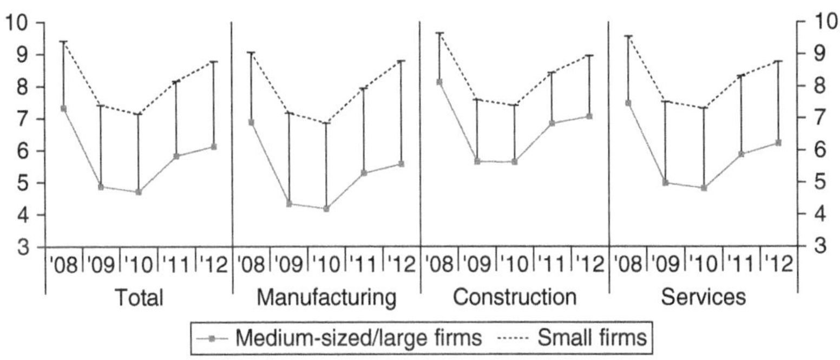

Figure 5.7 Interest rates on loans in relation to firm size (percent)
Source: Banca d'Italia 2013, Annual Report 2012, Figure 14.9.

Table 5.7 Trends in lending in relation to creditworthiness^ of firms, in Italy: 12-month percentage change

	Sound (%)	**Vulnerable** (%)	**Risky** (%)
Dec 2010	4.1	1.5	–6.5
Dec 2011	4.1	1.0	–5.4
Dec 2012	–3.1	–1.7	–7.2

^ The data refer to a sample of some 340,000 firms, distributed among the different risk classes on the basis of to their Z-scores (assigned by CERVED on the basis of a number of balance-sheet indicators). Firms are defined as 'sound' with Z-scores of 1 (high safety), 2 (safety), 3 (high solvency), and 4 (solvency); 'vulnerable' with Z-scores of 5 (vulnerability) and 6 (high vulnerability); and 'risky' with Z-scores of 7 (risk), 8 (high risk) and 9 (very high risk).

Source: Banca d'Italia, Financial Stability Report No. 5, April 2013.

be less specialized and not sufficiently equipped to assess the creditworthiness of companies, especially those operating in the most innovative sectors.

The crisis should finally provide the opportunity for the opening up new channels of financing, as an alternative to bank credit.

5.5 The exit strategies

In many European countries the restoration of a satisfactory flow of financing to firms, especially SMEs, is the essential precondition for escaping from the current recession. Alternative, non-traditional bank lending strategies are at the centre of the debate and of policy makers' attention, at both the national and the international levels. Italy is a special case for a number of reasons: the particularly high importance of bank lending, the relative underdevelopment of a number of elements of the financial system affecting firms' ability to access capital markets, high level of commercial credits outstanding in companies' favour from government bodies at all levels, and, last but not least, difficulties for banks arising from a sharp increase in NPLs and the consequent need for higher loan provisions, in a situation of squeezed margins.

Given this situation, it must be taken as read that in the short term the Italian banking system is not capable of restoring the flow of credit that companies need. Thus, it is clear that the slackening of financial constraints for firms, and for SMEs in particular, will have to pass through alternative channels, as the July 2013 IMF mission also stated. Therefore, supported by a wide-ranging debate, the policy makers[4] have been focusing for some time on measures designed to develop these channels, including tailor-made legislation. Some actions have already been taken and others are in the pipeline.

One initial measure is the repayment of the public sector's debt to Italian businesses, estimated at around 90–100 billion euro. In the last few years, the excessive public sector deficit was one of the main causes for the delay in these repayments. Repayments have now been scheduled over two or three years and this has been made possible, above all, by Italy's exit in June 2013 from the infraction procedure for excessive public sector deficit (the country has been below the critical 3 per cent deficit/GDP ratio since the start of 2013).

Below we offer an overview of the financial channels which may be used as an alternative, or in addition, to bank lending and the measures intended to encourage their development. We will then provide a more detailed discussion of the opportunities and obstacles relating to the birth and expansion of the bond market for SMEs (corporate bonds and securities generated through the securitization of credit to SMEs).

1. Bond market. The Italian government's 'Decree for Growth' (Decree Law 83/2012, art. 32) eliminated a number of fiscal and other constraints which discouraged the issue of corporate bonds by unlisted firms. The decree is related to the so-called 'mini bonds', or financing bills/commercial papers (CP) at 1–36 months (previously 3–12), and bonds with duration of at least 36 months. It envisages the involvement of a sponsor intermediary to provide assistance to issuers, market making and liquidity, and to certify the firm's latest financial statements and place the bonds with 'qualified investors' (as defined by art. 100 of the Consolidation Law on Financial Institutions). The issuer is able to benefit from a number of tax breaks typical of corporate bonds, and write off the interest paid against tax. The first issues by unlisted medium–large firms were large in size and in some cases acted as drivers for subsequent take-overs, as in the case of Cerved, acquired by CVC funds in February 2013. There are still significant barriers to the issue of instruments of this kind by smaller-sized firms, due to problems on both the demand and the supply sides, to be described in greater detail below.
2. The 'Fondo di Centrale di Garanzia (FCG)', or SME guarantee facility. The FCG has been in operation for more than ten years and is a public facility, backed up by government guarantees, which provides guarantees to banks and intermediaries on lending to financially sound SMEs in all areas of business. Since 2009 it has been beefed up through an increase in government resources and the gradual expansion of the categories of eligible beneficiaries to include firms in temporary difficulty (Bartiloro et al., 2012). However, many operators are unaware of its existence and it is underused. One possible way of extending its operations would be to enable the FCG to provide guarantees to investors in corporate bonds: this might encourage foreign investors, now already interested in the mini bond business, to increase their involvement in Italy.
3. Cassa Depositi e Prestiti (CDP). The CDP ('Bank for Savings and Loans') is a joint stock corporation principally owned by the Ministry of the Economy and Finance (MEF) (80.1 per cent) and by a group of banking foundations (18.4 per cent). Most deposits are in the form of post office savings accounts. Since 2009 it has been providing medium–long term loans to SMEs through the banking channel, in accordance with clearly defined ceilings; with other private investors, it established a private equity fund for SMEs (Fondo Italiano

d'Investimento) in 2010. Its operations to support SMEs could be reinforced both through participation in funds with the specific mission of investing in bonds issued by SMEs, or similar securitized instruments, and through the provision of guarantees on these securities.

4. The European Investment Bank (EIB) and the European Investment Fund (EIF). Lines of intervention are in operation on specific EU programmes to aid SMEs: loans, guarantees and equity financing. For the medium and long term (2014–2020 programme), the European Commission (EC) has put forward proposals for a new generation of both short and medium–long term financial instruments for SMEs, also involving loans, guarantees and equity financing. Italy's level of use of these facilities is relatively low compared to France and Germany and it is in this area that action is necessary in the immediate term. The European Commission and the EIB are also working on risk sharing instruments (European Commission and the European Investment Bank Group, 2013). The aim is to combine the lending capacity of the EIB and the EIF, as well as resources from national promotional banks, in order to finance special activities in EU priority areas (Draghi, 2013). Another hypothesis is the purchase of asset-backed securities by the EC and the EIB, with the added aim of revitalizing the market through these instruments.
5. Securitization and covered bonds to guarantee bank lending to SMEs. The aim is to revitalize a market which has traditionally been underdeveloped in Italy, but which has also been seriously penalized in other euro area countries by the subprime crisis. At the European level, there is the need for regulation of the factors that are hindering the recovery of the ABS market; this can be achieved through measures which promote transparent, useful securitization to benefit companies in general, including SMEs. The aim is to establish a uniform framework with other instruments, with regard to aspects such as risk, rating and duration (Draghi, 2013). In terms of these instruments, two aspects require monitoring in the immediate term: first, the scope for banks to use them for refinancing with the ECB. In the case of Italy, the second aspect is the provision of a specific system of guarantees which encourage institutional investors to buy bonds the underlying instruments of which are bank loans to small and medium enterprises. In Italy, work is under way on a proposal to amend the law on securitization (which dates back to 1999), in order to favour the development of instruments of this kind.
6. New credit intermediaries. The reference here is to credit funds, widely developed in a number of contexts, including the USA. These

funds provide credit to SMEs, subject to due diligence, and then securitize the credit for retail sale. The capital for the funds would have to be underwritten by institutional investors. Typically, credit funds form part of the shadow banking system, and before they can be introduced, legislation is required to establish the relevant regulatory perimeter. Legislation is currently being drafted on this, and if approved quickly it could have a high impact on the financing of businesses, by directing institutional deposits towards this area.

7. Venture capital and private equity. The Italian asset management industry is underdeveloped in general and in particular with regard to specialist vehicles for financing SMEs. This situation is partly explained by the fact that many small Italian companies are family owned, and by the extreme reluctance of family-based enterprises to open up their equity structures to outside investors. Another reason is companies' traditional high degree of dependence on bank lending: although the bank–firm relationship has been severely weakened during the last few years. In order to overcome this impasse, actions of various kinds are required: by policy makers, in order to introduce tax breaks to encourage institutional investors (problematical due to the parlous condition of government finances); by banks and other intermediaries, the CDP and the banking foundations, in order to promote specialist vehicles for financing SMEs; and by banks, to provide services that assist companies in their entry into the market, alongside their traditional lending operations. However, none of this will be effective unless firms accept the need to open up their ownership structures to outside investors.
8. Institutional investors. Compared to other countries, in Italy the role of institutional investors in the acquisition of corporate equity is very low. One of the reasons is firms' chronic reluctance to open up their equity capital to outside investors; significant cultural change is required in this area. The reinforcement of this role, to be achieved first and foremost through regulatory changes, could have a major impact for unlisted companies in the medium term, especially through the investment of the technical reserves of insurance companies. Amendments to the regulations of their supervisory body, the IVASS, to allow this are currently on the drawing board.
9. Crowdfunding. Italy was the first European country to adopt specific legislation for the development of crowdfunding platforms (Decree Law No. 179 of 18 October 2012, known as the Growth Decree 2.0). This was followed by Resolution No. 18592 dated 26 June 2013, issued by the Italian Stock Exchange Regulator (Consob), this regulation

covers equity crowdfunding (the raising of venture capital by innovative start-ups using online portals). These platforms are still in their infancy in Italy compared to other countries, but in the light of the new regulatory framework, the potential for the raising of venture capital for innovative start-ups is high.

Table 5.A2 in the Appendix summarises the main aims of the instruments/actions described above and specifies their implementation status and possible short term impact in reducing the credit crunch.

The majority of these actions (some of which still only exist on paper at the time of writing) aim to overcome the acknowledged weak points of the Italian financial system by aiming to extend the structure and complexity of markets, intermediaries and instruments, first and foremost in order to develop capital markets for SMEs, previously neglected due to the preference for traditional bank credit (Banca d'Italia, 2013b).

Below, we will assess the actions proposed for the development of equity and bond markets for SMEs, identifying the main obstacles and the specific actions to be introduced to overcome them. We will also outline the role that banks may play in establishing this bank–company–market linkage which, at present, is seriously lacking within the Italian banking system.

With the introduction of the new legislation (the so-called Decree for Growth described in point 5, at the beginning of this section) covering the issue of commercial papers and corporate bonds by unlisted firms, the volume of bonds issued by companies in this class has grown considerably. However, this only applies to medium–large firms. Mini bonds alone are unable to solve the problem of financing flow for smaller firms, the connective tissue of the Italian economy, due to factors affecting both the demand and the supply, which require precise measures to be implemented by a variety of players: firms, intermediaries and policy makers.

Supply

- *Obstacles*. The prerequisites for the issue of mini bonds actually exclude a large number of small firms: joint stock company status, turnover in excess of 2 million euro, rating, and financial statements certified by an auditing firm. With regard to this, a relevant negative factor is the high level of opaqueness of Italian SMEs, which is unlike anything found in other European countries.
- *Development actions*. The smaller-sized companies that are all-important to the Italian economy must realize that bank credit is a scarce resource and will continue to be so in the near future, and that they must therefore start to do everything needed to access the bond market,

by meeting the requirements set out above – especially the auditing of financial statements and the assignment of a credit rating.

Demand

- *Obstacles*. Mini bonds may only be purchased by 'qualified' investors, but in Italy there are very few investors that specialize in this type of security. Investors are generally in search of liquid securities, with credit ratings and low information-gathering costs, all lacking when the bonds that are issued by SMEs are generally smaller than the average of their European competitors. Therefore, mini bonds issued by most Italian SMEs will not be tempting for institutional investors, due to both their low liquidity and the high information costs involved.
- *Development actions*.
  - Creation of funds with the specific mission of investing in mini bonds. Some banks (e.g. Mediobanca) have already done this.
  - More active approach by Italian institutional investors. Some sectors are less developed in Italy than in other countries (e.g. pension funds). Regulatory measures would be beneficial to allowing these investors, especially insurance companies, to draw on their technical reserves in order to increase their investments in securities issued by unlisted firms.
  - Active role of the CDP and banking foundations in the creation of funds specifically to be invested in mini bonds and for direct investment.
  - Active role of banks in facilitating SMEs' access to the markets.
  - A segment of Borsa Italiana, ExtraMOT Pro, for the bonds and financing bills of unlisted companies, has been in operation since February 2013.

The possible role of banks requires more in-depth discussion. The development of the corporate bond market opens out excellent opportunities for banks in the advisory, underwriting and placement areas. The fees generated by these activities could potentially make a significant contribution to intermediation margins at this time of declining profitability. This requires the development of specific skills only rarely found in Italian banks. It should also be remembered that while on the one hand the development of these activities will help to restore the bank–firm relationship as part of the bank–company–market circuit, on the other hand there is the risk that the banks may be crowded out: the most suitable firms for bond issue projects are the ones with the best ratings, which are currently also the most desirable for bank loan operations.

Further, complementary actions should also be considered with regard to market instruments to simplify SMEs' access to financing. First and foremost, this means the revitalization of the ABS market, to allow the rating of products deriving from banks' securitization of tranches of SME loans. The creation of credit funds may also play an important role in the future.

5.6 Conclusions and recommendations

Our analysis reinforces the finding that in Italy the credit available to the real economy is insufficient in terms not only of quantity but also of quality. Italian firms' heavy reliance on bank credit compared to their international competitors means that the effects of the credit crunch are even more acute. This situation is affecting the types of firms which have the greatest difficulty in accessing alternative financing channels: the smallest companies, and consequently innovative firms as well; such firms have difficulty in demonstrating their financial sustainability and are therefore considered ineligible for bank credit even at normal times, especially in the initial stages of their life cycles. The situation is rendered even more dramatic by the recent indications of credit rationing in relation to companies with sound credit ratings.

The higher requirements imposed by Basel III on capital adequacy and also the introduction of liquidity ratios only partially justify this trend: structural factors peculiar to the Italian banking system have to be considered (Onado, 2013). In fact, while on the one hand the Italian banking system reacted better than those of other countries during the initial phase of the financial crisis (Venturelli, 2012) and proved itself to be relatively robust, on the other hand the persistence of the crisis is revealing structural problems within it, including increasing difficulty in distinguishing between creditworthy firms and the rest, and sustaining the growth of businesses. The reasons for the situation lie a long way back, when the restructuring of the Italian banking system led to the disappearance of institutions which specialized in assessing companies' financial soundness and investment prospects.

The whole scenario is aggravated by the continuing failure to develop channels of financing other than bank credit. The crisis has revealed the underdevelopment of the Italian financial market, the insufficient role of institutional investors, the embryonic state of the corporate bond markets and the virtual non-existence of CP markets; however, it could finally provide the opportunity for the development of these channels. This need is so pressing that when the EU confirmed the ending of the infraction procedure against Italy for the exceeding of deficit limits, its concluding recommendations included support for the creation of non-banking channels of financing.

Possible alternative sources include the new mini bond market, which requires three things if it is to take off as required: a higher level of financial disclosure by SMEs, investors interested in purchasing bonds of mini value, and a regulatory context that facilitates the process. With regard to the first factor, the decrease of the level of opaqueness also requires a cultural and managerial change among SMEs. Regarding the second factor, the CDP and many Italian banks and asset management firms are working to create specialized funds tasked with investing in mini bonds, which will therefore be able to indirectly finance Italian companies. Finally, new legislation for the creation of credit funds is needed. In more general terms, a solution is required to the problem of how to place the huge financing potential of the other institutional investors, especially the insurance companies, at the service of the real economy.

In view of the complexity and variety of the measures and instruments which must be brought into play in an approach of cooperation rather than competition, the directing role of the national policy makers (the Ministry for Economy and Finance (MEF) and the Ministero per lo Sviluppo Economico/Ministry of Economic Development (MISE)) is essential, and they will need to draw on the experience of the various foreign states where the different systems have been used most successfully in the past.

A number of countries have already implemented schemes of this kind. France established the Banque publique d'investissement, in 2012, which coordinates all programmes aimed at providing credit to small companies; more recently, it launched a proposal for further extending the finance to SMEs from insurance companies: it is estimated that the current 216 billion euro (30 more than in 2008) could be increased by a further 90 billion.

In some cases, these measures also need to link up effectively with those implemented by the European Commission and supranational organisations. Finally, the ECB's strategy on the characteristics that ABS and covered bonds are required to meet in order to be eligible for refinancing will also be highly significant.

We must always bear in mind that the specific situation of the Italian financial, economic and political systems could delay or impede the implementation and the effective working of the exit strategies. In particular, critical factors are the extremely small size of Italian SMEs, their opaqueness and their reluctance to accept risk capital injections; the delay in the modernization of the financial system and the simplification of the country's extremely complex bureaucracy; and banks' difficulties in adapting their business and lending model to the current economic and financial context.

Appendix

Table 5.A1 Breakdown of liabilities of European firms by size class

		Small	Medium	Large	Total
Capital and reserves as % of (liabilities + capital + reserves)					
Italy	2000	24.9	24.5	28.4	27.2
	2005	25.1	26.9	29.3	28.4
	2007	24.6	26.1	28.8	27.9
	2008	30.0	29.2	29.8	29.7
	2009	31.3	31.1	30.5	30.7
	2010	30.2	30.9	31.4	31.2
	2011	30.2	30.9	30.8	30.8
France	2000	32.1	30.9	24.6	27.1
	2005	32.0	33.5	31.4	31.9
	2007	31.5	33.4	32.2	32.3
	2008	31.6	33.7	30.2	31.0
	2009	32.4	33.6	30.5	31.3
	2010	32.7	33.6	32.8	32.9
	2011	31.0	33.8	31.1	31.5
Germany	2000	19.5	28.5	27.3	27.1
	2005	29.1	32.8	30.4	30.6
	2007	30.5	32.7	31.1	31.3
	2008	31.0	33.6	29.6	30.2
	2009	32.2	34.5	30.3	30.9
	2010	33.4	35.7	31.9	32.4
	2011	34.8	35.5	31.8	32.3
Spain	2000	39.1	44.2	39.5	39.9
	2005	40.2	42.1	36.3	38.1
	2007	40.3	40.1	35.4	37.2
	2008	41.6	42.0	34.3	36.5
	2009	42.5	42.1	35.1	37.8
	2010	44.4	40.7	35.8	38.6
	2011	46.8	40.7	35.2	38.5

		Small	Medium	Large	Total
Bank debt in % of total debt					
Italy	2000	31.4	31.4	21.9	25.0
	2005	33.1	31.5	18.6	22.8
	2007	35.3	33.8	18.2	23.0
	2008	37.0	34.5	19.3	24.2
	2009	37.3	34.4	18.2	23.2
	2010	37.7	34.5	18.6	23.5
	2011	37.7	35.0	19.0	23.5
France	2000	25.4	22.8	10.8	15.2
	2005	25.7	21.1	10.2	14.8
	2007	28.3	22.2	12.6	17.2
	2008	30.5	23.8	13.3	18.1
	2009	31.6	24.8	13.1	18.1
	2010	31.6	25.6	13.3	18.6
	2011	31.5	26.3	12.3	18.1

Continued

Table 5.A1 Continued

Germany	2000	44.1	43.5	13.7	19.0
	2005	45.6	40.6	11.0	17.0
	2007	44.4	37.8	11.2	16.5
	2008	45.5	39.1	12.5	17.5
	2009	45.8	39.2	12.0	17.2
	2010	45.9	38.7	11.6	16.7
	2011	47.9	41.7	11.5	16.1
Spain	2000	38.3	35.1	19.1	24.3
	2005	43.5	39.9	20.3	28.9
	2007	40.7	42.6	27.4	32.4
	2008	41.1	43.3	28.7	32.2
	2009	43.4	44.6	28.1	33.5
	2010	42.2	45.4	30.4	34.7
	2011	40.3	44.4	31.7	34.7

		Small	Medium	Large	Total
Short-term bank indebtedness as % of total liabilities to banks					
Italy	2000	69.5	73.9	67.5	69.6
	2005	63.5	65.7	47.8	55.4
	2007	62.8	65.4	48.2	55.6
	2008	62.0	66.3	48.6	55.9
	2009	58.2	61.2	43.4	50.9
	2010	57.7	60.0	45.1	51.4
	2011	59.3	62.1	48.5	53.8
France	2000	23.1	31.8	39.1	32.7
	2005	19.1	26.2	29.8	25.6
	2007	15.6	22.2	20.8	19.5
	2008	14.0	21.2	22.3	19.6
	2009	12.4	16.5	15.0	14.4
	2010	11.2	14.3	15.5	13.9
	2011	10.1	13.5	19.0	14.9
Germany	2000	39.0	30.6	34.0	33.6
	2005	36.9	28.7	28.4	29.9
	2007	27.6	25.4	35.0	31.1
	2008	27.1	24.4	32.6	29.5
	2009	26.3	22.2	26.3	25.1
	2010	25.6	22.5	23.8	23.7
	2011	25.0	23.7	24.8	24.5
Spain	2000	51.2	55.0	34.7	42.5
	2005	44.1	47.8	26.8	37.3
	2007	36.0	44.4	31.9	35.0
	2008	29.1	47.2	38.5	37.2
	2009	23.2	37.7	33.1	30.5
	2010	23.4	36.2	31.5	29.8
	2011	23.3	35.4	31.5	30.1

Source: Our processing of BACH data set.

Table 5.A2 Instruments and actions for the creation/reinforcement of financing channels for SMEs, other than bank loans

Targets of actions Actions/New instruments/ Intermediaries	Access to ECB refinancing	Credit	Guarantees	Corporate bond	Risk capital	Implementation status	Degree of efficacy in the short term on credit crunch	Potential impact on credit crunch
Corporate bonds – Mini bonds				X		Implemented by means of the Growth Decrees, 2012 (August) and 2.0 (October)	High for medium–large firms. Low for SMEs	Very high
SME guarantee facility			X			Reinforced since 2009. Further actions awaiting approval to amend eligibility criteria and extend geographical coverage	Medium	Very high
Cassa Depositi e Prestiti		X (through banking channel)	X (in the pipeline)		X (through participation in the Fondo Italiano di Investimento) Involvement in new funds being planned	Involvement already extended. Further expansion being planned with involvement in funds investing in securities issued by SMEs and the provision of guarantees on instruments of this kind	Medium	High

EIB/EIF			X		X	Reinforcement planned at EC level. Better use by Italy required	Low	High
Credit funds		X				In the planning stage	No one	Very high
Securitization, ABS and covered bonds	X	X		X		Amendments on the drawing board. ECB policy on eligibility for refinancing is completely independent.	Low	Medium
Venture capital and private equity					X	Actions and measures planned	Low	Very high
Institutional investors				X	X	Actions and measures planned (Amendment of IVASS Regulations)	No one	Very high, as for the technical reserves of insurance companies
Crowd funding					X	Legislation and regulations introduced	Low	High for innovative start-ups

Notes

1. The BACH (*Bank for the Accounts of Companies Harmonized*) database supplies harmonized information on the financial statements of non-financial corporations in 12 countries (Austria, Belgium, Czech Republic, France, Germany, Italy, Luxembourg, the Netherlands, Poland, Portugal, Slovakia and Spain). The data are grouped by area of business (NACE classification) and size of business (turnover), on the basis of a uniform accounting framework.
2. It should be remembered that the criteria for defining NPLs are stricter in Italy than in other European States (Banca d'Italia, 2013b, 2013c).
3. For a review of the structural difficulties faced by Italian and European SMEs in accessing finance, see Wagenvoort (2003a, 2003b).
4. Reference can be made to the countless articles on this topic that have recently appeared in the press. First and foremost, see http://www.ilsole24ore.com/.

References

Allen, F. and D. Gale (1995) 'A welfare comparison of intermediaries and financial markets in Germany and the US', *European Economic Review*, 39, 179–209.

Allen, F. and D. Gale (1999) *Comparing Financial Systems*, Cambridge: MIT Press.

Banca d'Italia (2013a) 'Financial Stability Report', No. 5, April.

Banca d'Italia (2013b) 'Annual Report 2012', Rome, May 31.

Banca d'Italia (2013c) 'La recente analisi dei prestiti deteriorati condotta dalla Banca d'Italia: principali caratteristiche e risultati', luglio.

Bartiloro, L., L. Carpinelli, P. Finaldi Russo and S. Pastorelli (2012) 'L'accesso al credito in tempo di crisi: le misure di sostegno a imprese e famiglie', Banca d'Italia, Questioni di Economia e Finanza, (Occasional Papers), No. 111, gennaio.

Cosma, S. and E. Gualandri (2012) 'The impact of the financial crisis on Italian banks', in Cosma, S. and E. Gualandri (eds) *The Italian Banking System and the Financial Crisis*, Basingstoke, England: Palgrave Macmillan Studies in Banking and Finance Institutions.

Cosma, S. and E. Gualandri (2014) 'The sovereign debt crisis: the impact on the intermediation model of Italian banks', in Lindblom, T., S. Sjögren and M. Willesson (eds), *Governance, Regulation and Bank Stability*, Hampshire, England: Palgrave Macmillan Studies in Banking and Financial Institutions.

De Mitri, S., A. De Socio, P. F. Russo and V. Nigro (2013) 'Le microimprese in Italia: una prima analisi delle condizioni economiche e finanziarie', Questioni di Economia e Finanza, (Occasional Papers), Banca d'Italia, No. 162, aprile.

Draghi, M. (2013) 'Hearing at the Committee on Economic and Monetary Affairs of the European Parliament. Introductory statement', by Mario Draghi, President of the ECB, Brussels, 8 July.

Draghi, M. (2012) 'The monetary policy of the European Central Bank and its transmission in the euro area', in Lindblom, T., sjogren, S. and M. Willesson (eds) Governance, regulation and bank stability, studies in banking and financial financial institution, Hampshire, England: palgrave Macmillan. Speech by the President of the ECB, Università Bocconi, Opening of the academic year 2012–2013, Milan 15 November.

European Commission and the European Investment Bank Group (2013) *Supporting small and medium-sized enterprises in 2012*, Joint report of EC and EIB, 2 May.

International Monetary Fund IMF (2013) 'Article IV Consultation with Italy concluding statement of the IMF Mission', July 4.

Onado, M. (2013) 'Credit crunch: quella regia ancora assente', *Il Sole 24 Ore*. 14 luglio.

Neri, S. (2013) 'The impact of the sovereign debt crisis on bank lending rates in the euro area', Questioni di Economia e Finanza (Occasional Papers), Banca d'Italia, No. 170, June.

Rajan, R. and L. Zingales (2003) 'Banks and markets: The changing character of European finance, European Central Bank', 2nd Annual Conference, Frankfurt.

Thakor, A. V. (1996) 'The design of financial systems: An overview', *Journal of Banking and Finance*, 20(5), 917–948.

Venturelli, V. (2012) 'Main features of the Italian financial system', in Cosma, S. and E. Gualandri (eds) *The Italian Banking System: Impact of the Crisis and Future Perspectives*, Basingstoke, England: Palgrave Macmillan Studies in Banking and Finance Institutions.

Wagenvoort, R. (2003a) 'Bank survey evidence on bank lending to SMEs in the European Union', EIB, Economic and Financial Report 2003/01.

Wagenvoort, R. (2003b) 'Are finance constraints hindering the growth of SMEs in Europe?', EIB Papers, Volume 8, No. 2.

6
Does the Team Manager Earn More than His Coached Players? Analysis of the Earnings of Italian Asset Management Companies, and their Portfolio Companies, in the Field of Private Equity

Elisa Giaretta and Giusy Chesini

6.1 Introduction

In association football, a team manager is responsible for running a football club and coaching the players. The team manager's responsibilities in a professional football club include selecting the players for matches, scouting for young, talented players, buying and selling players in the transfer market, planning strategies, delegating duties to the first team coach, facing the media in pre-match and post-match interviews and maintaining the profitability of the club.

Similarly, Italian asset management companies (AMCs) that invest in private equity should select the portfolio companies in which to invest, scout for young companies with high growth potential, buy and sell companies after the investment period, plan strategies, delegate certain duties to individual directors of the portfolio companies, release information on the companies' profitability and provide investors.

In this chapter, we aim to study whether the gain of Italian AMCs ('*the team manager*') is greater, or less, than that of the companies in which they invest ('the coached players').

The gains of AMCs do not derive directly from the performance of the portfolio companies. Indeed, the gains of AMCs derive from the commissions that they charge their customers for fund management. These commissions are composed by a fixed part, determined as a percentage of the assets under management and invested in portfolio companies, and a variable part, calculated as a percentage of the capital gains realized from the sale of the portfolio companies.

In this chapter, we analyse the performance of Italian AMCs that invest in private equity compared with that of the companies in which they invest. We use budget analyses to compare these two types of companies. To do this, we create a database of Italian AMCs operating in at least one private equity fund and a sample of private equity-backed Italian companies.

The results call into question the claim that Quindlen (2000) attributes to Arthur Rock: that, 'a great management team can find a good opportunity even if they have to make a huge leap from the market they currently occupy'.

The structure of this chapter is as follows: the second section discusses the literature about the AMCs and their investments, focusing on the Italian context; in the second section, we develop the research hypotheses. Then we describe the data collection process and the methodology of the research in the Section 6.4, and in Section 6.5, we report and discuss the results of the analysis. In the final section, we present the main conclusions, discuss the implications for entrepreneurs and provide recommendations for further research.

6.2 Literature review

The debate on private equity investments is a topic of current interest for both academics and practitioners. One of the most controversial issues is the profitability of fund managers that invest in private equity and the portfolio companies that they manage.

The main structure that governs the relationship between AMCs, portfolio companies and investors on a global basis, for private equity investments, is the structure of limited partnerships (Phalippou, 2007). The limited partners are investors (banks, insurance companies, foundations, pension funds, sovereign wealth funds, funds of funds and high net worth individuals) that provide private equity capital for investments; the general partners are AMCs: financial intermediaries who invest the capital of limited partners (and a small percentage, between 1–5 per cent, of their capital) in portfolio companies, monitor investments and establish appropriate strategies for investment exit. The portfolio companies are private equity-backed companies that receive capital from investments (Figure 6.1).

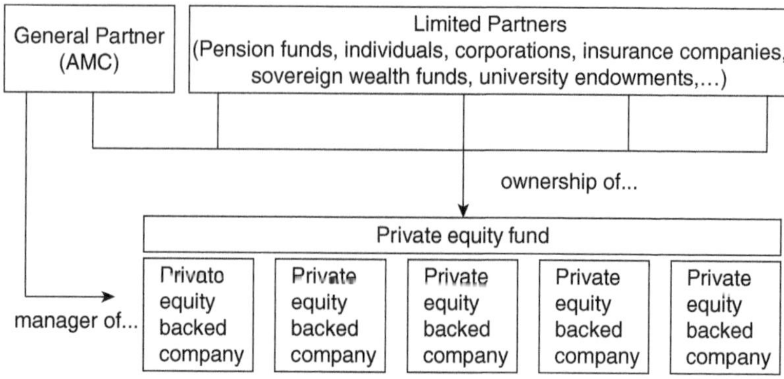

Figure 6.1 Limited partnership
Source: Authors' elaboration.

In international practice, the remuneration of the general partners is a percentage of the funds under management and a percentage of the capital gain realized from the investments. The standard compensation is known by the term 'two and twenty'. The 'two' refers to an annual management fee equal to 2 per cent of the capital under management. This fee covers the administrative costs, the monitoring costs, the operating costs and the salaries of managers. The management fee is fixed and therefore it does not depend on the performance of the fund. The 'twenty' refers to a percentage of the capital gain (20 per cent): this fee is also known as 'promotion', 'transport', or 'carried interest' and helps to align the incentives of the general partners and the limited partners. In fact, if the fund obtains high yields, the general partners earn more than the simple fixed fee. This fee acts as an incentive for the general partner to try to obtain higher capital gains for investors and therefore a higher carried interest for them. However, if the fund does not perform well, the only loss for the general partners is a loss of revenue. In principle, this mechanism of risk shifting leads the general partner to undertake high-risk initiatives to achieve higher performance. For this reason, the general partner must invest part of its capital into the fund and also suffer losses from these investments. The percentage of capital attributed to the managed fund usually ranges from 1 per cent to 5 per cent of the total managed fund (Fleischer, 2008).

Each category of fund managers has special characteristics in terms of investment choices and attitudes towards the undertaking concerned. In fact, companies operating in the private equity market tend to specialize in several types of portfolio companies on the basis of the sector and the geographical area of the companies, the types of transactions and the sizes of the investments, and the acquisition of majority or minority stakes.

The main fund managers that invest in private equity in Italy are AMCs, who managed approximately 20,233 million euro of capital in the private equity market in 2012. Italian AMCs are financial intermediaries that are authorized to carry out portfolio management services both on an individual and on a collective basis. They pursue the activity of collective portfolio management through the establishment and management of funds. Italian AMCs were established by the Italian Legislative Decree no. 58 of 1998, and they are subject to the rules contained in the 'Consolidated Law on Finance' (Testo Unico della Finanza (TUF)).

Italian AMCs that manage private equity funds operate with the goal of creating value in the portfolio companies by selling them at a greater price than the purchase cost, thus realizing capital gains for investors.

In line with international practice, the gains of Italian AMCs derive from the commissions they charge to their customers for the management of the funds. These commissions are composed by a fixed part, determined as a percentage of the capital under management, and a variable part, calculated as a percentage of the capital gain realized.

To build their investment portfolios, Italian AMCs use specific management tools: asset allocation, stock pricing and market timing. Asset allocation consists of the distribution of the capital of funds between different asset classes. More precisely, it consists of identifying the activities to include in the investment portfolio in order to optimally allocate financial resources, taking into account the preferences of investors in terms of risk and return, the time horizon and the set of activities available in the market. Stock pricing is the selection of individual securities to buy or sell in different areas on the basis of fundamental analysis and technical analysis. Stock pricing is also the main activity of specialized fund managers. Market-making activity is the choice of the optimal moment for the purchase and sale of securities in order to obtain the greatest possible return for the investor.

To exercise this activity, Italian AMCs are required to take the form of joint stock companies and are therefore required to draw up balance sheets.

The structure of the balance sheet – the income statement and the statement of assets and liabilities – for AMCs is regulated by the Bank of Italy in the Decision of 13 March 2012 also known as 'Instructions for the preparation of financial statements and returns of financial intermediaries'.

The structure of the income statement is homogeneous for each Italian AMC. The content of the income statement is summarized in Table 6.1.

In the first row of the income statement, there is the fee and commission income. This item includes all fees related to the portfolio management services. This item also includes all the fixed and variable fees that AMCs charge their customers for the management of portfolio companies. This value corresponds to the revenues from sales in non-financial companies. The ratio of the commission income to total assets corresponds to a value of return on assets (ROA).

The net commission income is the fee and commission income net of any commissions that AMCs are paid, in the case of the management of the funds being delegated to other financial intermediaries. It follows that in the absence of any commission expense the net commissions correspond to the fee and commission income.

Table 6.1 Typical income statement for Italian AMCs

	Fee and commission income
–	Passive commission
=	Net commission income
+	Dividends
+	Interest income
–	Interest expenses
+/–	Net income from trading activity
+/–	Net income from hedging activity
+/–	Net income from financial assets and liabilities at fair value
+/–	Profit (loss) from the sales or buyback of financial assets and liabilities
=	Intermediation margin
–/+	Net losses / recoveries from impairment of financial assets
–	Management costs
–	Value adjustment to tangible assets
–	Value adjustment to intangible assets
+	Net income from evaluation at a fair value of tangible and intangible assets
–	Net provisions for risks and charges
+/–	Other management income and provisions
=	Operating result
+/–	Profit (Loss) from investments
=	Profit (Loss) from current activity before taxes
–	Income taxes
=	Profit (Loss) from current activity after taxes
+/–	Profit (Loss) from assets held for sales after taxes
=	Profit (Loss) for the period

Source: Bank of Italy.

The intermediation margin includes all revenues and expenses that AMCs obtain from the activity of fund management. In addition to the fees included in the above items, it includes any dividends and capital gains received from the investments. The intermediation margin is therefore a useful measure of the overall profitability of the operator in the management of private equity-backed companies. This value consists of a gross margin analogous to the EBITDA for non-financial companies.

Despite the increased interest in private equity investments and their potential importance for the economy as a whole, most of the literature focuses on the profitability of private equity funds and not on the profitability of the fund managers themselves. In addition, the few academic studies on the profitability of fund managers focus on the individual amounts of commissions and capital gains rather than on annual budgetary measures. As mentioned above, in the present paper, we prefer to study measures of annual budget along with the same financial ratios exhibited by the portfolio companies, in order to compare the profitability of fund managers to the profitability of the companies they manage.

Among the studies on the managers of private equity funds is the work of Gompers and Lerner (2000), which showed that the performance of larger and older fund managers is greater than that of other fund managers active in private equity. According to this study, larger and older fund managers receive a percentage of capital gains that is 1 per cent greater than the share of their counterparts. Another important study is by Kaplan and Schoar (2005), which demonstrated that general partners who underperform are likely to repeat this performance. Cumming and MacIntosh (2006) show that higher fixed fees for fund managers are associated with lower fund risk and lower fund returns.

Marquez, Nanda and Yavuz (2010) argue that fund managers tend to manipulate the variable fees, and thus their profitability, in order to provide stable returns to investors over time and to manipulate investors' beliefs about their managerial ability to add value.

The analysis by Christoffersen (2001) showed that private equity fund managers voluntarily waive the fees they earn. As a result, the effective fee charged is substantially less than indicated in expense ratios and may vary over the course of a year despite a constant contractual fee. Fund managers use fee waivers and reduce their profitability to strategically adjust fees according to the fund's performance and expected cash flows.

Metrick and Yasuda (2009) studied the performance of fund managers in relation to the investors' demand for funds. Their study shows that the supply curve from investors shifts depending on the performance of the funds. In response to this increased supply of capital, the general partners may increase the size of the funds managed or create new funds. However, the increase in the size of funds or the creation of new vehicles increases costs and reduces the overall profitability for investors and fund managers.

Achleitner, Betzer and Gider (2009) argue that managers of private equity funds are exempted from several regulatory obligations that are usually applied to investment companies because their client base is solely made up of sophisticated investors. As a result, fund managers are allowed to make risky investments with high returns in case of success and without losses in the case of failure.

However, there is a strong gap in the literature. Studies about the profitability of fund managers analyse the amount of the individual fees and commissions rather than indices of budgets. Therefore, these studies cannot be applied to portfolio companies. This compels us to further investigate this phenomenon. To the best of our knowledge, there are no studies that cover all aspects of the performance of private equity fund managers, while particularly focusing on Italian AMCs. It should be noted that we have chosen to focus only on Italian AMCs because the structures of the private equity fund managers are heterogeneous and can lead to investments in different portfolio companies and different performances. In fact, the reasons for the existence of different types of private equity fund managers on the international scene are varied, which impacts on the efforts they devote to the portfolio companies. The investment horizon varies considerably between different fund managers, which results in a number of different incentives and varying profitability for investors, portfolio companies and fund managers (Luukkonen et al., 2011).

This analysis differs from the existing literature because it uses an original sample and deepens the study of the performance of Italian AMCs in relation to the performance of portfolio companies. In other words, we aim to carry out a comparison of the earnings of the manager and those of the managed.

The research question that we want to investigate can be summarized by the following: what is the performance of Italian AMCs that invest in private equity in comparison to that of the companies that they manage?

6.3 Research hypotheses

In this section, we develop hypotheses for the performance of Italian AMCs that manage private equity funds. The hypotheses are derived from the academic literature and are tested in Section 6.5.

The main research hypothesis aims to compare the performance of the 'team managers' (Italian AMCs) with the performance of the 'coached players' (the portfolio companies). It is assumed that the performance of the former is better than the performance of the latter.

> H_1: Italian AMCs show better performance than their portfolio companies.

Second, we aim to analyse the relationships between the performance of the fund managers and the characteristics of the investments they manage. In fact, the capital invested per portfolio company, for example, has a positive effect on investments. A greater amount invested encourages the development of new technologies and new products, supports extraordinary finance operations or strengthens the financial structure of the portfolio companies. It follows that AMCs that sell at higher values obtain higher yields and also higher carried interests on the capital gains. For this reason, we expect a positive relationship between the capital under management and the performance of the capital. In addition, we study the effects of the specialization of fund managers on one, or several, types of portfolio companies.

> H_2: Italian AMCs show different performance depending on the characteristics of the portfolio companies they manage.

6.4 Data description and methodology

The data collection process and the sample selection are described in this section. In this section, we provide descriptive statistics for the samples analysed and discuss the research methodology.

With this analysis, we aim to answer the main research question: we compare the performance exhibited by Italian AMCs that invest in private equity and the main characteristics of their portfolio companies.

6.4.1 Data description

The samples analysed are described in this section. The first sample consists of Italian AMCs that manage private equity funds (Sample AMC). Data on Italian AMCs are taken from the Italian Association of Private Equity and Venture Capital (AIFI) and are matched with the financial information taken from the Italian Chamber of Commerce. We study the performance of Italian AMCs that in 2011 had managed at least one private equity fund. The data set includes 37 Italian AMCs.

The second sample includes companies that were the subject of private equity investments between 2006 and 2010. We study only the investments made by private fund managers in unlisted companies, considering the initial funding made by private equity managers, but not the second round of investment. In addition, we only consider investments in companies that have passed the start-up phase. Therefore, the study does not include the following types of investment transactions:

- Operations carried out by public institutions;
- Seed and start-up operations;
- Second-round investments.

Data is obtained from the database of the Private Equity Monitor observatory (PEM) and matched with the information contained in the AIDA database produced by Bureau Van Dijk. The sample (Sample PE) is composed of 333 companies. The distribution of private equity-backed companies in the years studied is shown in Table 6.2.

For both samples, we studied variables from 2008 to 2011. Table 6.3 shows the descriptive statistics of Italian AMCs and the private equity-backed Italian companies in the period under study.

From Table 6.3, we can see that the amount of revenue for portfolio companies is higher than that of fund managers, when considering the mean and median values. The average value of the EBITDA of portfolio companies is twice the value exhibited by the fund managers. However, when considering the median values, the EBITDA is similar for the two types of companies, and the AMCs show higher values. The portfolio companies have a mean value of the total assets that is almost ten times the value expressed by AMCs. We can even find a similar situation when considering the median values. This is because – unlike industrial

Table 6.2 Distribution of private equity-backed companies in the years studied

Years	Number of deals	Distribution(%)
2006	68	20.42
2007	82	24.62
2008	95	28.53
2009	42	12.61
2010	46	13.81
Total	333	100.00

Source: Private Equity Monitor (PEM).

Table 6.3 Descriptive statistics of Italian AMCs and portfolio companies in the period 2008–2011

Variables	Sample AMC	Sample PE	*t*-test
Revenues	4,038,189 (2,082,410)	63,853,567 (25,114,643)	(<0.0001)***
EBITDA	3,926,772 (2,154,318)	6,707,924 (1,919,592)	(<0.0001)***
Profit	738,245 (143,374)	–2,621,883 (–742)	(<0.0001)***
Total assets	5,355,385 (3,179,118)	34,676,651 (34,676,652)	(<0.0001)***
Equity	1,808,338 (1,250,000)	35,328,459 (8,370,806)	(<0.0001)***
ROA	0.7139 (0.7163)	–1.6751 (1.9350)	(0.0350)**
ROE	0.4870 (0.0729)	–3.48691 (0.7400)	(0.0001)***

Descriptive statistics for variables analysed from 2008–2011. Samples include 37 Italian AMCs (Sample AMC) and 333 portfolio companies (Sample PE). The variable definitions and data sources are described in the Appendix (Table 6.A). The mean and median values (median values in brackets). Student's t-test.

* Significant at 10% ** Significant at 5% *** Significant at 1%.

companies – AMCs do not require a high amount of assets to carry out their activities. Similarly, the value of the equity of portfolio companies is higher than the value of the equity of AMCs. Note that the average values of ROA and ROE are positive for Italian AMCs and negative for portfolio companies. However, when considering the median values, the ROA and ROE ratios are both positive, and in both cases, the greatest value is expressed by the portfolio companies.

The results of Student's *t*-test show that all the differences between portfolio companies and AMCs are statistically significant for the variables analysed.

6.4.2 Methodology

In this section, we describe the research methodology and discuss the variables chosen to analyse the performance of Italian AMCs and portfolio companies.

We decided to analyse some variables from the balance sheet to explain the main features of private equity investments. This is due to the choice of using public data available for all companies and not using questionnaires and interviews. In addition, annual balance sheet data is a measure that can be easily used to compare different types of companies. In fact, we cannot compare these two types of companies by directly studying the gains from individual private equity transactions put into place by the managers.

First, we implement a comparison of the performance of AMCs and their portfolio companies to verify whether the profitability of the fund manager is higher than the return on the invested companies. The period of analysis is 2008–2011 (panel data). The study is carried out using a probit model. The dependent variable is a dummy variable that takes the value of 1 if the company is a portfolio company and 0 otherwise – for the purpose of comparing these samples the other company is an AMC. The independent variables are performance variables for the two samples and are selected to reflect the traditional performance evaluation within the limits of data availability. The specific constructs are found in the Appendix (Table 6.A). These variables are chosen to compare the performance between the portfolio companies subject to private equity and the Italian AMCs who manage them. We expect that AMCs should show higher returns than portfolio companies do. In precise terms, we study the following probit model:

$$PROB_{PE} = \beta_0 + \beta_1 PRO + \beta_2 TAS + \beta_3 ROA + \beta_4 EBI + \beta_4 ROE + \beta_4 EQU \quad (6.1)$$

where

PROB_PE: *dummy* variable explaining the membership to the PE sample (1 portfolio company, 0 AMC);
PRO: profit or loss for the period;
TAS: total assets;
ROA: return on assets;
EBI: EBITDA;
ROE: return on equity;
EQU: equity.

The analysis continues by using a regression model with the ordinary least squares (OLS) method. Within the regression, we seek to analyse the performance of Italian AMCs according to the characteristics of the investment implemented. The regression used in the analysis is the following:

$$Y = \beta_0 + \beta_1 CAP + \beta_2 MIN + \beta_3 FUN + \beta_4 POR + \beta_5 EUR + \beta_6 ITA + \beta_7 IND \quad (6.2)$$

where[1]

CAP: capital under management;
MIN: the minimum amount invested per portfolio company;
FUN: the number of funds managed;
POR: the number of portfolio companies;
EUR: investment specialization in Europe;
ITA: investment specialization in Italy;
IND: no industrial specialization.

The independent variables indicate the types of portfolio companies in which AMCs have chosen to invest. In fact, the specialization of the investment made by AMCs in one, or several, types of portfolio companies is not randomly chosen but it is selected from the same AMCs and specified in the contract subscribed to by the investors. In using these regressions, we aim to investigate whether the specialization of the investments in a few types of portfolio companies leads to higher returns for AMCs. The impact of private equity investments on the performance of Italian AMCs is directly analysed through balance sheet analysis in order to understand the fundamental characteristics of the investments. We analyse the percentage changes of 12 financial ratios, which are used as dependent variables. We study the profit or loss for the period as well as the revenues from fees, both gross (fee and commission income) and net (net commission income), and we aim to study the overall profitability resulting from management (intermediation margin). These measures are studied both in absolute and weighted values. The measures of liabilities that are used as the denominator for weighted values are the total amount of assets and equity capital. In addition, we study the impact of these two measures of the variables by using them as dependent variables. As a result, the indices used as the dependent variables are as follows: total assets (TAS), equity capital (EQU), the intermediation margin (INT), net commission income (NET), fee and commission income (FEE), intermediation margin/equity (INT/E), net commission income/equity (NET/E), fee and commission income/equity (FEE/E), intermediation margin/total assets (INT/A), net commissions/total assets (NET/A), fee and commission income/total assets (FEE/A), and profit or loss (PRO). Through the analysis, we seek to answer the main research question: we aim to compare the performance exhibited by Italian AMCs and the performance of the portfolio companies.

6.5 Results

In this section, we first report the results of the analysis and subsequently discuss the results, taking into account the research hypotheses formulated in Section 6.3 in relation to the previous academic literature.

It should be noted that in this research, with data from the report of the PEM observatory database and the AIDA Bureau Van Dijk database, we created a sample of the portfolio private equity-backed companies for the period 2006–2010, which includes 333 companies in total. The second sample is composed of 37 Italian AMCs that had managed at least one private equity fund in 2011. Data on Italian AMCs is taken from the Italian association of venture capital and private equity (AIFI) and matched with balance sheet data from the Italian Chamber of Commerce database.

The analysis begins by comparing the performance of Italian AMCs with their portfolio companies through the use of a probit model. The dependent variable is a dummy variable that takes the value of 1 if the company is a portfolio company and 0 if the company is an AMC. The independent variables are the profit or loss for the period, total assets, ROA, EBITDA, ROE and equity. The results are reported in Table 6.4.

All of the variables are statistically significant. The coefficients related to profit, total assets, equity and ROA are positive, while the coefficients relative to EBITDA and ROE are negative. This means that portfolio companies show values higher than AMCs for profit, total assets, equity and ROA but lower values than AMCs for EBITDA and ROE.

The analysis continues with an OLS regression model (6.2). We aim to analyse the performance of Italian AMCs according to the characteristics of the investment implemented. The performance of Italian AMCs is measured by 12 indicators: total assets (TAS), equity capital (EQU), intermediation margin (INT), net commission income (NET), fee and commission income (FEE), intermediation margin/equity (INT/E), net commission income/equity (NET/E), fee and commission income/equity (FEE/E), intermediation margin/total assets (INT/A), net commissions/total assets (NET/A), fee and commission income/total assets (FEE/A), the profit or loss (PRO). The results of the regressions with the dependent

Table 6.4 Probit model

Variable	**Coefficient**
PRO	4.45E-07 (0.00002)***
TAS	1.78E-07 (0.00233)***
ROA	0.0831356 (<0.00001)***
EBI	−9.34E-07 (0.00001)***
ROE	−0.0124433 (0.0006)***
EQU	9.54E-08 (0.00005)***
CONST	0.296434 (0.00152)***

Probit model. The sample consists of 37 Italian AMCs (Sample AMC) and 333 portfolio companies (Sample PE). The dependent variable is a dummy variable that indicates the membership of the Sample PE. The independent variables are profit or loss, total assets, ROA, EBITDA, ROE and equity, as defined in the Appendix (Table 6.A). P-values in brackets.

* Significant at 10% ** Significant at 5% *** Significant at 1%.

variables TAS, EQU, INT, and NET are summarized in Table 6.5; those of the regressions with the dependent variables FEE, INT/E, NET/E, and FEE/E are summarized in Table 6.6; and those of the regressions with the dependent variables INT/A, NET/A, FEE/A, and PRO are summarized in Table 6.7.

The variables are statistically significant in most regression models. The capital under management recorded a coefficient with a positive sign in all statistically significant regressions: total assets, equity intermediation margin, net commission income, fee and commission income, intermediation margin/equity, net commission income/equity, fees/equity, and profit. Therefore, there is a positive relationship between assets under management and the performance of AMCs. The regressions that had as dependent variables the ratio of total assets, the intermediation margin/ total assets, net commission income/total assets, and fee and commission income/total assets are not significant.

The minimum amount invested is statistically significant for all dependent variables except for the regression with the amount of equity. In all statistically significant regressions, the coefficients showed positive values. This means that a large amount of capital invested by AMCs also leads to an increased profitability for the fund managers themselves.

The number of funds managed has a positive coefficient in all models in which the regression is significant: total assets, equity, intermediation margin, net commission income, fee and commission income, intermediation margin/equity, net commission income/equity, fee/ equity, and profit. The number of funds managed is not significant for models that had as dependent variables fee and commission income and the ratio of total assets, the intermediation margin/total assets, the net commission income/total assets, and the fee and commission income/total assets.

In this study, we demonstrate a negative relationship between the number of portfolio companies managed and profitability variables except for the intermediation margin/total assets, the net commission income/total assets, and the fee and commission income/total assets, which are not significant. It follows that a smaller number of companies in the portfolio leads to greater profitability for AMCs.

The variable EUR, which represents Italian AMCs that invest in Europe, presents a positive coefficient in some models and a negative coefficient in others. A negative sign is related to the regressions which have dependent variables that are equity and total assets, while a positive sign is present in the regressions that have these variables in the denominator or regressions with dependent variables of the

Table 6.5 OLS regressions – dependent variables: TAS, EQU, INT and NET

	TAS	EQU	INT	NET
CAP	8,314 (0.00001)***	1,005 (0.05318)*	8,283 (<0.00001)***	8,161 (<0.00001)***
MIN	239,094 (0.00041)***		272,866 (06)***	272,054 (<0.00001)***
FUN	900,192 (0.00182)***	113,871 (0.07902)*	418,743 (0.06769)*	386,583 (0.08919)*
POR	−60,995 (01)***	−13,371 (0.00011)***	−29,892 (0.0006)***	−27,800 (0.00658)***
EUR	−4,150,000 (0.03132)**	−2,070,000 (0.00374)***		
ITA	−4,710,000 (0.01376)**	−2,180,000 (0.00138)***	−1,170,000 (0.00384)***	
IND				
CONST	4,620,000 (0.0088)***	3,310,000 (<0.00001)***		

The sample consists of 37 Italian AMCs from 2008 and 2011. The dependent variables are total assets (TAS), equity capital (EQU), the intermediation margin (INT), and the net commission income (NET). Variable definitions are described in the Appendix (Table 6.A). P-values are in brackets.
* Significant at 10% ** Significant at 5% *** Significant at 1%.

Table 6.6 OLS regressions – dependent variables: FEE, INT/E, NET/E and FEE/E

	FEE	INT/E	NET/E	FEE/E
CAP	8,022 (<0.00001)***	0.0018 (0.03619)**	0.0017 (0.03806)**	0.0016 (0.06482)*
MIN	269,885 (0.00007)***	0.1550 (0.00002)***	0.1550 (0.00001)***	0.1591 (<0.00001)***
FUN		0.3661 (0.0304)**	0.3402 (0.03714)**	0.3121 (0.06199)*
POR	−26,679 (0.00242)***	−0.0163 (0.03633)**	−0.0149 (0.04826)**	−0.0131 (0.0946)*
EUR		0.7338 (0.07219)*	0.8142 (0.047)**	0.8053 (0.04958)**
ITA	−1,410,000 (0.02091)**			
IND				
CONST				

The sample consists of 37 Italian AMCs from 2008 and 2011. The dependent variables are fee and commission income (FEE), intermediation margin/equity (INT/E), net commission income/equity (NET/E), and fee and commission income/equity (FEE/E). Variable definitions are described in the Appendix (Table 6.A). P-values are in brackets.
* Significant at 10%** Significant at 5% *** Significant at 1%.

Table 6.7 OLS regressions – dependent variables: INT/A, NET/A. FEE/A and PRO

	INT/A	NET/A	FEE/A	PRO
CAP				1,970 (0.0001)***
MIN	0.0156 (0.04575)**	0.0159 (0.03998)**	0.0162 (0.03302)**	81,370 (0.00019)***
FUN				171,014 (0.0959)*
POR				–9,031 (0.04105)**
EUR	0.2454 (0.01096)**	0.2679 (0.00554)***	0.2410 (0.01233)**	
ITA				
IND	–0.1763 (0.0847)*	–0.1818 (0.07465)*		
CONST	0.5973 (0.00003)***	0.5669 (0.00012)***	0.6127 (0.00005)***	–497,595 (0.05941)*

The sample consists of 37 Italian AMCs from 2008 and 2011. Dependent variables are the intermediation margin/total assets (INT/A), net commission/total assets (NET/A), fee and commission income/total assets (FEE/A), profit or loss (PRO). Variable definitions are defined in the Appendix (Table 6.A). P-values are in brackets.

* Significant at 10% ** Significant at 5% *** Significant at 1%.

intermediation margin/equity, net commission income/equity, fee and commission income/equity intermediation margin/total assets, net commission income/total assets, and fee and commission income/ total assets. It should be noted that in these regressions, the variable ITA concerning the focus of investment in Italy has values that are not statistically significant. However, these values are significant with negative signs for other regressions: total assets, equity intermediation margin, and fee and commission income.

The relationship between the lack of focus on a particular industry and the profitability of Italian AMCs is statistically significant only in two models – the intermediation margin/total assets and the net commission income/total assets – and in both cases, it has a negative sign.

6.6 Conclusions

6.6.1 Discussion and implications

This analysis studied the performance of 37 AMCs that managed at least one Italian private equity fund in 2011. As we have seen, the first analysis was performed by using a probit model, comparing the portfolio companies and the managers of private equity funds. In the analysis, we found that the profit, total assets, ROA and equity of the portfolio companies are greater than those of AMCs. However, we found that the performance expressed in terms of EBITDA and ROE is greater for AMCs compared to that of their portfolio companies. This means that it is more profitable to invest in AMCs than to invest in private equity, in comparison to investing in companies that are private equity-backed. The performance of the fund managers is better than the performance of the companies they manage.

In the second part of the analysis, we investigated the performance of AMCs in relation to the type of investments made through an OLS model. The independent variables relate to the type of portfolio company in which Italian AMCs decided to invest, while the dependent variables are financial ratios that measure the performance of AMCs, namely: total assets (TAS), equity capital (EQU), intermediation margin (INT), net commission income (NET), fee and commission income (FEE), intermediation margin/equity (INT/E), net commission income/ equity (NET/E), fee and commission income/equity (FEE/E), intermediation margin/total assets (INT/A), net commissions/total assets (NET/A), fee and commission income/total assets (FEE/A), and the profit or loss (PRO). The regression results confirmed the research hypotheses. The performance of Italian AMCs is higher for companies that invest more in each portfolio company.

First, we found a positive relationship between the capital managed by AMCs and their economic performance. In fact, the greater the assets under management, the greater the resources that are available for each company and, consequently, the greater the growth of the company invested in should be. This result is in line with the work of Ewans, Jones and Rhodes-Kropf (2003), which showed that the size of the private equity funds is related to the size of the investments, and it follows that for the same reasons given previously, the size of the funds should lead to a higher return for AMCs. Similarly, a positive relationship was found between the minimum amount of capital invested per portfolio company by AMCs and their economic performance.

In addition, we found that the number of funds managed positively correlates with the performance of AMCs. This is in contrast with the study by Metrick and Yasuda (2009), which showed that the creation of new private equity funds involves additional costs and reduces the overall profitability of investors and fund managers. Indeed, there are diseconomies of scale in the number of funds managed that lead to lower returns for investors and managers themselves.

We also showed that the number of companies in the portfolio of each manager of private equity funds is positively related to the performance of the managers. This confirms the findings of Gompers and Lerner (2000), who asserted that in general, the performance of the managers of private equity funds is positively related to the number of portfolio companies. According to the authors, the optimal number of portfolio companies for private equity fund managers is equal to two dozen companies over three years. These results, however, are in contrast with the statement made by Ewans, Jones and Rhodes-Kropf (2003), who argued that because a long time is required to manage a project, only a small number of investments can be supervised by the fund managers. In any case, we found a positive relationship between the number of companies in the portfolio and the performance of AMCs.

Subsequently, we analysed the relationship between specialization in one, or several, countries and the performance of AMCs. We found that the managers who focus on Italy have a lower performance than companies that do not focus on one country. AMCs taking the European market as reference, however, show better performance in more cases. In fact, the fee structure should lead to an overinvestment in countries that show greater historical performance and an underinvestment in other countries (Axelson, Strömberg and Weisbach 2009). It follows that the overinvestment reduces the possible returns and decreases the performance of fund managers. In addition, institutional investors show a substantial preference for companies located in countries where they themselves reside, which means that they lose the opportunity to seize investment opportunities in other countries (Hochberg and Rauh, 2013). As a result, investors who do not focus on a single country should obtain higher yields.

In addition, we found that the specialization of investment companies in an industry is negatively related to the performance of AMCs. In fact, the managers of private equity funds often specialize in one industry so that they can better understand the reality of the field in which they invest and the process of value creation. However, managers of private equity funds may choose to invest in companies outside their field of specialization in order to expand their investment opportunities or diversify their portfolio (Huyghebaert, Priem and Van de Gucht, 2010).

In general, we conclude that there is evidence that Italian AMCs show superior performance compared to their portfolio companies. We also show that the performance of fund managers is higher for companies that invest more, as they have a greater amount of capital under management or a greater amount invested per portfolio company and a greater number of managed funds.

6.6.2 Limitations of the research and directions for future analyses

We conclude this work by analysing the limitations of the study and suggesting some possible directions for further research.

The first limitation of this study is the statistical significance of the constants in the regression model. This means that some factors affecting the profitability of Italian AMCs and portfolio companies are not included in the models.

A further limitation of the analysis is that the sample of Italian AMCs does not have the same sample size as the sample of portfolio companies. This may lead to a slight distortion in the comparison between the two samples.

In addition, this phenomenon can be further analysed through the use of other statistical methods and other performance variables.

Finally, it may be interesting to extend the research question to other European countries.

Appendix

Table 6.A Variable definitions and data sources

Variable	Definition	Data Source
Minimum (MIN)	Minimum amount of money invested per portfolio company by the asset management company	AIFI
Funds (FUN)	Number of funds managed by the asset management company	AIFI
Capital (CAP)	Capital under management by the asset management company	AIFI
Portfolio (POR)	Number of portfolio companies	AIFI
Italy (ITA)	Dummy variable that indicates investment specialization in Italy (1 Italy, 0 otherwise)	AIFI
Europe (EUR)	Dummy variable that indicates investment specialization in Europe (1 Europe, 0 otherwise)	AIFI
Industry (IND)	Dummy variable that indicates no industrial specialization (1 no industrial specialization, 0 otherwise	AIFI
Fee and commission income (FEE)	Fee and commission income for the study period	AIDA Bureau Van Dijk
Net commission income (NET)	Net commission income for the study period	AIDA Bureau Van Dijk
Intermediation margin (INT)	Intermediation margin for the study period	AIDA Bureau Van Dijk
Fee and commission income/total assets (FEE/A)	Fee and commission income/total assets for the study period	AIDA Bureau Van Dijk
Net commission income/total assets (NET/A)	Net commission income/total assets for the study period	AIDA Bureau Van Dijk
Intermediation margin/total assets (INT/A)	Intermediation margin/total assets for the study period	AIDA Bureau Van Dijk
Fee and commission income/equity (FEE/E)	Fee and commission income/equity for the study period	AIDA Bureau Van Dijk
Net/equity (NET/E)	Net commission income/equity for the study period	AIDA Bureau Van Dijk
Intermediation margin/equity (INT/E)	Intermediation margin/equity for the study period	AIDA Bureau Van Dijk
Revenues (REV)	Revenues from sales and services for the study period for private equity-backed companies and fee and commission income for AMCs	AIDA Bureau Van Dijk
EBITDA (EBI)	Earnings before interest, taxes, depreciations and amortizations for the study period for private equity-backed companies and the intermediation margin for AMCs	AIDA Bureau Van Dijk
Profit (PRO)	Profit (Loss) for the study period	AIDA Bureau Van Dijk

Continued

Table 6.A Continued

Variable	Definition	Data Source
Total assets (TAS)	Total assets – total receivables from shareholders for the study period	AIDA Bureau Van Dijk
Equity (EQU)	Shareholders' funds for the study period	AIDA Bureau Van Dijk
Return on equity (Roe)	Profit/equity * 100 for the study period	AIDA Bureau Van Dijk
Return on assets (Roa)	Revenues/total assets * 100 for the study period	AIDA Bureau Van Dijk
PROB_PE	Dummy variable that explains the membership of the sample of portfolio companies (1 for PE-backed companies, 0 for asset management companies)	AIFI

Note

1. Variable definitions are in the Appendix (Table 6.A).

References

Achleitner, A., A. Betzer and J. Gider (2009) 'Investment rationales of hedge funds and private equity funds in the German stock market', Working Paper, http://dx.doi.org/10.2139/ ssrn.1292896.

Axelson, U., P. Strömberg and M.S. Weisbach (2009) 'Why are buyouts levered? The financial structure of private equity funds', *Journal of Finance*, 64(4), 1549–1582.

Christoffersen, S. E. K. (2001) 'Why do money fund managers voluntarily waive their fees?', *Journal of Finance*, 56(3), 1117–1140.

Cumming, D. J. and J. G. MacIntosh (2006) 'Crowding out private equity: Canadian evidence', *Journal of Business Venturing*, 21(5), 569–609.

Fleischer, V. (2008) 'Two and twenty: Taxing partnership profit in private equity funds', *New York University Law Review*, 83(1), 1–59.

Gompers, P. and J. Lerner (2000) 'Money chasing deals? The impact of fund inflows on private equity valuation', *Journal of Financial Economics*, 55(2), 281–325.

Hochberg, Y. V. and J. D. Rauh (2013) 'Local overweighting and underperformance: Evidence from limited partner private equity investments', *Review of Financial Studies*, 26(2), 403–451.

Huyghebaert, N., R. Priem and L. Van de Gucht (2010) 'Incidence and structure of European buyout syndicates: The relationship between target companies and lead buyout investors', Working Paper.

Ewans, M. C.M., Jones, and M. Rhodes-Kropf (2003) 'The price of diversifiable risk in venture capital and private equity', Columbia University, Working Paper.

Kaplan, S. N. and A. Schoar (2005) 'Private equity performance: Returns, persistence, and capital flows', *Journal of Finance*, 60(4), 1791–1823.

Luukkonen, T., M. Deschryvere, F. Bertoni and T. Nikulainen (2011) 'Importance of the non-financial value added of government and independent venture capitalists', 7th European Framework Programme (Grant Agreement No. 21748).

Marquez, R., V. Nanda and M. D. Yavuz (2010) 'Private equity fund returns: Do managers actually leave money on the table?', http://dx.doi.org/10.2139/ssrn.1571180.

Metrick, A. and A. Yasuda, (2009) 'The economics of private equity funds', *Review of Financial Studies*, 23(6), 2303–2341.

PEM, Private Equity Monitor Report (2003–2009).

Phalippou, L. (2007) 'Investing in private equity funds: A survey', http://dx.doi.org/10.2139/ ssrn.980243.

Quindlen, R. (2000) *Confessions of a Venture Capitalist: Inside the High-stakes World of Start-up Financing*, New York: Hachette Digital Inc.,Warner Books.

7

Does 'Political Bias' Undermine the Korea Investment Corporation?

Andrea Paltrinieri, Flavio Pichler and Stefano Miani

7.1 Introduction

In recent years sovereign wealth funds (SWFs) have become increasingly important as institutional investors, both in numerical terms and in terms of assets under management (Aizenman and Glick, 2007; Jen, 2007; Kern, 2007, 2008). In particular, since 2007, when many banks needed to recapitalize because of the subprime financial crisis, the number of SWFs has continuously increased to reach 65 investment vehicles in December 2012, with total assets under management equal to more than $5 trillion (Sovereign Wealth Fund Institute, 2013).

Thus far, the academic research has proposed different definitions of SWFs (Rozanov, 2005; Blundell-Wignall, Wei Hu and Yermo, 2008; Kimmitt, 2008; International Monetary Fund, 2008; Truman, 2008).

For the purposes of this chapter, we can define SWFs as those investment vehicles that: (1) are established and controlled by a sovereign state or by a confederation of states; (2) raise funds mainly through transfers of surplus financial assets in foreign currency; (3) can issue explicit liabilities to increase financial leverage;[1] and (4) whose asset allocation and time horizon differ in relation to their institutional objectives.

With regard to institutional objectives, SWFs can be classified into: stabilization funds, that serve to isolate state budgets from the excessive volatility of commodity prices; savings funds, that ensure intergenerational transfers of national wealth; sovereign pension reserve funds (SPRFs), that cover potential future pension deficits;[2] and reserve investment corporations, whose aim is to manage those currency reserves in excess of the ones managed by the central bank, in order to maximize the risk–return relationship.

In terms of funding, we could distinguish between commodity funds, that raise capital from the sale of non-renewable commodities extracted from national soil (e.g. oil, copper, gas) and non-commodity funds, whose funding comes from transfers of currency reserves generated by current account surpluses, that is, an export-led strategy associated with an exchange rate pegged to a major currency.

Following the above definition, we identify a data set of 56 SWFs, with total assets under management (AUM) of about $5.5 trillion, according to SWF Institute (in Table 7.1 we summarize the top twenty SWFs in terms of AUM).

The aim of this chapter is to carry out a case study on the Korea Investment Corporation (KIC), a non-commodity fund established in 2005 and classified as a reserve investment corporation; the KIC had a total AUM of $57 billion as of June, 2013, placing it the 17th in the Sovereign Wealth Fund Institute ranking.

Our specific interest in the Korea Investment Corporation stems from both macro- and micro-economic reasons. First of all, South Korea is one of the most important economies among the so-called emerging markets. *The Economist* magazine (2011) stated that South Korea is a model of growth, even more so than China, which is too vast to copy, Taiwan, Singapore or Hong Kong. Second, the KIC was among the first SWFs to re-entrust financial resources to external managers, with important implications in terms of corporate governance and geographical asset allocation. Third, it was one of the first SWFs to invest in alternatives, in terms of managing excess reserves, consistent with the form of reserve investment corporations. Finally, KIC provides some information on its functioning. Even though its degree of disclosure is not as high as the top SWFs, KIC's Linaburg–Maduell Index is equal to 9 out of 10, steadily over time, and the Truman scoreboard is equal to 51 per cent, higher than all other Middle-East SWFs. Therefore, we have been able to get information about KIC's corporate governance, investment strategies and asset allocation, unlike other SWFs in the top twenty ranking (e.g. Abu Dhabi Investment Authority, SAFE Investment Company, Saudi Arabia Monetary Agency).

Our study makes two important contributions to the existing literature. First of all, we would like to contribute to an emerging body of literature dealing with case studies on individual SWFs. Other similar studies include Goldstein (2008) and Balding (2012), who investigate Temasek, a Singaporean SWF; Clark and Monk (2010), who focus on the other Singaporean SWF (Government of Investment Corporation (GIC)); and Chesterman (2008), who analyses the Norway Government

Table 7.1 The top twenty SWFs for assets under management (June, 2013)

State	Sovereign Wealth Fund	Starting date	Funding	Assets under management (US $billion)
Norway	Government Pension Fund Global	1990	Commodity	737.2
U.A.E. (Abu Dhabi)	Abu Dhabi Investment Authority	1976	Commodity	627
China	SAFE Investment Company	1997	non-commodity	567.9
Saudi Arabia	SAMA	1952	Commodity	532.8
China	China Investment Corporation	2007	non-commodity	482
Singapore	Government of Singapore Investment Corporation	1981	non-commodity	247.5
Russia	National Welfare Fund	2008	Commodity	175.5
China	National Security Fund	2000	non-commodity	160.6
Singapore	Temasek Holdings	1974	non-commodity	157.5
Qatar	Qatar Investment Authority	2005	Commodity	115
Australia	Australian Future Fund	2006	non-commodity	88,7
Algeria	Revenue Regulation Fund	2000	Commodity	77.2
U.A.E. (Dubai)	Investment Corporation of Dubai	2006	Commodity	70
U.A.E. (Abu Dhabi)	International Petroleum Investment Company	1984	Commodity	65.3
Libya	Libyan Investment Authority	2006	Commodity	65
Kazakhstan	Kazakhstan National Fund	2000	Commodity	61.8
South Korea	Korea Investment Corporation	2005	non-commodity	57
U.A.E. (Abu Dhabi)	Mubadala Development Company	2002	Commodity	53.1
Iran	National Development Fund of Iran	2011	Commodity	49.6
USA	Alaska Permanent Fund	1976	Commodity	46.8
Total				4,437.5

Source: Data are collected from the Sovereign Wealth Fund Institute.

Pension Fund Global. Woochan (2011) gives a detailed account of the creation and evolution of the Korea Investment Corporation. The author emphasizes several problems with the fund, including that: i) its mission statement is unclear and has evolved over time; ii) it exhibits a clear conflict of interest between the central bank and the Ministry of Finance and Economy; and iii) it favours bureaucrats and politicians.

In this respect, as our work is complementary to Woochan's study, we try to expand the existing literature on SWFs 'political bias', by examining the KIC's investment process, asset allocation and portfolios.

Therefore, we investigate whether KIC aims to maximize the risk/return relationship on the portfolio, given that it is subject to the pursuit of specific institutional goals. To this end, we evaluate the KIC's investment strategies for the period 2005–2012 (i.e. from its inception) by using benchmark as well as asset allocation analyses. Our results suggest that the KIC tries to meet financial objectives.

Since Dyck and Morse (2011) point out that SWFs' portfolios are explained by taking into account both 'financial and state industrial planner objectives', and Paltrinieri and Pichler (2012) show that in the medium- to long-term SWFs pursue financial objectives (while in the short term they are influenced by 'external political bias'), we also deepen the analysis of the investment process and the corporate governance of the funds. We find evidence that the maximization of the risk/return relationship coexists with political bias.

Our findings may be useful to policymakers for the definition of a regulatory framework in order to supervise SWFs in a similar way to other institutional investors (Mezzacapo, 2009), that is, without introducing any new requirements (Kimmitt, 2008; Epstein and Rose, 2009; Barbary and Bortolotti, 2011), or, alternatively, with the introduction of tighter regulation (Gilson and Milhaupt, 2008). Our chapter might also be helpful to Asia–Pacific central banks that have a large amount of foreign reserves, should they wish to establish a new sovereign wealth fund (India, Thailand), or to transfer the excess reserves into an existing one (China, Indonesia, Malaysia).

The rest of the chapter is structured as follows. Section 7.2 provides a brief literature review on SWFs' asset allocation and political bias. Section 7.3 offers a view on the KIC's framework. Section 7.4 focuses on data and methodology. Section 7.5 analyses the KIC's asset allocation and investment process. Finally, Section 7.6 presents our main conclusions and indicates possible directions for future research.

7.2 A brief literature review on SWFs' investment strategies

The growing importance of SWFs in financial markets has spawned an expanding body of research that examines their investment strategies and overall portfolio. Some studies focus on the impact of SWFs on the target firm's performance. For example, Bortolotti et al. (2010), Dewenter, Han and Malatesta (2010); Knill, Lee and Mauck (2010), among others, investigate the stock price reaction of target firms around acquisitions from SWFs. They show that financial markets expect these institutional investors to improve the target firms' performance, given the positive price reaction in a short window. However, the authors note that, in a longer time horizon (from one to two years), SWFs are not able to improve both target firms' performance and stock prices through acting as passive investors.

Other studies analyse the portfolio of SWFs and their asset allocation. Balding (2008) investigates the portfolios of seven SWFs in a single year and shows that they have a preference for low risk/return asset classes, such as investment grade bonds and liquidity. Even in the case of equity investments, they tend to buy large cap shares, with a low level of risk; the same conclusions are reached by Chhaochharia and Laeven (2008). In contrast, Fernandez and Eschweiler (2008) show a more aggressive asset allocation by SWFs, as they overweight equities and alternatives. Kunzel et al. (2011) compare the portfolios of SWFs across time, around the subprime financial crisis: the authors divide SWFs into four groups – stabilization, saving, sovereign pension reserve fund and reserve investment corporations – and show the importance of both the institutional objective and the time horizon for strategic asset allocation.

The academic interest in SWFs has recently shifted towards investigating the presence of political bias, or the influence of political motivations in SWFs' investment strategies. For example, Balding (2008) and Avendaño and Santiso (2009) find no evidence of political bias, suggesting that SWFs behave similarly to other institutional investors in terms ofmaximizing the risk/return relationship of the overall portfolio. In contrast, Bernstein, Lerner and Schoar (2009) highlight how SWFs' investment strategies are influenced by political motivations, especially when a fund's board of directors includes politicians and a fund's management is not entrusted to external managers. The authors, speculating about the influence of the politicians on a fund's corporate governance and investment strategies, mainly refer to 'internal political bias'.

Knill, Lee and Mauck (2012) demonstrate that SWFs follow non-financial objectives in their investments and that they 'are more likely to invest in nations with which they have relatively weaker political relations', instead of maximizing the overall portfolio. Paltrinieri and Pichler (2012) show that, in the short term, SWFs investment strategies are influenced by political reasons, which they label 'external political bias': they argue that the influence of macro-economic factors related to internal financial systems leads SWFs to deviate from portfolio maximization.

7.3 The Korea Investment Corporation's framework

Before carrying out the case study, we would like to provide an overview of the Korea Investment Corporation's background. One of the peculiarities of the Korean economy concerns capital flows (Woochan, 2011; Lee and Rhee, 2012). During the 1997–1998 East-Asian crisis, Korea faced a huge financial account deficit, but, at the same time, the Korean Won (KR₩) began to weaken against dollar, with the beneficial effect that Korean exports became cheaper.

As a consequence, after the Asian financial crisis, both current and financial account surpluses, along with a lingering Korean Won depreciation against the US dollar (Jo, 2011), fostered a substantial build-up in foreign reserves, probably well above any precautionary level needed to counteract sudden financial shocks (IMF, 2003; Jinyong and Yong-Cheol, 2005; Aizenman, Lee and Rhee, 2007). In 1997 foreign reserves were $9 billion, at the end of 2003 they reached $155 billion and at the end of 2007 they increased to $262 billion, which was equivalent to 137 per cent of short-term external debt (IMF, 2012).

About $65 billion of these reserves were then used, during the subprime financial crisis in 2007–2008, in order to ensure foreign exchange liquidity and to provide liquidity to the entire financial system. After that, the reserve accumulation process reached the pre-crisis amount in 2009 ($269.9 billion: equivalent to 146 per cent of short-term external debt) and peaked at $304 billion in 2011.

Since the reserves are often held in safe assets, the opportunity costs are not negligible (Lee and Rhee, 2012); hence the idea of establishing a sovereign wealth fund, to manage the excess reserves in a more lucrative way than those managed by the Bank of Korea.

The Korea Investment Corporation was established in 2005 by the Korea Investment Corporation Act with the aims of managing national wealth, which is entrusted by both the government and the Bank of

Korea, and helping to develop South Korea's financial system. Consistent with its legal form of reserve investment corporation, that is, a SWF made up of excess reserves, the KIC aims to maximize the risk/return relationship when managing resources, while the Bank of Korea faces restrictions in managing foreign exchange reserves, because they have primarily invested in highly liquid assets, cash and debt securities (IMF, Balance of Payments Manual).

The KIC has its own legal personality because it was set up by the Ministry of Finance and Economy as a corporation, with an initial equity capital of KRW 200 billion (about $200 million), and was not established as a pool of assets, such as, for example, SAMA. It is also an asset management company that oversees the assets entrusted to it by the Bank of Korea and the Foreign Exchange Stabilization Fund. Originally, these assets amounted to $20 billion, equivalent to 13 per cent of total foreign reserves (Woochan, 2011): the Bank of Korea provided $17 billion at the end of the first quarter of 2007 and the Foreign Exchange Stabilization Fund contributed the remaining $3 billion in October, 2007.

Information is scarce about how and when financial resources would be provided by the government and/or the central bank and under which conditions withdrawals from the fund would be possible. As regards funding, no threshold for foreign reserves exists that promotes their transfer to the KIC (e.g. if they exceed three months of imports or total short external debt), nor are there specific provisions for the issuance of new debt to increase financial leverage. It seems that issuing new domestic bonds could amplify the sterilization effect previously examined and raise concerns about the fund's performance, due to the high KRW interest rates they could suffer. Therefore, no bond issuance has been made yet.

As regards withdrawals, the Presidential Enforcement Decree states that the Bank of Korea can withdraw financial resources from the KIC if: 1) the size of reserves falls by more than 10 per cent in two consecutive months; 2) Korea's sovereign rating falls below the investment level rating for at least two rating agencies; 3) the KIC breaches the investment management contract and does not ratify such a breach within a month. Until now, no confirmation exists of the fact that the KIC was involved in the subprime financial crisis, despite the use of Korea's international reserves to support domestic banks. Only a couple of newspapers speculated that the KIC would support Korean banks when they were forced to roll over their external debt (Woochan, 2011).

As of June, 2013, the KIC had assets under management of $57 billion, but it aimed to raise this to $200 billion by 2020 (see Annual Report of KIC, 2012).

The KIC's governance structure is made up of four bodies and three divisions, with a two-tier board system: the steering committee, the Investment Subcommittee, the risk management committee and the board of directors. The steering committee is the governing body for the KIC and is composed of the Ministry of Finance and Economy and the governor of the Bank of Korea (the institutions that entrusted assets exceeding KRW 1 trillion), the CEO of the KIC and six external experts from the asset management industry ('civil members'). This composition is intended to represent all the institutions that gave rise to the fund and to ensure autonomy and independence from public authorities, thanks to the six external experts. As regards the latter, the KIC accurately defines the necessary requisites to be eligible as civil members, that is, a background in of financial systems and corporate management, but not an actual working knowledge of the asset management industry.

The steering committee has responsibility over the most important issues regarding the KIC, such as strategic asset allocation, medium- to long-term investment strategies, increases and/or decreases in the fund's assets under management, the appointment of external managers and governors, approval of the financial statement and the evaluation of performances.

The three other bodies (the Investment Subcommittee, the risk management committee and the board of directors) form the KIC's governance structure. The Investment Subcommittee implements the decisions taken by the governing body, defines the tactical asset allocation in agreement with the chief investment officer, plans investments on an annual basis and makes decisions on all the issues relating to asset management posed by the steering committee. This body is quite similar to the asset allocation committee in a mutual fund.

The board of directors is a body with almost purely executive powers. It is formed by the CEO and all the governors appointed by the CEO after consultation with the steering committee. The CEO is directly appointed by the President of the Republic of Korea, on recommendation from the Ministry of Strategy and Finance and after approval from the steering committee.

In contrast, the number of governors is not fixed: there is no information on their current number or on the range within which they can vary. The key functions of the board of governors are the use of emergency funds (although no explanation is given as to why these might be used), the arrangement of an estimated budget, the adoption of internal regulations and all other issues the steering committee asks it to decide on.

Finally, the corporate governance structure includes three strictly operational and managerial divisions. The first one is the investment management division, headed by the chief investment officer (CIO). It is divided into different subdivisions according to asset classes (fixed income, equity) and strategies (investment strategy group and private markets group). The CIO implements measures adopted by the steering committee and, is particularly focused on tactical asset allocation, short-term investment policy, portfolio management and performance monitoring. He is accountable to both the board of governors and the steering committee.

The corporate management division is chaired by the chief operating officer (COO). Its key functions are medium- to long-term planning, arrangement of annual business plans and IT support to investment management through the information technology team. The risk management division is chaired by the chief risk officer (CRO). This division is responsible for the risk management of the fund's activity, the supervision of risk factors and the performance of investments.

According to the Korea Investment Corporation Act, independence from the management internal audit function is also present in the form of the statutory auditor. The auditor is appointed by the Ministry of Strategy and Finance, after consultation with the steering committee, and performs the typical auditing functions of being an accountant to the board of governors and arranging the audit reports. The statutory auditor appoints the external auditors responsible for the audit of the fund's financial statement.

From the above analysis we can evince that the governance structure of this SWF seems to ensure independence from political interferences, thanks particularly to the presence, in the steering committee, of the six external experts in asset management issues who should have no links with public authorities. However, two open issues remain: on the one hand, the role of members such as the minister of strategy and finance and the governor of the Bank of Korea in the definition of the guidelines or the implementation of specific investments; on the other hand, the possibility that the President of the Republic of Korea decides not to appoint specific members to the steering committee.

7.4 Data and methodology

Having outlined the Korea Investment Corporation's origins and corporate governance, and in spite of multiple changes to its mission statement over time, we carry out our case study in order to investigate whether the KIC aims to maximize its portfolio's risk/return relationship, given that it is subject to the pursuit of specific institutional goals.

To this end, we evaluate the KIC's investment strategies and overall portfolio. We collected data for the period 2005–2012 (i.e. from its inception) from the KIC's annual reports (the first one that we considered was in 2006, the last was in 2013). We also checked the KIC's and the Bloomberg's website to gather control data on investment strategies provided by the annual reports. We were able to get aggregate data on different asset classes (bonds, equities, alternatives) and the regional breakdown for single asset classes, but not the individual stocks or bonds held by the KIC.

We are aware that our analysis suffers from a major limitation due to the lack of data on sovereign wealth funds, since they are not regulated, as hedge funds are, and the KIC is not an exception: this issue could lead to a biased analysis.

Even though its degree of disclosure is not as high as the top SWFs, the KIC's Linaburg–Maduell Index is equal to 9 out of 10 and it is steady over time (Woochan, 2011, assumes a score of 6), according to the Sovereign Wealth Fund Institute; in comparison, the China Investment Corporation has a Linaburg–Maduell Index equal to 8 while the Government of Singapore Investment Corporation is equal to 6. The Truman scoreboard is equal to 51 per cent, higher than most East-Asian non-commodity SWFs and Middle-Eastern commodity SWFs.

After gathering data, the first step of our study is to analyse the benchmarks, in order to make an *ex ante* evaluation of the overall portfolio, before performing a strategic asset allocation analysis. Since we assume that the KIC's first goal is to manage the excess foreign reserves in a more lucrative way than the Bank of Korea, the first hypothesis is that time horizon is a key driver in strategic asset allocation: the longer the time horizon and holding period, the higher the risk tolerance (Siegel 1998). As Damodaran (2010) demonstrated, this is related to equity risk premium. As regards the KIC, we expect a higher proportion of equities over bonds and liquidity in its asset allocation (Gollier 2007), given that it would also be the 'premier sovereign wealth fund for future generations' (KIC Vision, Annual Report 2012).

The second hypothesis is that the KIC, given the long time horizon, seeks to invest in illiquid assets, such as private equity, hedge funds and real estate, in order to exploit the illiquidity premiums, or the extra return required by investors for the holding of a less liquid asset (Brandt and Kavajecz 2004, Khandani and Lo 2009).

The second step is to analyse geographical asset allocation. Regarding this, there are two opposing thrusts: on the one hand someone could expect a preference for domestic/regional assets, the so-called 'home bias', which characterizes institutional investors (Chan, Covrig and Ng, 2005; Ke, Ng and Wang, 2006) and which could be related to an internal political bias (Bernstein et al., 2009); on the other hand a ban on investment in KRW-denominated assets (Woochan, 2011) reduces the probability for investment inside Korea, but cannot rule out investments in countries with similar cultural origins (Chhaochharia and Laeven, 2008).

Our third hypothesis is that the KIC avoids home and cultural bias and invests abroad, outside the Asia–Pacific area.

The third step is to investigate political bias. Since Bernstein et al. (2009) show that SWFs are affected by internal political bias when the fund's management is not entrusted to external managers, because of the presence of politicians in the Board of Directors, we analyse the KIC's investment process. We argue that if most of the investment strategies were implemented by external managers, it would mean that the KIC avoids any form of internal political bias.

7.5 The KIC's investment strategies

7.5.1 The analysis of benchmark and strategic asset allocation

The first method we use to understand the KIC's investment strategies is the benchmark analysis for the period 2005–2012 (see Table 7.2).

Table 7.2 shows the difficulty in identifying the KIC portfolios through this type of analysis: the first benchmark (Morgan Stanley Capital International All Country (MSCI World)) was introduced in 2007, in

Table 7.2 Benchmark for asset class (December 2007–December 2012)

Asset Class	Benchmark	Introduction
Equity	Morgan Stanley Capital International All Country	2007
Bonds	Barclays Capital Global Aggregate	2008
Inflation-linked bonds	Barclays Capital Global Inflation-linked	2009
Hedge funds	G7 Inflation +5%	2010
Private equity		
Real estate		
Commodity	S&P GSCI Light Energy	2010

Source: 2010–2012 KIC Annual Reports.

relation to the equity component. With reference to the bond component, in September 2008, Barclays Capital Global Aggregate substituted Lehman Brothers Global Aggregate Bond Index after Lehman Brothers failed; at the end of 2009, Barclays Capital Global Inflation-linked was established to identify inflation-linked bonds as a stand-alone asset class. Finally, in 2010, two benchmarks were introduced as regards the alternative asset class: S&P GSCI Light Energy index is related to commodities, while hedge funds, private equity and real estate got a target return, equal to G7 Inflation plus five per cent.

Overall, there is a single benchmark for each asset class: the equity and bond components are represented by a global index, while the alternative asset class has one sectorial index (S&P GSCI Light Energy index) and one target return.

The absence of any weight for each index makes it difficult to identify the KIC's portfolio and leads us to investigate the strategic asset allocation (see Table 7.3).

To analyse the strategic asset allocation, we divided the KIC's portfolios into four asset classes, namely: cash, fixed income, equity and alternatives. We included inflation-linked bonds in the fixed-income asset class, while investments in private equity, hedge funds, real estate and commodities were included in the alternatives asset class, as in Kunzel et al. (2011).

Looking at Table 7.3, we find evidence that the Korea Investment Corporation opted for an aggressive strategic asset allocation; furthermore, the weight of the riskiest asset classes, such as equity and alternatives, has increased over time.

Indeed, after the first investment in bonds was made in November, 2006, there has been a progressive growth of the equity component. In December 2007, $14.8 billion out of the $20 billion entrusted by the Foreign Exchange Stabilization Fund and the central bank were invested: $10.3 billion (71 per cent) in bonds and $4.5 billion (29 per

Table 7.3 KIC strategic asset allocation (December 2006–December 2012)

	2006 (%)	2007 (%)	2008 (%)	2009 (%)	2010 (%)	2011 (%)	2012 (%)
Cash	0	0	0	0	2	2	2
Fixed-income	100	71	71	49	49	40	39
Equity	0	29	29	44	43	52	53
Alternatives	0	0	0	7	6	6	6

Source: 2007–2012 KIC Annual Reports.

cent) in equities, and this asset allocation did not change in 2008. However, in 2009 major changes occurred regarding the KIC's portfolio, since its assets under management had increased to $30 billion by December of that year. The strategic asset allocation shifted towards a higher risk/return relationship: at the end of 2009, equities were, in fact, 47 per cent of the total traditional portfolio. Furthermore, in the second half of 2009 the Ministry of Finance and Economy, through the Foreign Exchange Stabilization Fund, entrusted additional assets to the KIC. In total, $3 billion was provided to make 'special investments' and $2 billion to be invested in alternatives. The former were used to buy a $2 billion stake in Merrill Lynch, the latter to implement investments in the alternatives asset class, up to just under 7 per cent of the overall portfolio at the end of 2009.

In 2010, the assets under management amounted to $37.5 billion and were divided into three different portfolios: 90.8 per cent was invested in traditional asset classes, 5.5 per cent in the alternatives asset class and 3.7 per cent was directed to special investments. While the percentage of risky assets has remained almost unchanged in the traditional portfolio, as regards special investments, the KIC has aimed at building a diversified portfolio through acquiring shares in leader firms at a global level. By the end of 2010, these special investments were related to four firms of the financial and energy sectors: for the former, Bank of America–Merrill Lynch, where the KIC's shares already amounted to more than 7 per cent as of end 2008, for the latter, Chesapeake Energy, with an interest in natural gas production, Laricina Energy and Osum Oil Sands Corp., both active in the oil sector.

In 2011, as the assets under management increased to $42.9 billion, thanks to the additional resources provided by the government and the Bank of Korea, investments in the traditional asset classes increased to 91.1 per cent, at the expense of special investments. High volatility in the global financial markets due to different factors, such as the eurozone debt crisis, the downgrading of the US economy and the slowdown of the Chinese economy, did not imply changes in the KIC's investment policy. On the contrary, it increased the weight for higher risk activities – possibly consistent with the new mission of the SWF 'to be the premier sovereign fund for future generations' – which boosts a long-term time horizon for investments.

Consequently, investments in fixed income decreased from 49 per cent of the overall portfolio in 2010 to 41 per cent in 2011, while equities increased from 43 per cent of the overall portfolio in 2010 to 51 per cent in 2011. Investments in alternatives remained unchanged. As regards special investments, the KIC did not disclose information for 2011.

In 2012, additional injections of financial resources to the fund resulted in another substantial increase in the assets under management, which reached $57 billion at the end of the year through 'increased exposure to stocks and credit to enhance returns' (Annual Report 2012, CEO Message:8). Indeed, in December 2012 the equity component amounted to 53 per cent of the total portfolio, with a stable 6 per cent of the alternative asset class.

Looking at the shift in the strategic asset allocation over time (in 2007, only 29 per cent of the total assets under management was invested in equities; in 2012 this percentage was equal to 53 per cent, with another 6 per cent of alternatives), we can observe that time horizon is an important key driver in the KIC's investment strategies. In particular, strategic asset allocation changed substantially in 2009, probably because of the impact of the subprime crisis on the fund's performances (see Table 7.5 for an overview). The Steering Committee then decided to implement a 'contrarian strategy', increasing investments in equities and alternatives and therefore decreasing those in bonds.

Given that this shift proved to be permanent, we support the hypothesis that the KIC tries to maximize the portfolio risk/return relationship, with a higher proportion of equities over bonds and liquidity in order to exploit equity risk premium. At the same time, the KIC tries to invest in alternatives in order to exploit illiquidity premiums. This would be consistent with the nature of the fund ('reserve investment corporation'), but also with its last mission (to 'increase national wealth by maximizing risk/adjusted returns and invest for the benefit of future generation'). From this analysis, we can then evince that the Korea Investment Corporation pursues financial objectives.

7.5.2 The analysis of geographical asset allocation

The next step is to analyse geographical asset allocation. Since information is only available for 2010 and 2011, on one hand, we divided the total portfolio into three asset classes (equities, bonds and alternatives) and, on the other hand, we considered four geographical areas, in which each asset class can be invested (America, Europe, Asia–Pacific and emerging markets – ex-Asia). Table 7.4 shows the KIC's geographical asset allocation for the period 2010–2011.

Looking at Table 7.4, we can argue that geographical asset allocation does not seem to be influenced by a strong home bias, that is, a preference for domestic/regional assets. As regards, for example, the geographical

Table 7.4 KIC geographical asset allocation (December 2010–December 2011)

Korea Investment Corporation				
	America (%)	**Europe (%)**	**Emerging markets (ex-Asia) (%)**	**Asia–Pacific (%)**
Geographical area (2010)				
Equities	47	25	12	16
Bonds	46	32	3	19
Alternative assets	60	19	18	3
Geographical area (2011)				
Equities	40	19	28	13
Bonds	49	30	8	13
Alternative assets	52	24	13	11

Source: 2010–2011 KIC annual reports.

asset allocation of the equity component in 2010, 47 per cent was invested in America and 25 per cent in Europe. These weights were not so very different from their benchmark, namely MSCI World, where US weights were 48 per cent and Europe weights were 25 per cent.

This trend is confirmed by the other asset classes in 2010 and 2011: bond issues in Europe have a higher weight than equities in both years and in 2011 the weight of emerging markets – ex-Asia equities increased from 12 per cent to 28 per cent. The Asia–Pacific area has a less than 20 per cent weight on the overall portfolio in 2010 (about equal to zero in alternatives), and less than 15 per cent in 2011.

Overall, we can say that the KIC tends to avoid home bias, since its geographical asset allocation demonstrates that it invests mainly outside the Asia–Pacific region and it is overweight in American assets.

Therefore, through the geographical asset allocation analysis we can rule out any form of political bias, as the KIC tries to pursue financial objectives, under its institutional goal of maximizing the excess reserve risk/return relationship, and avoids any form of home bias by investing outside the Asia–Pacific region.

7.5.3 The 'internal political bias' analysis

It is also interesting to go deeper inside the investment process, as Woochan (2011) underlines that 'the case of KIC effectively shows how a sovereign wealth fund can be operated in a way that favours the bureaucrats and the politicians'. In particular, we want to dwell on the role of internal or external managers in the KIC's portfolio management.

At the end of 2007, almost all financial resources were re-entrusted to external managers: indeed, they had to manage $4.5 billion in equities and $8 billion in bonds (out of $14.8 billion (85 per cent) of the assets under management). The remaining $2.3 billion was internally invested in bonds. Investments carried out by internal managers have steadily increased over the years. In 2008, 35 per cent of the fund's financial resources were internally managed; and this percentage grew to 65 per cent at the end of 2009, to reach 70.3 per cent in 2010 and 71.9 per cent in 2011. At the end of 2012, there was a decline to 66.7 per cent.

The steady increase of in-house investments can have different explanations. As Woochan (2011) notes: the more resources are internally managed, the less relevant is the double-fee payment made by the Bank of Korea (one for the KIC and the other one for the KIC's external managers). At the same time, this choice does not attract foreign asset management companies into Korea and thereby does not contribute to the development of Korea's financial industry (one of the KIC's missions). If we follow results from Bernstein et al. (2009), the more in-house managed resources there are, the more the probability of internal political bias.

To verify whether external managers did not get positive results, due to double-fee payments and in order to justify the choice to manage financial resources in-house, we also check for the KIC's performance (see Table 7.5).

According to the table, there is no strong evidence that, over time, internal management of financial resources has been better than external management. In terms of the total return rate against the benchmark, there are three years of underperformance (2007, 2008, 2011), but in the annual reports, there is no disclosure regarding the presence of internal or external managers.

Table 7.5 Korea Investment Corporation performance

	2007 (%)	2008 (%)	2009 (%)	2010 (%)	2011 (%)	2012 (%)
Total rate of return	7.40	−13.71	18.67	8.46	−3.32	11.83
Versus benchmark	−0.25	−0.66	+1.42	+0.05	−0.90	0.66
Equities	5.19	−41.43	31.96	11.71	−10.26	16.20
Versus benchmark	−1.19	−0.11	−0.23	−0.68	−0.99	+0.01
Bonds	9.91	3.81	8.56	5.60	3.94	7.76
Versus benchmark	+0.09	−1.36	1.71	0.35	−0.71	+1.24

Source: 2008–2012 KIC annual reports.

Nevertheless, in 2007 and 2008 the KIC showed an underperformance against the benchmark in both the equities and bonds investments, which was also due to the higher fees paid to the external managers. Only in 2012 was there an over-performance against the benchmark in both the equities and bonds investments, with 66.7 per cent of internally managed total assets under management. Overall, the total annualized return for the period 2005–2012 was 4.32 per cent, with a slight underperformance against the benchmark of -0.07 per cent.

Since there is no strong evidence that internal managers were better than external managers, we tend to support the explanation of Bernstein et al. (2009): since the KIC was among the first SWFs to delegate the management of part of its portfolio to external managers in order to ensure independence and lessen political influence, the reversal of the process raises doubts about the presence of internal political bias.

7.6 Conclusion

In this chapter we carried out a case study on the Korea Investment Corporation, a non-commodity sovereign wealth fund, with total assets under management of $57 billion and placed 17th in the Sovereign Wealth Fund Institute ranking. We contextualized the KIC within the Korean economy, since the emergence of a new SWF in Korea occurred after the Asian financial crisis of 1997–1998. In the first years of the 2000s, Korea experienced a long period of both current and financial account surplus, during which a large amount of foreign reserves were accumulated. As a result, the idea to establish a SWF emerged and it was classified as a reserve investment corporation, with the aim of managing these excess reserves in a more lucrative way than the Bank of Korea was able to achieve.

After giving an overview of the fund's corporate governance, we tried to assess if political bias undermines the KIC's management, through the analysis of the KIC's asset allocation and investment process.

Our results suggest that the KIC tends to manage financial resources by pursuing the maximization of the risk/return relationship, since strategic asset allocation has shifted towards riskier asset classes, such as equities and alternatives, with the aim of exploiting the equity risk premium and the illiquidity premium. In this sense, we can argue that time horizon is a key driver of strategic asset allocation, as the KIC tries to be 'the premier sovereign wealth fund to future generations'. At the same time, geographical asset allocation does not seem to show a strong home bias, as the KIC overweighs US and Asia–Pacific areas, in both the bonds and equity components of its portfolio.

However, a deeper analysis of the investment process shows that it has been reversed over time, even though the KIC was among the first SWFs to delegate the management of part of its portfolio to external managers in order to ensure independence and lessen political influence. Since most of the KIC's financial resources are managed in-house, we cannot completely rule out the presence of an internal political bias, that is, the influence of political motivations on investment strategies.

Overall, we support the hypothesis that in the Korea Investment Corporation both financial and political objectives coexist, as Dyck and Morse (2011) and Paltrinieri and Pichler (2012) show, but in contrast to Balding (2008) and Avendaño and Santiso (2009). We also support the hypothesis of Bernstein et al. (2009) that SWFs investment strategies are influenced by political factors, especially when the fund's management is not entrusted to external managers.

Notes

1. This is in contrast with prevalent literature (Jen 2007, Monk 2008, Monitor Group and ENI Enrico Mattei Foundation 2008). However, it permits us to take into account an important characteristic of SWFs, that is, to raise funds through bond issues (consider Temasek Holdings or Dubai World).
2. It is important to distinguish between sovereign pension reserve funds (SPRFs) and social security reserve funds (SSRFs), the latter have the same objective as the SPRFs, but their financial resources accrue principally from the payroll taxes of employees and employers. SSRFs are not considered SWFs for the purposes of the present study, and neither are the activities of central banks in managing foreign exchange reserves to achieve macro-economic objectives, not even the state owned enterprises

References

Aizenman, J. and R. Glick (2007) 'Sovereign wealth funds: Stumbling blocks or stepping stones to financial globalization?' Federal Reserve Board of San Francisco, Economic Letter, December 14.

Aizenman, J., Y. Lee and Y. Rhee (2007) 'International reserves management and capital mobility in a volatile world: Policy considerations and a case study of Korea', *Journal of Japanese International Economies*, 21, 1–15.

Avendaño, R. and J. Santiso (2009) 'Are sovereign wealth funds' investments politically biased? A comparison with mutual funds' Working Paper, OECD Development Centre 283, 1–50.

Balding, C. (2008) 'A portfolio analysis of sovereign wealth funds', Working Paper, University of California, 1–64. SSRN eLibrary.

Balding, C. (2012) 'A brief research note on Temasek Holdings and Singapore: Mr Madoff goes to Singapore', Working Paper, 1–12. SSRN eLibrary.

Barbary, V. and B. Bortolotti (2011) 'Taming Leviathan: Foreign investment, political risk and a regulatory framework for sovereign wealth funds', Paolo Baffi Centre on Central Banking and Financial Regulation, Bocconi University, Working Paper, 1–27.

Bernstein, S., J. Lerner and A. Schoar (2009) 'The investment strategies of sovereign wealth funds', National Bureau of Economic Research, Cambridge, Massachusetts, Working Paper 14861, 1–53.

Blundell-Wignall, A., Y. Wei Hu and J. Yermo (2008) 'Sovereign wealth and pension fund issues', OECD Working Papers on Insurance and Private Pensions 14, 1–18.

Bortolotti, B., V. Fotak, W. Megginson and W. Miracky (2010) 'Sovereign wealth fund investment patterns and performance', Working Paper, University of Oklahoma, 1–62. SSRN eLibrary.

Brandt, M. and K. Kavajecz (2004) 'Price discovery in the U.S. Treasury market: The impact of order flow and liquidity on the yield curve', *Journal of Finance*, 59(6), 2623–2654.

Chan, K., V. Covrig and L. Ng (2005) 'What determines the domestic bias and foreign bias? Evidence from mutual fund equity allocation worldwide', *Journal of Finance*, 60(3), 1495–1534.

Chesterman, S. (2008) 'The turn to ethics: Disinvestment from multinational corporations for human rights violations – the case of Norway's sovereign wealth fund', Working Paper, 2008. SSRN eLibrary.

Chhaochharia, V. and L. A. Laeven (2008) 'The investment allocation of sovereign wealth funds', Working Paper, 1–44. SSRN eLibrary.

Clark, G. L. and A. Monk (2010) 'Government of Singapore Investment Corporation. (GIC): Insurer of last resort and bulwark of nation-state legitimacy', *The Pacific Review*, 4, 429–451.

Damodaran, A. (2010) 'Equity Risk Premium (ERP): Determinants, estimation and implications – The 2010 Edition', Stern School of Business, 1–89.

Dewenter, K.L., X. Han and P. H. Malatesta (2010) 'Firm values and sovereign wealth fund investments', *Journal of Financial Economics*, 98, 256–278.

Dyck, A. and A. Morse (2011) 'Sovereign wealth fund portfolios', Working Paper, University of Toronto and University of Chicago, 1–36. SSRN eLibrary.

Epstein, R.A. and A. M. Rose (2009) 'The regulation of sovereign wealth funds: The virtues of going slow', *The University of Chicago Law Review*, 76(111), 1–24.

Fernandez, D. G. and B. Eschweiler (2008) 'Sovereign wealth funds: A bottom-up primer', JP Morgan Research, 1–100.

Gilson, R. J. and C. J. Milhaupt (2008) 'Sovereign wealth funds and corporate governance: A minimalist response to the new merchantilism', Law and Economics Working Paper, February, 1–35.

Goldstein, A. (2008) 'Temasek: fondo sovrano o reincarnazione dell'IRI nello stretto di Malacca?', Osservatorio Monetario, No.3, Milano, Università Cattolica del Sacro Cuore.

Gollier, C. (2007), 'Intergenerational risk-sharing and risk-taking of a pension fund', Cesifo Working Paper, April, 1–52.

International Monetary Fund (2003) 'Three current policy issues in developing countries', *World Economic Outlook*, September, 65–111.

International Monetary Fund (2008) 'Sovereign wealth funds: A work agenda', Monetary and Capital Markets and Policy Development and Review Departments, February 29, 1–38.

International Monetary Fund (2012) 'Republic of Korea, 2012 Article IV Consultation', September.

Jen, S. (2007) 'How big could sovereign wealth funds be by 2015?' Morgan Stanley Research Global, May 3.

Jinyong, K. and K. Yong-Cheol (2005) 'The monetary stabilization bond spread as a signal for financial crisis', 1–29. SSRN eLibrary.

Jo, G. J. (2011) 'Analysis of international reserve hoarding in Korea', *Pacific Economic Review*, 16(2), 154–167.

Ke, D., L. Ng and Q. Wang (2006) 'Home bias in foreign investment decisions', Working Paper, 1–45. SSRN eLibrary.

Kern, S. (2007) 'Sovereign wealth funds – state investment on the rise', Deutsche Bank Research, September 10.

Kern, S. (2008) 'SWFs and foreign investment policies – an update', Deutsche Bank Research, October 22.

Khandani, A. E. and A. W. Lo (2009) 'Illiquidity premia in asset returns: An empirical analysis of hedge funds, mutual funds, and US equity portfolios', Working Paper, June, 1–59.

KIC (2012) 'Korea Investment Corporation Annual Report 2012', www.kic.go.kr/en/.

Kimmitt, R. M. (2008) 'Public footprints in private markets: Sovereign wealth funds and the world economy', Foreign Affairs, 87, 1, January/February.

Knill, A., B. Lee, and F. Mauck (2010) 'Is sovereign wealth funds investment destabilizing?', Working Paper, Florida State University, 1–42.

Knill, A., B. Lee, and F. Mauck (2012) 'Bilateral political relations and sovereign wealth fund investment', *Journal of Corporate Finance*, 18, 108–123.

Kunzel, P., Y. Lu, I. Petrova, and J. Pihlman (2011) 'Investment objectives of sovereign wealth funds: A shifting paradigm', International Monetary Fund, IMF Working Paper, WP/11/19, 1–17.

Lee, H. and C. Rhee (2012) 'Lessons from the 1997 and the 2008 crises in Korea', *Asian Economic Policy Review*, 7, 47–64.

Mezzacapo, S. (2009) 'Law & Economics dei c.d. "Fondi Sovrani" d'investimento nell'ordinamento comunitario e nazionale', *Diritto della Banca e del Mercato Finanziario*, 22(1), 55–90.

Monitor Group and Eni Enrico Mattei Foundation (2008) 'Weathering the storm: Sovereign wealth funds in the global economic crisis of 2008', SWF Annual Report, 1–96.

Monk, A. H. B. (2008) 'Recasting the Sovereign Wealth Fund Debate: Trust, legitimacy and Governance', University of Oxford, 1–34.

Paltrinieri, A. and F. Pichler (2012) 'Are sovereign wealth funds different?', Fourth Joint World Bank/Bank for International Settlements, Public Investor Conference on Central Banks, Sovereign Wealth Funds and Public Pension Plans, Washington DC, 1–37.

Rozanov, A. (2005) 'Who holds the wealth of nations?' *Central Banking Journal*, 15, (4), May 20.

Siegel, J. (1998) *Stocks for the Long Run*, New York, Irwin.

Sovereign Wealth Fund Institute (2013), 'Fund Rankings', http://www.swfinstitute.org/fund-rankings/.

Truman, E. (2008) 'The rise of sovereign wealth funds: Impacts on foreign policy and economic interests', Testimony before the Committee on Foreign Affairs, US House of Representatives, Washington, May 21.

Woochan, K. (2011) 'Korea Investment Corporation: Its origin and evolution', KDI School Working Paper series, 1–44, SSRN eLibrary.

8

Regulating High-frequency Trading: An Examination of European, US and Australian Equity Market Structures

Giusy Chesini and Elisa Giaretta

8.1 Introduction

Equity trading in the world is dramatically changing and at the same time raising doubts as to both its quality (liquidity, price efficiency and volatility) and its integrity; the change is mainly due to two factors: the first is fiercer competition, both among trading venues and between trading venues and intermediaries; the second is the increasingly significant role of technology in trading processes. Fiercer competition has primarily been the result of regulation. The second factor, technology, is significant in so far as the algorithms used by some traders have changed the operating procedures underlying the execution of orders. While advances in technology are a natural evolution of the market, they have a major impact on market structures. In particular, in the event of network outages or flash crashes, doubts arise in relation to the market integrity and the existence of a level playing field, since technology is expensive and not equally accessible to all traders.

High-frequency trading (HFT) is commonly defined as a subset of algorithmic trading where, in particular, a large number of small orders are sent to the market at high speed, with round-trip execution times measured in microseconds. Programs running on high-speed computers analyse massive amounts of market data, using sophisticated algorithms to exploit trading opportunities that may open up for milliseconds or seconds. High-frequency traders are constantly taking advantage of very small price imbalances; by doing that at a high rate of recurrence, they are able to generate sizeable profits. Typically a high-frequency trader would not hold a position open for more than a few seconds.

Even if HFT is just a way of trading, it has been widely blamed for the May 2010 flash crash when the Dow Jones Industrial Average dropped by nearly 9 per cent in a matter of minutes before recovering. That crash was just the first of a series of market disruptions caused by electronic trading over the past few years. In 2012 technical glitches also disrupted Facebook's IPO and were blamed for the collapse of brokerage firm Knight Capital.

With HFT being a relatively new phenomenon in securities markets, regulators strive to collect information in order to decide on potentially new provisions which might become necessary if HFT proves to present a risk to capital market quality or integrity. If HFT causes some serious risks to the financial system, managing and mitigating these risks has become a highly relevant and intensively discussed issue for all market participants and regulators.

While some of the HFT tactics are the same as those used in the past, the new challenge is how the orders are executed. Algorithm-driven traders post thousands of quotes in microseconds across numerous trading platforms, including 'dark pools' that are off-exchange. The authorities have a hard job because unless there is evidence of intent to manipulate, it is hard to derive intent from raw trading data. Furthermore, among the challenges authorities face, there is a lack of comprehensive market data to work from.

The topic is relevant because the rules being decided in the coming months may shape the industry for decades and could determine which markets, and which parts of these markets, succeed or fail.

Even if the phenomenon is quite clear and widespread, basic differences between American, European and Australian market structures still exist and are analysed in this chapter in order to better understand the relative differences between regulatory approaches.

The aim of this chapter is to shed more light on a relevant twofold question that still remains unanswered: what is the impact of HFT and, in particular, how might different regulations impact on market structures?

The logical organization of this chapter is as follows: after a review of the literature, the third section summarizes the main risks and proposed policy measures; the fourth section examines the main pieces of regulation around the world; next, the fifth section proposes a critical analysis of the relation between different market structures and different regulation of HFT. The final section comprises the conclusions of the study. The findings relate largely to the period from late 2008 to late 2013.

8.2 Literature review

Existing evidence related to the impact of high-frequency trading on certain market quality and efficiency indicators is, so far, inconclusive. Even though, to date, the substantial majority of the empirical research has concluded that HFT has had a measurable beneficial impact on a variety of core market quality metrics, including increased liquidity, tighter spreads, more efficient price formation, reduced transaction costs for market users and lower market volatility in most circumstances, doubts still exist on some issues relating to market integrity.

The main issues analysed in the literature so far are the impact of HFT on liquidity, price formation and volatility. With regard to liquidity, many papers have demonstrated that high-frequency trading is beneficial to the financial markets. According to Zhang (2010), who analysed US equities from 1993 to 2009, with HFT in use, trading costs declined, bid-ask spreads narrowed and available liquidity increased. Jarnecic and Snape (2010) analysed HFT versus other trades by using LSE equity markets data from April to June 2009: they demonstrated that HFT improved liquidity and was unlikely to have increased volatility. Menkveld (2013) analysed Dutch equities traded on Chi-X and Euronext in 2007 and discovered that a single high-frequency trader played an important role in the development of a competitive market centre, resulting in better liquidity and lower trading costs. Hasbrouck and Saar (2013) analysed US equities, in particular the full NASDAQ order book from June 2007 to October 2008. In this research low latency automated trading was associated with lower quoted and effective spreads, lower volatility and greater liquidity. Riordan and Storkenmairm (2012) used the Xetra high-speed trading system on Deutsche Börse in 2007. They found that higher system speeds led to increased liquidity and improved price discovery. Hendershott and Riordan (2009) considered automated trades versus other trades on Deutsche Börse equities in January 2008. They concluded that automated trades made prices more efficient and did not contribute to higher volatility.

As regards price transparency, Hendershott, Jones and Menkveld (2011) studied the automated quoting facility for NYSE equities in 2003.

They found that automated trading narrowed bid-ask spreads, lowered trading costs, and improved price efficiency. Hendershott and Moulton (2011) analysed the NYSE TAQ database, plus others, from 1 June 2006 to 31 May 2007; they discovered that the introduction of automation via the NYSE hybrid system improved price discovery and made prices more efficient. Brogaard (2013) analysed HFT versus other trades, in US equities on NASDAQ, during various periods from 2008. In this case HFT helped to narrow bid-ask spreads, improved price discovery and may have reduced volatility. HFT activity tends to decrease idiosyncratic and intraday volatility.

In contrast, following the flash crash, the SEC and the CFTC (Commodity Futures Trading Commission) presented a joint report entitled 'Findings regarding the market events of May 6, 2010', which describes the sequence of events that led to the collapse of the DJ index in a matter of minutes. The report highlighted the ability of high-frequency traders to amplify the volatility of the market in particularly turbulent conditions. Also, Boehmer, Fong and Wu (2012) documented that algorithmic trading systematically increased volatility, which imposed costs on other market participants. They suggested that market observers should take this effect into account when evaluating the costs and benefits of algorithmic trading in markets dominated by HFT. Finally, Jarrow and Protter (2011) also provided a model, with no bid/ask spreads and perfect liquidity, in which the introduction of high-frequency trades both increased market volatility and generated abnormal profit opportunities for the high-frequency traders at the expense of the ordinary traders.

Even though they tackle a slightly different topic, it is useful to mention Hagströmer and Nordén (2013), who analysed high-frequency trading strategies on NASDAQ OMX Stockholm; they compared the behaviour of the market making HFT to opportunistic HFT and found that market makers constitute the majority share of HFT trading volume and limit order traffic. Interesting findings were also shown by Gomber et al. (2011), who published a report which included many survey papers that highlighted beneficial aspects of HFT, while noting that perceived problems are largely a result of the US market structure.

Finally, it is worth mentioning that in October 2012 the UK Foresight Committee released a comprehensive report 'Foresight: the future of computer trading in financial markets' which provides a valuable insight for policymakers, legislators and regulators undertaking work related to computer trading.

8.3 Market factors contributing to the rise of high-frequency trading (HFT)

In the past few years regulatory changes and technological innovations have presented many implications for market structures around the world.

In terms of regulatory changes, the Regulation National Market System (Reg. NMS) in the US, the Markets in Financial Instruments Directive (MiFID) in Europe and, later, the Market Integrity Rules in Australia all prompted the birth of new trading venues which soon began to compete with incumbent stock exchanges.

At present, trading in the same securities takes place simultaneously on various different trading platforms and this has created new market making and arbitrage potential for some traders and the fragmentation of order flows, both issues of concern for all market participants and for regulators (Menkveld, 2013).

It is of particular interest that there is substantial market fragmentation in the US and a growing level of fragmentation in the EU, particularly in the United Kingdom. In these regions, traditional exchanges compete for order flow with several non-exchange market trading systems (ATSs and MTFs) and also OTC trading systems. In Australia, the phenomenon started much later and most of the trading is still consolidated within a single domestic exchange.

In order to understand the different levels of development of market fragmentation, Figure 8.1 illustrates Fidessa data on the market share of the main indices. To be specific, the Fidessa Fragmentation Index (FFI) measures fragmentation of trading in a particular stock (and by aggregation, in an index) across lit trading venues. The higher the number, the more fragmented trading has become. If the index has a value of 1, it means that the stock is still traded at one venue. Increases in the FFI indicate fragmentation of trading across multiple venues and, as such, any firm wishing to effectively trade that security must be able to execute across several venues. Once a stock's FFI exceeds 2, liquidity in that stock has become fragmented to the extent that it no longer 'belongs' to its originating venue. Since the FFI is calculated as a single number, it provides a useful tool to measure, track and compare how fragmented an index really is. The Australian S&P ASX 200 has an FFI equal to 1.1 while the Dow Jones has an FFI of more than 4. In the middle there are the main European indexes, of which the FTSE 100 is the index most affected by fragmentation in Europe.

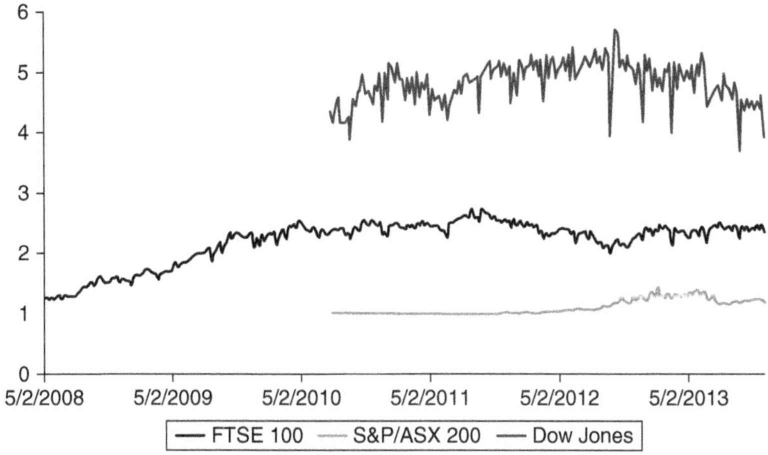

Figure 8.1 Fidessa Fragmentation Index from 2008 to 2013
Source: Our elaboration from Fidessa data.

Regarding fragmentation, the 2001 IOSCO Report had already identified a number of concerns raised by market fragmentation, including: (1) the duplication of costs, which also covers 'search' operating and regulatory costs; (2) the introduction of trading methods and business practices that may diminish efficiency and not be in the interests of the market as a whole; (3) the dispersion of liquidity that could result in less efficient price formation and in higher volatility.

The second point is very relevant for our analysis because it concerns the integrity of the financial markets. In other words, if we add to fragmentation the recent technological innovations that have accelerated the speed of trading, the problem of maintaining a level playing field for every trader becomes very apparent.

It is evident that trading strategies used by high-frequency traders are generally the same as those used in the past, but the speed is very different and not every trader can afford the expenses related to the new technology.

It is noteworthy that, as a result of this higher speed, traders have emerged who tend to trade a complete cycle (in its simplest form, buying and then selling the same security) over very short time periods – seconds, or even parts of seconds, rather than minutes, hours or days. The speed with which these traders can react to detailed changes in market conditions is important to making a success of this type of trading. Both absolute speed and speed relative to others attempting to use the same strategies are important and, as a result, very small changes in speed become critical. The reactions to changing market conditions lead to traders sending a very high levels of orders to trading venues, and then cancelling a fairly high proportion of these orders before they are actually executed (for some of the techniques used, only one in about 500 orders sent to the venue will be executed).

Coming back to the relevance of the regulation, new pieces of regulation in the US and in Europe have made it easier for new marketplaces to compete with incumbent exchanges and this has had the intended effect of improving fee and service execution among trading venues, but also the unintended effect of a changing the pricing policies of execution fees in the market. It is notable that the maker-taker pricing model has been introduced as a new pricing structure, whereby firms that provide liquidity to the trading platform are rewarded with a rebate, instead of a fee. This model was initially introduced in the US stock market in the late nineties, when electronic communications networks (ECNs) began to compete with the US stock exchanges (Stoll, 2006). In particular, the need to divert the abundant liquidity of the big stock exchanges that were poorly responsive to market changes urged ECNs to attract orders to their trading platforms by offering a maker-taker pricing model (Angel, Harris and Spatt, 2010). Given the success of major ECNs – such as BATS trading, which diverted a large number of trades from the NYSE – their European counterparts, once they had gone live, immediately embraced the maker-taker pricing model. The model, in fact, provided an incentive structure that helped European MTFs to accrue the crucial seed capital liquidity necessary to gain traction quickly.

In a bid to bolster their share of secondary market trading, even the main incumbent stock exchanges began to court high-frequency order flows through pricing policies, such as the maker-taker model, in order to prop up their flagging market share. Furthermore, HFT flows also bring additional revenues through co-location, the practice whereby a broker locates a server within the exchange's data centre in order to gain a speed advantage and access to other technological services. But, as it has been noted, the creation of this industry segment has brought some problems: in particular, high-volume data-intensive HFT strategies – which can involve sending a hundred orders to execute one trade, due to the need to continuously update prices – represent a major technical challenge. Exchanges effectively opened the floodgate to HFT on account of competition issues, but HFT's success in attracting flow is putting a considerable strain on their technology. Increasingly, exchanges have to update to stay ahead, but the economics of these investments are questionable. Ultimately, exchanges only get paid if an order is executed, so the huge volume of message data created by HFT is a massive deadweight on the system (Chesini, 2012); because of that, the maker-taker model has recently become an issue of concern for many regulators. In addition, the race for improved technology is blamed by some scholars (Harris, 2012)

Lastly it must be considered that the increasing slicing of orders has also had a major impact on the average transaction size. The average lit transaction size in the shares listed on the main indexes has dramatically dropped. This is because automated, or electronic, trading has sliced orders into ever-smaller sizes; in particular, with algorithmic trading it is necessary to disguise traders' intentions, in order to avoid giving clues to the rest of the market, by splitting orders into smaller and smaller baskets.

Figure 8.2 illustrates the decrease in average trade size by looking at the stock exchanges most affected by competition in Europe (LSE, Deutsche Boerse, NYSE Euronext and NASDAQ OMX Nordic), in the US (NASDAQ OMX and NYSE Euronext US) and in Australia; for example for the London Stock Exchange the average trade size order has dropped from 33,000 dollars to 10,000 dollars in six years (from 2007 to 2013). Also the Australian stock exchange (ASX) decreased from an average trade size of 23,000 dollars to less than 5,000 dollars.

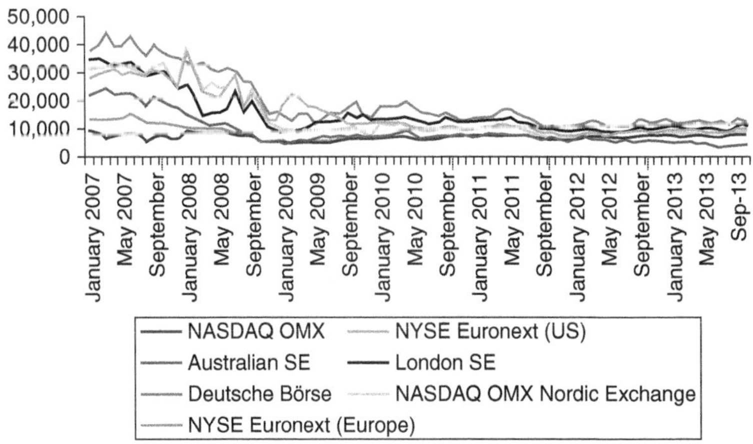

Figure 8.2 The decline in the average trade size in the regulated markets (in $)
Source: Our elaboration on WFE statistics.

This trend is even more evident for dark trading venues; in this case the increase in the number of trades was much higher than the corresponding increase in trading volumes, resulting in a larger decrease in trade size. It is particularly significant that, in the major dark pools, trade size is under 10,000 dollars: therefore the average trade size for lit and dark trading venues is converging. These changes have taken place since MiFID and Reg.NMS were introduced; not only can dark pools execute large orders with exemption from pre-trade transparency requirements, but they are also allowed to execute smaller size orders if they are matched at mid-point with a set of bid and ask prices. As a result, most trades executed in the dark venues are similar in size to those performed in the lit venues. Consequently, dark venues are a rapidly growing market segment, with significant implications in terms of price formation.

Figure 8.3 summarizes the market factors contributing to the rise of HFT.

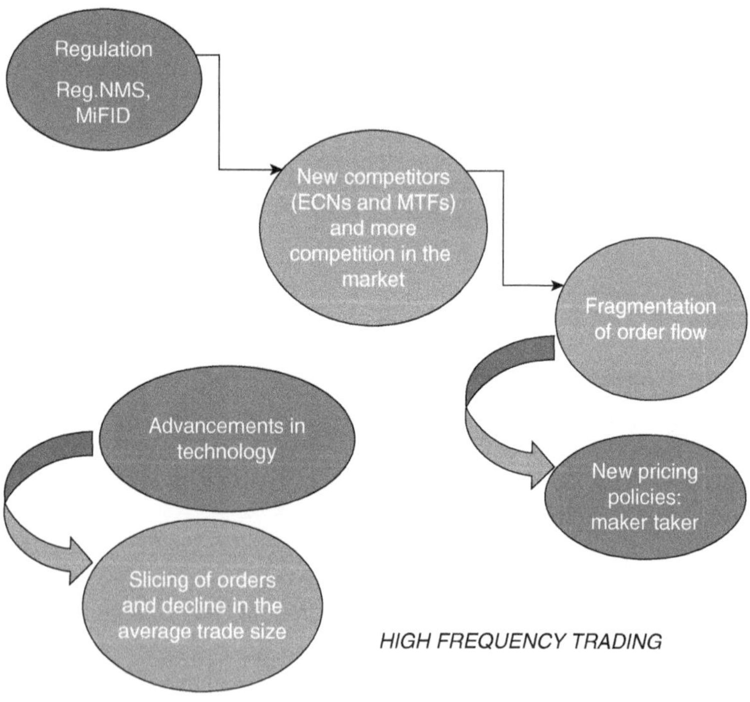

Figure 8.3 Summary of market factors contributing to the rise of HFT

8.4 Main risks and proposed policy measures to mitigate them

Different kinds of risk can arise in highly automated markets. Even though HFT represents the rational evolution of electronic markets, as participants adapted to new market structures and leveraged advancements in technology and telecommunications, it is still blamed for increasing risk, mainly because it does not serve long-term investors and hinders regulators in their role as market supervisors.

So the main question that arises is the following: does HFT pose significant risks to the integrity of the equity market structure?

In defining risks associated with HFT, it must be considered that the use of extraordinarily high speed and sophisticated quantitative and algorithmic computer programs for generating, routing and executing orders is very significant. To be specific, it requires speedy market data delivery from trading centre servers to the server of HFT firms; speedy decision processing in the HFT firm's trading engine; speedy access to trading centre servers; and speedy order execution by the trading centres. Hence, an extremely low latency, which is defined as the time which passes between the entry of an order until it is executed and the transaction is processed, is vital for high-frequency traders (Cvitanic and Kirilenko, 2010); because of this they are mainly proprietary traders (i.e. they utilize their own capital for trading activities and do not usually conduct HFT on an agency basis).

As we mentioned earlier, to facilitate this way of trading, market operators offer speed-sensitive market participants the opportunity to install their trading engines adjacent to their own infrastructure. This co-location of servers in close physical proximity to the market operator's systems minimizes network latencies between the matching engine of the trading venue and the servers of the market participants. Further characteristics of HFT firms include real-time data analysis in order to produce automatic trading decisions and very short time-frames for establishing and liquidating positions, resulting in the submission of numerous orders that are often cancelled shortly after submission (cancellation rates of greater than 80 per cent are common). Moreover, HFT firms end the trading day 'delta-neutral' (i.e. in as close to a flat position as possible, to avoid carrying significant, unhedged positions overnight).

Even though HFT hase some characteristics which seem to minimize risks to the financial markets (Martinez and Rosu, 2013), it may cause new types of serious risks and, as will be outlined later on, managing and mitigating these risks is actually a very appropriate activity for market participants and regulators worldwide (Sornette and Von der Becke, 2011).

To be specific, HFT involves changes to order books which are so fast that from the moment when an investor places his order and the moment when an order is executed, the book has already moved on many times (Harris, 2013). This permanent instability is a source of concern among investors. Consequently two evident problems caused by HFT arise: 1) the possibility that traditional investors will quit the markets and 2) the fact that increasing amounts of messaging damage the operation of trading platforms and can undermine market integrity (Frino and Lepone, 2012).

Regarding the first issue, regulators are aware that the ongoing development of algorithmic trading and HFT may deteriorate investors' confidence in the efficiency and integrity of the market and, possibly, reduce traditional market participants' willingness to trade. In fact, the presence of high-frequency traders can discourage traditional traders from participating as they feel an inherently disadvantaged by the superior technology. For example, some traditional institutional investors, who, as fundamental investors, are supposed to base their trading decisions on the perceived fundamental value of securities, could be prompted to withdraw, reflecting a loss of faith in the integrity of the market; consequently, the information content of public market prices might be altered, as a knock-on effect. This has the potential to produce a less efficient price formation process and possibly cause others to trade in markets with different characteristics, such as the dark execution venues.

In terms of the second issue, the increased messaging that has come with extensive use of algorithms raises costs for many participants, including marketplaces and regulators.

Beyond the two issues just mentioned, which are intrinsic to the activity of high-frequency traders, other more common risks could undermine the efficiency and the integrity of a financial market: systemic risk, market risk, counterparty risk and operational risk.

As regards systemic risk, the spread of automated trading surely deserves regulatory attention. It must be said however that HFT generates an audit trail that could be analysed. Furthermore, new technologies are being developed and deployed to effectively manage this risk. It is particularly important to continue to look for ways to improve the management of systemic risk and, for this purpose, uniform circuit breakers – both volume and price related – should be prioritized. Moreover, current debate regarding the use of kill switches – both within investment firms and at the execution/clearing level – is surely appropriate.

Regarding market risk, HFT strategies are largely market neutral and high-frequency traders have more advanced risk management practices than traditional, non-automated firms. Theoretically, in terms of market risk, HFT does not introduce any new market issues that did not exist previously in the markets.

In terms of counterparty risk, while settlement failure is a potential threat, HFT only occurs in electronic markets covered by central counterparty (CCP) operations. In this respect, sponsored access is a widely used trading tool, and should be monitored by regulators because it can generate big risks. Regulators are considering this problem: in the US, with the SEC Rule 15c3-5,[1] and in Europe with the proposals for MiFID II.

Finally, as regards operational risk, it has been shown that improper usage or failure of algorithms can lead to a disruption. Significant uncertainty usually spreads as a result of outages at primary market centres. In general, a lack of capacity to handle market data, message traffic and orders can lead to an interruption of trading systems. In this respect, it is important to implement more robust testing environments for market participants and exchanges, and ESMA's Guidelines, as described later on, are an appropriate and helpful foundation for facing this risk.

All these risks demand that exchanges and other market participants employ effective quality management systems and sophisticated risk mitigation controls that are adapted to these new dynamics in order to successfully face potential threats to market stability arising from technology malfunctions or episodic illiquidity (Easley, de Prado and O'Hara. 2011).

The major exchanges of the world have enacted many safeguards to ensure orderly markets and regulators are reacting to concerns about HFT with new measures as well, which will be discussed presently.

It is noteworthy that exchanges have adapted to the dynamic changes in financial markets by significantly investing in technology too, not only to support more highly efficient and scalable markets, but also to enhance the reliability, stability and integrity on the markets.

Regarding regulators, in order to mitigate the risks of HFT on equities markets, they are analysing many policy measures that can curb the spread of the activity and, in particular, reduce negative externalities. The problem is to find a fair balance between the rules and the innovation fostered by the advances in technology. In some cases rules sound very much like an attempt to ban technology from financial markets.

Technology drives innovation and sometimes innovation creates new problems, but the answer should never be to ban technology.

There are two questions here: are some of the proposed regulatory measures able to erode the benefits that technological progress has delivered to investors? And: do regulatory changes do more harm than good to financial markets?

Some rules might certainly contain the spread of the phenomenon and above all reduce any negative impact. Basically, the aims of the rules can be divided into two groups: (1) more information to be provided to the authority regarding the operations conducted on the markets by high-frequency traders and by all other market participants; (2) improvements in the characteristics of market microstructure mainly put into operation by trading venues and sometimes stated by regulators. Furthermore, improvements in risk management systems should be suggested and implemented by all market participants.

There are eight primary policy measures to be considered in the HFT debate; of these, the mandatory notification of algorithms is part of the first group while the other policy measures mentioned below belong to the second group, and these are: obligations for market makers, circuit breakers, kill switches, limitations on the minimum tick size, minimum resting time, order-to-trade ratios, and abolition of the maker-taker pricing model. The main characteristics of all these measures are synthesized in the box below:

- *Mandatory notification of algorithms:* the imposition of obligations for operators who make use of algorithmic trading to notify the authorities of the characteristics of the algorithms used and the related systems of risk management. On the one hand, this notification helps to promote the establishment of risk management systems more rigorously,through intermediaries and, on the other hand, it would improve the authorities' understanding of the phenomenon, making the supervisory action more effective.
- *Obligations for market makers:* high-frequency traders are not required to make two-sided markets, as traditional market makers are required to do. Regulators are still evaluating the possibility of tightening market maker obligations on HFT firms.
- *Circuit breakers:* these are used by exchanges to limit or stop trading when certain conditions occur. The purpose of these measures is to reduce the risk of sudden and large movements in prices induced by a cascading sequence of negotiations. These mechanisms can be designed in different ways. They are effective mechanisms for

monitoring the impact on prices of contingent phenomena unrelated to the underlying fundamentals. Moreover, the numerous studies presented in the literature do not provide clear guidance because it is not possible to carry out counterfactual analysis (i.e. to determine what would happen in the market if, upon the occurrence of certain conditions, trading was not interrupted).

- *Kill switches:* limits set by exchanges on the categories of activities that an investment firm is allowed to engage in, with an automatic shutdown implemented if it exceeds those limits. In this way it is possible to limit the total exposure each firm has to the market. They were proposed after Knight Capital flooded the New York Stock Exchange with thousands of money-losing orders on 1 August 2012. The SEC, concerned about the integrity of the marketplace, asked stock exchanges to make sure such an event did not happen again. The exchanges recognized that there was a big hole in their risk management systems: the presence of single stock circuit breakers and 'clearly erroneous' trading rules that allow the exchanges to counteract bad trades did not prevent the kind of runaway algorithm generated by Knight Capital. Apart from being used at the execution level, kill switches can also be put at clearing level, as well aswithin the risk management systems of investment firms.
- *Limitations on the minimum tick size:* determining the magnitude of the optimal tick size is complex as it affects, in an ambiguous way, liquidity. Empirical evidence shows, in fact, that the lowering of minimum tick size not only reduces the bid-ask spread but also the depth of the trading book, as it makes it less expensive to place orders at prices improved on those already on the market, therefore discouraging the participation of operators that provide liquidity to the market. In fact, in the different trading venues, the priority of orders depends on the time an order is placed and the price. Therefore, a new order can override those already on the market only if it is done at an improved price (buy or sell). The reduction in the minimum tick size makes this operation less expensive, thereby discouraging entry limit order.
- *Minimum resting time:* HFT strategies provide for the cancellation of orders entered in a very short period of time, thereby increasing the cost of monitoring the market for all participants and generating the phenomenon of so-called ghost liquidity, with negative impacts on the quality of the market. To discourage these effects it is therefore necessary to define a minimum time in the trading book for all orders placed. Such a measure could be uniform or differentiated depending

on the market conditions and the type of instrument traded. The introduction of a minimum time for orders to rest in the order book allows for mitigation of the phenomenon of share stuffing, making it shiny transparent to the actual depth of the book and the underlying process of placing orders. In addition, the reduction in message traffic to the platform of trading activities reduces the risk of technological problems related to congestion of the information systems that must receive and process them. The measure could have, however, negative consequences on the process of price formation and liquidity. By imposing a minimum time for orders to rest in the order book, any new information on the fundamentals of the securities aspect of the order is not immediately incorporated into its price, because market participants may only react to such news with a lag.

- *Order-to-trade ratios (OTR):* this is another measure that tends to discourage the frequent cancellation of orders on the part of market participants. It aims to impose an upper limit on the ratio of orders placed and those executed.
- *Different commission schemes (maker vs taker):* this is a pricing model that tends to encourage HFT. In fact, high-frequency traders – due to their better operating speed – are able to place their orders at the top of the queue, thereby having the advantage over traditional market makers. A commission structure that rewards, at the time of the order, the liquidity provider, may encourage high-frequency traders to implement this strategy with increasing frequency, discouraging, in this way, the participation of traditional market makers, making the market more exposed to the work activity of high-frequency traders and to phenomena of temporary illiquidity.

8.5 Regulatory measures around the world: the state of the art

The growing relevance of high-frequency trading is shown in Figure 8.4; in 2012 in particular,HFT was estimated by the TABB Group to make up 51 per cent of equity trades in the US and 39 per cent of traded value in the European markets. This data clearly highlights that HFT is a major component of regulated markets even if the trend is flat to down among the earliest markets to adopt HFT. In other markets, such as the Australian one, HFT still appears to be growing relatively rapidly, albeit from a smaller base, in correlation with advances in technology. In fact, HFT in Australia is dominated by a small group of trading entities with

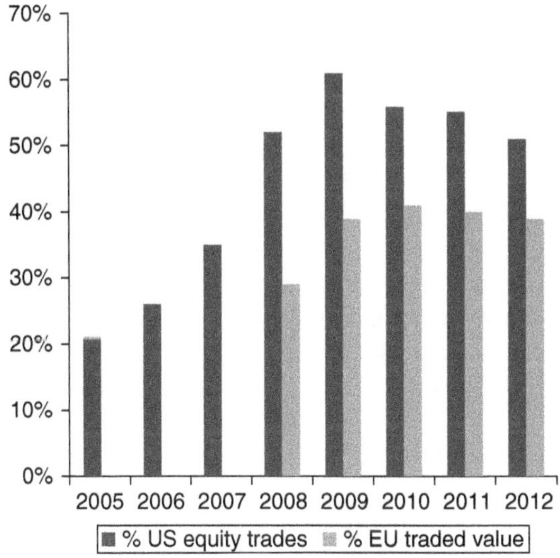

Figure 8.4 HFT market share in the US and in Europe
Source: Our elaboration from TABB Group estimate.

the 20 largest entities accounting for about 80 per cent of all HFT turnover (or 22 per cent of total equity market turnover).

In light of the growing importance of HFT and its allegedly harmful effects in the event of adverse market conditions, regulators are currently putting strong emphasis on subjecting high-frequency traders to prudential and organizational requirements and to supervision by a competent authority. Consequently, regulators have to identify the critical risks and the related effective, balanced solutions that can enhance the safety of markets without compromising the quality of markets. It is particularly important that they do not impose policies that would damage market liquidity or limit other market quality benefits provided by automated trading and HFT.

8.5.1 Supranational level organizations

At a supranational level many recommendations and guidelines have been issued by IOSCO and ESMA. The arrangement of these organizations has been addressed directly to regulators so that they can properly supervise the operation of trading venues and market participants. To be specific, in November 2010 the IOSCO received from G20 the request to develop some recommendations to promote integrity and efficiency of markets and to mitigate the risks posed to the financial system by the latest technological developments. Consequently, in October 2011 the IOSCO issued a final report entitled 'Regulatory issues raised by the impact of technological changes on market integrity and efficiency' in which a number of recommendations to the regulators are outlined, of these the fourth and the fifth focused specifically on HFT.[2]

Although there are still relevant differences in market structures and different regulations in the financial centres around the world, the IOSCO report represents an important starting point for analysing the surveillance of high-frequency trading and the related micro-structural issues. It explicitly addresses the need for regulators to continuously evaluate the regulatory challenges related to new and evolving trading strategies.

More recently, in April 2013, the IOSCO issued another final report entitled: 'Technological challenges to effective market surveillance: Issues and regulatory tools'. In this report the new challenges that technological changes pose to regulators during their market surveillance are outlined with a particular focus to two processes: 1) the fragmentation of markets and the resulting dispersal of trading information; 2) the increased speed of trading and regulators' ability to gather and process the increased volume of trading data. The first point has been analysed in Section 8.3; in terms of the second point, the issues involve this question: can surveillance databases handle the volume of information generated by HFT, and are surveillance alerts suitable (and suitably calibrated) for this type of trading?

The main evidence as synthesized in the report – is that in some jurisdictions market authorities conduct real-time surveillance and the latter receive alerts relating to looping algorithms, order-to-trade ratios, unusual orders and trade alerts, and pattern recognition. Furthermore, recently, in some jurisdictions, there have been new regulatory requirements which: 1) place more responsibility on those using algorithms to trade; 2) require more information to be provided to market authorities on algorithms and their strategies; 3) introduce more requirements for trading venues relating to fair and orderly trading.

As far as Europe is concerned, in February 2012 the European Securities and Market Authority (ESMA), the supranational organization in which Europe's national regulators are represented, published 'Guidelines on systems and controls in an automated trading environment for trading platforms, investment firms and competent authorities' with the aim of ensuring common, uniform and consistent application of the MiFID and the Market Abuse Directive (MAD).

The guidelines are meant to reinforce incoming revisions of the main European directives and they affect any market member involved in electronic trading, having a 'common sense' approach rather than outright bans in certain activities, such as HFT. To be precise, in these guidelines ESMA[3] considers separately regulated markets, multilateral trading facilities and investment firms, and it recommends organizational requirements for the electronic trading systems of each of them. The guidelines also cover other relevant issues, such as fair and orderly trading in an automatic trading environment, the prevention of market abuse (in particular, market manipulation) and the provision of direct market access (DMA) and sponsored access (SA) by trading platforms and investment firms respectively. Synthetically, these guidelines attempt to prepare the necessary safeguards in order to minimize the potential negative effects of automated trading on secondary markets. All EU countries have confirmed their intention to adopt these guidelines.

Continuing at a supranational level, in September 2011, in the light of the financial crisis, the European Commission adopted a proposal for a financial transaction tax (FTT), or Tobin tax. Since governments have had to bail out numerous financial institutions, the argument goes that it is only fair that the financial industry as a whole should contribute to the recovery by paying a tax. An FTT could be just another cost component of trading. From a financial intermediary's perspective nothing much changes, except that its clients may very well trade less as a result of the higher costs. But if all intermediaries were to pass these additional costs on, everyone who trades securities would eventually pay the price. Ultimately, this includes everyone who is investing in some way and for this reason the tax was not welcomed and was considered more harmful than good.

To be specific, the Commission proposed a broad-based FTT taxing transaction on securities and derivatives. After a number of consultations, in 2012 it became clear that there was no unanimity on the Commission's FTT proposal, but a number of member states expressed support for a move towards the use of enhanced cooperation. Following the Economic and Financial Affairs Council of the European Union (Ecofin), on 22 January 2012, at which the Council adopted a decision authorizing 11 member states to proceed with the introduction of an FTT through enhanced cooperation, the Commission published a formal legislative proposal on 14 February. The Commission proposal is largely based on its earlier draft of September 2011. As a result of the proposal all 27 member states may take part in the deliberations, but only those participating in the enhanced cooperation procedure have voting rights.

8.5.2 European directives

As it has been noted, there are two main European directives, which consider HFT activity in detail. The first one is the revision of the MiFID, enacted in 2007 under EU law in order to harmonize regulation for investment services across Europe. When the directive came into effect it had already been decided that a review should take place three years later. In effect, the review process, which led to MiFID II, started in 2010 with a consultation by the European Commission. Later, on 20 October 2011, the European Commission adopted proposals for a revised MiFID and a new regulation called MiFIR. In terms of HFT, specific risk controls are addressed to those asset managers or investment firms that use any form of algorithmic (or high-frequency) trading. The definition of algorithmic trading is wide and covers any trading of financial instruments determined by computer algorithms other than order routing systems. MiFID II also aims to manage the risks the Commission sees as inherent in the substantial and controversial increase in algorithmic and HFT volumes. In fact, the proposals introduce specific controls relating to investment firms providing direct electronic access (DMA) to markets. The intention is to ensure that persons using the DMA service are properly qualified and that risk controls are imposed on the use of the service. Both investment firms and trading venues must ensure that robust measures are in place, to ensure that automated trading does not create a disorderly market and cannot be used for abusive purposes. Trading venues should also ensure their trading systems are resilient and properly tested in order that they can deal with increased order flows or market stresses, and that circuit breakers are in place to temporarily halt trading if there are sudden unexpected price movements.

Furthermore, pursuant to the Commission's proposals, firms engaging in algorithmic trading should be authorized by member states and should deploy a series of risk control measures, including business continuity arrangements. Similarly, regulated markets should be expected to provide effective systems, controls and circuit breakers to prevent market disruption from algorithmic trading.

The most debated aspect of the new rules is the requirement that algorithmic trading strategies must be in continuous operation during trading hours and must post firm quotes at competitive prices. Consequently, all electronic traders would be required to act as market makers and provide liquidity irrespective of market conditions. In October 2012, the European Parliament's Economic and Monetary Affairs Committee (ECON Committee) voted to limit this requirement to high-frequency traders solely because it wanted to put the brakes on such traders; hence two contentious measures applying to all HFT firms were proposed: market making obligations and minimum resting time.

With regard to the minimum resting time, the ECON Committee proposed a resting period of 500 milliseconds for all trading. It must be outlined that in the context of HFT, half a second is a substantial restriction.[4] Some high-frequency traders replied that, as a result of this resting period, liquidity might drop and the spread might rise, leading to additional costs for investors and the real economy. Indeed some of these proposed measures might erode the benefits that technological progress has delivered to investors up until now. In fact there is no scientific evidence that the minimum resting time is able to achieve anything, according to a well-known UK study (UK Government Office for Science's Foresight project, 2012), even if some academics in the US have recently supported this policy measure (Harris, 2013).

Regarding the second directive, in October 2011 the European Commission published its long-awaited proposals to update the existing Market Abuse Directive (MAD). Similar to MiFID II, this piece of regulation is also split into a directive (MAD II) and a regulation (MAR).

In relation to the latter directive, the strategies used in HFT are not considered to be anything new. As long as people pursue legitimate strategies, there is no ground for treating high-frequency traders any differently from other market participants. If, however, the strategies are designed to abuse the markets, it is necessary to take action but in itself, HFT cannot be equated with market abuse.

To be able to act effectively against possible illegal and/or undesirable behaviour by market participants, it is essential that regulators make additional investments in technological know-how, expertise and resources. The information systems currently available in Europe are not adequate for supervisors to obtain a coherent and complete picture of the behaviour of individual players. A more intense exchange of information between international regulators and further harmonization of international supervision are needed.

The proposals for MAD II seek to adapt EU rules to the new market reality, notably by extending their scope to financial instruments only traded on new platforms and over the counter (OTC) – currently not covered by EU legislation – and adapting rules to new technology.

Consequently, the regulatory framework provided by the original MAD has been outpaced by the growth of new trading platforms, OTC trading and new trading characteristics, such as those of HFT. In particular, the European Commission, labelled a number of practices, said to be linked to HFT, as being specifically abusive in that they constitute prohibited market manipulation; these include trading strategies such as quote stuffing, which consists of submitting orders without an intention to trade, but instead to disrupt a trading system (Egginton, Van Ness and Van Ness, 2014).

Under MAD II there will presumably be a number of compliance checks that have to be carried out and which can be broken down into three categories: (1) insider dealing checks; (2) DMA market abuse checks; (3) principal dealing checks.

The indications are that MAD II will be implemented by member states during the course of 2015 at the earliest, together with MiFID II.

8.5.3 US regulation

Not long before the flash crash, the SEC conducted a broad review of the US equity market structure. The review included an assessment of equity market structure performance in those years and an evaluation of whether market structure rules have kept pace with, among other things, changes in market technology and practices. To further help its review, in 2010 the SEC published a concept release to invite public comment on a wide range of market structure issues, including high-frequency trading, order routing, market data linkages and undisplayed or dark liquidity. The Commission wanted to understand whether regulatory initiatives to improve the current equity market structure were needed and, if so, the specific nature of such initiatives.

In view of the flash crash and of the need for the supervisory authority to acquire a source of useful data for the control and prevention of irregularities (Kirilenko et al., 2011), in July 2011 the SEC adopted a regulatory approach designed to track the activities of market participants that are able to influence market prices because they trade large quantities of securities.

The SEC approach concerning HFT relies on the inclusion of high-frequency traders in the category of large traders. In other words, high-frequency traders are understood as a subset of large traders and their activity is regulated in the context of regulations for large traders. This regulatory approach aims to quickly improve SEC's ability to identify and collect information on the most relevant trading activities.

In particular, the information requirements cover two levels of disclosure: a) the registration of large traders at the SEC; b) the registration of trades and information, and surveillance requirements for broker-dealers of large traders. Consequently, according to a large trader reporting system, brokers are required to tag, in real-time, the trades of firms that execute substantial trading volume.

It is worth underlining, moreover, that the Financial Stability Oversight Council (FSOC), a council of regulators established under the Dodd–Frank Act, recommended in July 2012 that the SEC and the Commodity Futures Trading Commission (CFTC) consider establishing error controls and standards for exchanges, clearing houses and other market participants that are relevant to high-speed trading.

More recently, in March 2013, the SEC proposed a rule that should have proven instrumental in bolstering investor confidence, protecting investors and maintaining fair and orderly markets. The proposed rule, called Regulation SCI (systems, compliance and integrity) would require entities essential to the smooth functioning of the US securities markets to have comprehensive policies and procedures regarding their technological systems. In particular the rule is designed to assure that: a) these systems have adequate capacity, integrity, resiliency, availability and security; b) such systems operate in the manner intended; c) these entities are well positioned to take prompt and appropriate corrective action when problems arise.

8.5.4 Australian regulation

Australian regulators have raced ahead of their European and US counterparts, who were still engaged in extensive discussions on whether or not to restrict automated trading; meanwhile, at the end of 2012 the Australian Government unveiled new proposals for curbing automated trading and preserving Australia's market integrity.

To be specific, in Australia, on 20 November 2012, the Australian Securities and Investments Commission (ASIC) introduced new market integrity rules to address risks emerging from developments in market structure, including growth in automated trading and the changing nature of dark liquidity. The key changes are: (1) volatility controls for extreme price movements were amended to introduce a market-wide two-minute pause. The controls were extended to apply to the ASX SPI 200 index futures contract, from May 2014, in order to minimize cross-product contagion; (2) automated trading rules require direct and immediate control over filters and orders (i.e. kill switch capabilities) and existing rules were amended to require annual reviews of the systems. These take effect in May 2014. Revised guidance clarifies ASIC's expectations on trading system controls, testing of systems and minimum standards for direct market access; (3) regulatory data for supervision rules requires additional data on orders and/or trades including: (a) identification of dark pools; (b) flagging whether a participant is acting as principal or agent; (c) a client identifier or reference; (d) identification of licensed intermediaries; (e) flagging of direct market access.

The government also launched further inquiries into high-frequency trading and so-called dark pool trading, which allows shareholders to trade among themselves away from the main 'lit' market without revealing their identity or displaying prices.

In March 2013 ASIC released a report and a consultation paper that examined the impact of dark liquidity and high-frequency trading on Australia's financial markets. The documents focus on the quality of the market for capital raising and long-term investment, and thus Australia's competitiveness as a regional financial centre.

They are the results of the analysis of two internal taskforces: the dark liquidity task force and the HFT task force; the latter particularly addressed concerns about disorderliness and unfairness.

The HFT task force did not find systematic manipulation or abuse of markets by high-frequency traders, but it found that their trading strategies are commonly adopted by many other algorithmic traders, including institutions.

ASIC has dropped the idea of implementing a shorter order-resting time. Its new ruling will force operators of crossing networks to disclose information, in order to avoid malpractice.

The task force found that the order-to-trade ratio in Australia was moderate compared to overseas markets and that the average holding time was 42 minutes, not seconds. Most traders, whether high-frequency traders or not, had order-to-trade ratios below 4:1 while the market average was approximately 10:1.

8.5.5 Other regional regulation in Europe

Looking at the regulatory landscape in Europe, several reforms, laws and taxes are being implemented in different countries, all with the aim of restructuring the market and making it less attractive for HFT strategies. Several European statutory regulators are also conducting studies which attempt to examine and measure the impact of HFT on market integrity and quality, including volatility (AFM, 2010).

In some countries new regulation concerning HFT has been recently adopted, even if EU financial rules – such as MiFID II – once approved, will take precedence over domestic regulations.

To correspond with the European Commission proposal concerning a financial transaction tax (FTT), France introduced its own domestic FTT on 1 August 2012. The French FTT includes a tax on the acquisition of shares in listed French companies with a market capitalization of over one billion euros; a tax on the acquisition of uncovered CDS on EU sovereign debt; and a tax on cancelled or modified orders, in order to capture HFT activity. This HFT tax, in particular, targeted algorithmic computer trades executed within half a second.

In Italy, a domestic FTT was also enacted and came into force on 1 March 2013. From March onwards, the FTT taxed the transfer of equity securities, while it was planned that from September it would have taxed the transfer of equity derivatives as well; however, in June, Italian lawmakers stated that there would be a delay in the introduction of the latter by at least two months, reflecting growing uncertainty over the levy which was being closely watched ahead of a proposed transaction tax across 11 European member states in 2014.

According to Reuters, the launch of the FFTs in France and Italy has hit demands for stocks, offering a glance of the impact a pan-European levy might have on a recovery in market volumes; to be specific, Thomson Reuters Equity Market Share Reporter data showed that since the taxes on trades were introduced in France and Italy, their market shares have fallen as much as 30 per cent and 45 per cent, respectively. That means that Italy and France could end up with a smaller amount than was projected by their governments. Moreover, going them lone, before a broader tax was agreed, France and Italy have both lost some trades to other countries, such as Germany. They have also pushed some cash-market trade into other, untaxed parts of the market.

At the moment there has been a lot of back-pedalling from certain EU countries after the initial Italian and French FTT results, as it seems that HFT activities will be impacted the most by an FTT and the risk of proprietary firms relocating to a more lucrative financial centre is high.

More interestingly, in Germany, on 26 September 2012, the Federal Government adopted a specific regulation concerning HFT. Unlike the French and Italian FTT, the German HFT Act is not a tax law, as such, but a licensing requirement that forces trading venues to implement automatic trade ratio limits and firms to communicate details of their trading strategies (Moosa, 2013).

On 28 February 2013 the German parliament, in a pre-emption of the rules under MiFID II, approved the act (the Hochfrequenzhandelsgesetz),

Table 8.1 Main pieces of regulation concerning HFT

Regulator	Title	Date
International Regulation		
OICV-IOSCO Technical Committee of the International Organization of Securities Commissions	Regulatory issues raised by the impact of technological changes on market integrity and efficiency, final report	October 2011
OICV-IOSCO Technical Committee of the International Organization of Securities Commissions	Technological challenges to effective market surveillance: Issues and regulatory tools, Final Report,	April 2013
European Regulation		
ESMA European Securities Markets Authority	Final report: guidelines on systems and controls in an automated trading environment for trading platforms, investment firms and competent authorities	December 2011
ESMA European Securities Markets Authority	Systems and controls in an automated trading environment for trading platforms, investment firms and competent authorities, guidelines	February 2012
European Commission	Proposal for a Financial Transaction Tax (FTT)	February 2012
European Commission	Proposal for a directive of the European Parliament and of the Council on market in financial instruments repealing Directive 2004/39/EC of the European Parliament and of the Council	October 2011
European Parliament	Amendments on the proposal for a directive on the European Parliament and the Council on markets in financial instruments repealing Directive 2004/39/EC	October 2012
European Council	Compromise text of MIFID II and MIFIR	June 2013
European Commission	Proposal MAD II and MAR	October 2011
European Parliament	Amendments on the proposals MAD II and MAR	October 2012
US Regulation		
SEC (Securities and Exchange Commission)	Concept release on equity market structure (Release No. 34–61358)	February 2010
SEC (Securities and Exchange Commission)	Large trader reporting (Release No 34–64976)	July 2011
SEC (Securities and Exchange Commission)	Regulation systems compliance and integrity, proposed rule and form (Reg SCI)	March 2013
Australian Regulation		
ASIC	Report 215 Australian equity market structure	November 2010
ASIC	Report 311 Draft market integrity rules and guidance	November 2012
ASIC	Report 331 Dark liquidity and high-frequency trading	March 2013

Source: Own elaboration

and it was subsequently approved by the Federal Council on 22 March 2013. The act imposes:

1. an authorization requirement for firms undertaking high-frequency trading on a German regulated market or multilateral trading facilities; in practice, the HFT Act requires that a proprietary trading company using HFT strategies must obtain a license from the BaFIN. Consequently, they will be obliged to comply with the general regulatory framework of the German Banking Act and the German Securities Trading Act, including minimum capital requirement, organization and risk management requirements. Furthermore, algorithmic trading strategies must be approved by BaFIN or the trading venue where they will be put to practice.
2. requirements that trading venues set order-to-trade ratios and minimum tick sizes; also a minimum resting period for trades is under consideration. Additional fees must be introduced by trading venues for excessive cancellations, and they have also to put in place flagging systems for algorithmic orders.
3. a transitional period of six months (for domestic firms) or nine months for foreign firms to apply to the German Federal Financial Services Supervisory authority (BaFin) for authorization.

Finally, in August 2013, in the UK, a group of politicians (the Business Select Committee) called for the re-examination of the introduction of a tax on high-frequency trading activities, thus reopening the case of an HFT tax. This happened despite the fact that the UK was widely opposed to the European FTT and it demonstrated the enormous uncertainty about the proper regulation to adopt.

Table 8.2 Regional regulation concerning HFT

Country	**Regulator**	**Title**	**in force since**
France	French Parliament	Article 6 of 2012 Finance Bill	1 August 2012
Germany	German Parliament	Hochfrequenzhandelsgesetz, the HFT Act	28 February 2013
Italy	Italian Government	Decree of the Minister of Economy and Finance, 21 February 2013	1 March 2013

Source: Our elaboration.

8.5.6 A Regulatory comparison concerning different market structures

The market structure can be defined as the trading rules and the trading systems used by a market. These rules in general determine who can trade, how they can trade and what, where and when they can trade (Harris 2003:89). While market structure profoundly affects trader behaviour, it also contributes towards determining whether markets are liquid, whether prices are informative and which traders trade profitably.

An appropriately balanced market structure is also the focus of market regulator because it should provide for strong investor protection, foster fair and efficient capital markets and confidence in those markets, and enable businesses to raise capital for the benefit of the overall economy.

Very relevant in any new development in financial markets is its impact on transaction costs. If transaction costs are low, market participants are better able to invest in the securities most suited to them, and informed participants are more able to buy and sell the securities, based on their private information, and to impound the information into asset prices (Brogaard et al., 2013)

The issue is also relevant because the fragmentation of trading has meant that the landscape has changed dramatically for HFT strategies, and the clear-cut distinctions between investors, intermediaries and trading venues are being replaced by a very different framework. The main question here is whether the new market structure answers well to the recent market changes.

As shown in Figure 8.5, in Europe, but also in the US and in Australia, the monopolies of national stock exchanges have been broken and

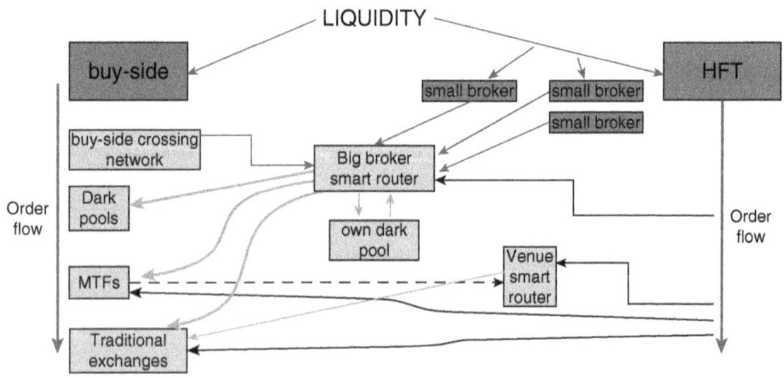

Figure 8.5 The new liquidity landscape in Europe

the interaction between all market participants has become blurred. Liquidity flows from the buy-side between different sized intermediaries, dark pools, MTFs/ECNs and primary market centres in a much more interrelated way. The impact of the HFT community can also be seen in terms of electronic liquidity provision on and between alternative trading systems, ATSs and primary market centres. In Europe, some MTFs (such as BATS Europe) also act in a 'broker' capacity by offering onward routing services for any orders that fail to match on their own lit and dark order books.

The new market paradigm can also be viewed in terms of participants fighting for their place in the liquidity queue. Small brokers run the risk of being disintermediated if they cannot afford to invest in the appropriate smart routing technology. Venues of all types are looking at ways to 'jump the queue' by offering either new business models or onward routing services to attract order flow to their venue first.

Meanwhile brokers are looking at how to legitimize their own non-lit matching activities and how to potentially aggregate them so as to increase the likelihood of matching client order flow.

As a result, strictly one-directional, linear trading that flows from the buy-side blotter, through the sell-side trading desk, on to the traditional exchange, and then on to a central clearing house, will become a thing of the past. Instead, orders will be broken up and traded across more than one venue. Ultimately they could also then be cleared through a number of clearing and settlement providers. Either way, the constituent parts of the order will then need to be reassembled to reflect a complete and unified picture back to the end customer. With more options between trader and final execution, orders may get filled in any number of ways.

Finding the best route is also complicated by the fact that different trading venues will typically offer rebates for posting liquidity (passive orders) and charge for taking or removing liquidity (aggressive orders). In this way, venue execution analysis (ECA) goes hand in hand with transaction cost analysis (TCA).

All things considered, complexity has become the hallmark of the new electronic landscape, whether it is in the form of a multitude of venues and participants or the advanced algorithms that many of them are using to analyse incoming market data.

The process by which orders are handled, routed, and executed can be very complex because of the fragmented nature of the equity market and the reliance on advanced technology and speed. Firms use algorithms to route different portions of an order to different venues in various sequences, taking into account such factors as minimization of market impact, minimization of information leakage, immediacy of execution versus cost of execution in various pools, and other factors that provide the most efficient executions possible.

Complex systems can also spin out of control in unexpected ways and, in fact, the incidents are becoming more and more common.

Even though these processes are spreading worldwide, many key features still differentiate the US market system from the European and the Australian set-up. To be precise, the US Reg NMS codified the national best bid best offer (NBBO). To calculate the NBBO, marketplaces are obliged to distribute their best bid and best offer, for securities they are listing, through a securities information processor (SIP). The processor aggregates the quotes coming from marketplaces and ascertains the NBBO from the nationwide best bid and offer in a given security. This system has been implemented to enable market participants to trade on the best available prices in the US.

To guarantee that trades are always executed at the best available price, Rule 611 Reg NMS implemented the trade-through rule, which bars marketplaces from trading at prices that are worse for their customers than the NBBO. If a marketplace is not able to match an incoming order at the NBBO or better a price, it is forced to route the order to the trading venue that is currently offering the best price (which requires inter-linkage of all markets) or cancel the order instead of routing it away. The necessity to execute incoming orders at the NBBO or better prices changed the landscape of the US market system. Since the relevant price is now the most important factor when determining where a given trade is executed, new marketplaces displaying aggressive quotes can attract orders from other exchanges.

In this context, specifically in terms of HFT, US authorities are facing an uphill battle to combat potential market manipulation, from incomplete records to interpreting the volume of trades executed in milliseconds. In particular, the SEC has been investigating possible manipulative trading strategies since the 2010 'flash crash' and has hired more than a dozen quantitative analysts across three of its divisions. As noted, since 2011, high-volume traders are required to report their equity trade data to the SEC, which in its turn began using tools from Tradeworx, a high-frequency trading group, at the end of 2012 to provide it with a real-time glimpse into stock trading.

Even if the plan to build a so-called consolidated audit trail is not expected to be completed for several years, the SEC's team of quantitative analysts can help decipher the data received from the high-volume traders. Recently the FBI also joined up with the Securities and Exchange Commission to focus on high-speed, algorithmic trading.

In Europe, MiFID introduced a principles-based best execution regime in contrast to the rules-based US approach. Instead of establishing a pan-European best price like the NBBO, MiFID requires investment firms to: '... take all reasonable steps to obtain, when executing orders, the best possible result for their clients taking into account price, costs, speed, likelihood of execution and settlement, size, nature or any other consideration relevant to the execution of the order' (European Commission, 2004). The second key difference, in comparison to the US market structure, is the fact that best execution is an obligation relating to investment firms in Europe, while it is outsourced to the market venues in the US. However, the actual implementation of best execution is not codified in Europe. Therefore, there are two basic ways for financial institutions to implement this obligation. The first one would be to implement best execution as a process (i.e. to establish an order execution system which routes orders to execution venues that have been proven to provide best execution results on a consistent basis). The second way would be to determine the best execution venue on an order by order basis. This approach – which goes beyond the minimum regulatory requirements of MiFID – relies on access to real-time market data in order to determine where to route and execute an incoming order, thereby providing customers with the best possible execution results on a trade-by-trade basis (Gomber et al., 2009). However, SOR comes at a cost and is not yet available to all market participants.

In Australia there are various types of trading spaces. We can distinguish exchanges, non-exchange trading market systems and OTC trading systems. While in the EU and in the United States there are specific regulatory regimes that apply for each type of trading space, in Australia there are not distinct regulatory frameworks because the development of trading spaces is a relatively recent phenomenon.

In Australia, financial regulation over financial markets is developed by Australia's corporate, markets and financial services regulator: ASIC. ASIC assumed responsibility for market supervision and real-time surveillance of trading from ASX on 1 August 2010. In Australia the transfer of market supervision from the ASX to ASIC paved the way for alternative trading venue Chi-X to open its doors in the fourth quarter of 2011.

ASIC now supervises Chi-X Australia, which commenced operations on 31 October 2011. ASIC supervises also compliance with market integrity rules, compliance with the Corporations Act 2001 and ensures that Australian license conditions for financial services are met by market participants.

In Australia, a best execution rule was introduced in 2011, as part of the new market structure that permits competition between exchange markets. It is a similar principle-based model to the one in the EU. There is also a rule to prioritize the treatment of displayed orders over dark orders at the same price in an order book.

The uptick in technology-guided market monitoring is not restricted to American regulators. In fact, in Australia, ASIC has partnered with First Derivatives to build a market surveillance system that will employ technology used by high-frequency traders.

The new Australian market surveillance system will monitor markets so as to avoid 'market events' such as flash crashes and other outages. Ideally, the First Derivatives surveillance system would allow its regulatory body to monitor a breadth of products and venues while it rapidly works its way through large quantities of data. This means that the monitoring technology used by regulators is essentially the same technology that requires monitoring.

In general, among the challenges authorities face, there is a lack of comprehensive market data to work from. For example, until recently,

Table 8.3 The main characteristics of market structures

	Europe	US	Australia
Main regulation	MiFID	RegNMS	Market integrity rules
Main authority	ESMA	SEC	ASIC
Dispersion of trading	– 47 exchanges – 156 MTFs – 13 systematic internalizers	– 16 exchanges – 31 ECN – 16 dark pools – more than 200 brokers/dealers	– 1 exchange – 1 ATS
Model of regulation	Principles-based model	Trade-through model	Principles-based model
Trading in fragmented markets	Sell-side and buy-side best execution policies are not obliged to consider every venue	Market centres are connected to one another and prevent trade-through (market participants can opt out and use an SOR to create the linkages)	Market participants' best execution policies are not obliged to consider every venue
Market data	Consolidated post-trade tape anticipated under MiFID II	Consolidated pre-trade and post-trade data	Consolidation left to third parties
Tick size	Non-standardized	Standardized	Standardized
Clearing system	More providers but low interoperability	Single provider (DTTC)	Single provider (ASX Clear) for the moment

the Securities and Exchange Commission (SEC) had relied on official trade confirmations from what is known as the 'consolidated tape', a record of all transactions executed that does not include cancelled orders. So, once trades are executed, they are immediately reported to the consolidated tape – the mechanism for the provision of public post-trade transparency. In Europe the consolidated tape does not exist and the EU Parliament has contemplated it in the proposals for the new Markets in Financial Instruments Directive (MiFID II).

8.6 Conclusions

HFT is the result of a series of recent innovations in financial markets pushed to the fore mainly by previous changes in the regulations. The goal of more competition in the financial markets has brought fragmentation, reduction in trade size and more trading outside regulated markets, in dark pools and OTC venues. These results together with the advances in technology have contributed to the birth of HFT strategies.

It is evident that regulation cannot keep pace with technological innovation and that in its bid to harmonize markets, regulation around the world has encouraged the HFT phenomenon which itself is now at the heart of so much regulatory debate.

At present, HFT accounts for too much equity trading volume – about 50 per cent in the US, 40 per cent in Europe, 22 per cent in Australia – to be left to self-regulate.

Academic studies on the effects of HFT have demonstrated that this practice is not harmful to the markets and in particular, liquidity, spreads and volatility can improve. However the increasingly frequent glitches and outages in the trading venues lead to the conclusion that HFT could be very harmful to the integrity of financial markets. This suggests that the practice should be governed by rules that put some brakes on high-frequency traders.

The solution seems to be to block the damaging episodes without blocking the overall activity of high-frequency traders, because the latter is the result of progress and innovation. Technological advances in every business area are able to change operating models and in this case they are going to change market structures forever.

However, it must be highlighted that up until now the worst trading outages have occurred in the United States, while in Europe the incidents have been smaller in size and in Australia the phenomenon is more recent and has not yet resulted in any relevant damage. The action of the regulators, however, seems strongest where the phenomenon is less present. In Australia the authorities are concerned that the phenomenon could harm and marginalize their financial markets and therefore they are very active to block the negative effects of HFT before they cause damage to the market. Also in Europe, the revision of MiFID and MAD shows that the prevention of the negative effects of HFT is being taken very seriously. Conversely, in the US, the SEC, despite having to deal with the most damaging episodes, has a very cautious approach, which is basically aimed at structuring of data collection. It is evident that in the US they are very careful not to stifle innovation with too harsh regulations. But everyone knows that the most extensive damage (such as the subprime financial crisis) have, so far, emanated from the US, which at the moment seems to have a weak approach to the regulation of HFT; at present the main concern in the US is with the gathering of information about these phenomena.

It must also be considered, moreover, that the damages, flash crashes, outages and glitches inflame doubts among ordinary investors that the financial markets are fragile and susceptible to sudden shocks. For the retail investor, this evidence leads to confusion and undermines confidence. Repeated crashes could undermine confidence in the financial markets.

The glitches highlight the fragility of market structures. After every glitch the industry requires a higher level of robustness in market structures. In effect, the regulation has encouraged the creation of multiple trading venues because it was thought that competition would lower trading costs and be good for markets. There is a cost to everything and the costs are shown through these glitches.

In particular, trading halts call into question the system in general, because the outages show that the structure of the equity market, which has changed in recent years amid an onslaught of computerized trading firms and increasing automation on the part of exchanges and other intermediaries, needs to be rethought. Fundamental market structure reforms should be considered.

Moreover, markets around the world are at different stages of development with respect to HFT. But markets are interconnected, so international cooperation among market operators is important in order to accelerate shared learning and promote high standards for enhancing the safety and integrity of markets. In general, the internationalization of the financial markets has resulted in increased complexity. A more intense exchange of information between international regulators and a further harmonization of European regulation should both be pursued.

For example, ongoing European discussion around the introduction of a FTT is uncertain and protracted. Theoretically, with two models of FTT already in place (the French and the Italian), the negotiations should have been much easier, but practically speaking it has become a real issue with regard to what will be actually taxed.

Because of the interconnection of the markets, the drastic European proposals might influence the American rules, which are still at an early stage of research and are not yet formulated. The degree of influence on the US might depend on the results of the European regulatory process, because currently there is no guarantee that the European regulators are going to get the results they are looking for.

Notes

1. In November 2010 the SEC banned naked access, preventing unregistered HFT customers from accessing exchanges and alternative trading systems without passing through pre-trade risk controls.
2. Recommendation 4 – 'Regulators should continue to assess the impact on market integrity and efficiency of technological developments and market structure changes, including algorithmic and high-frequency trading. Based on this, regulators should seek to ensure that suitable measures are taken to mitigate any related risks to market integrity and efficiency, including any risks to price formation or to the resiliency and stability of markets, to which such developments give rise.' Recommendation 5 – 'Market authorities should monitor for novel forms or variations of market abuse that may arise as a result of technological developments and take action as necessary. They should also review their arrangements (including cross-border information sharing arrangements) and capabilities for the continuous monitoring of trading (including transactions, orders entered or orders cancelled) to help ensure that they remain effective.'
3. In April 2010, the CESR (now ESMA) issued a call for evidence on microstructural issues in European equity markets (CESR/10-142), with the aim to gather information on high frequency trading and on sponsored access. After many consultations with the industry ESMA in July 2011 issued a consultative paper about 'Guidelines on systems and controls in a highly automated trading environment for trading platforms, investment firms and competent authorities', ESMA/2012/122, 24 February (final paper).
4. To be specific, the Committee proposed a mandated half-second resting time for all trading orders, not only in equities, but every market, including fix income and other asset classes. The proposed rules could apply to any entity dealing on their own account and have a proportion of orders cancelled exceeding 20 per cent, a common characteristic of high frequency trading. If HFT firms do not meet the 20 per cent cancellation threshold the rule would be drawn to capture them anyway, by adding to the criteria the co-location of its servers at exchanges, or having a daily portfolio turnover of at least 50 per cent or having the majority of its position unwound within the same day.

References

AFM (2010) 'High-frequency trading: The application of advanced trading technology in the European marketplace', Netherlands Authority for the Financial Markets Report, December.

Angel J., L., Harris, C. S. Spatt (2010) 'Equity trading in the 21st century', Working Paper, http://dx.doi.org/10.2139/ssrn.1584026.

Boehmer, E., K. Y. L. Fong and J. Wu (2012) 'International evidence on algorithmic trading', AFA 2013 San Diego Meetings Paper, available at SSRN: http://ssrn.com/abstract=2022034.

Brogaard (2013) 'High-frequency trading and price discovery', ECB Working Paper No. 1609, http://ssrn.com/abstract=2341037.

Brogaard J. A. et al. (2013) 'High-frequency trading and the execution costs of institutional investors', FSA Occasional Paper Series, No.43, January.

CESR (ESMA) (2010) 'Call for evidence "Microstructural issues of the European equity markets"', 10–142, April.

CFTC and SEC (2010) 'Findings regarding the market events of May 6, 2010', Joint Advisory Committee on Emerging Regulatory Issues Report.

Chesini G. (2012). 'The Effects of competition on the fee structures of the major stock exchanges'. *World Review of Business Research*, 2(6), 100–118.

Cvitanic, J. A. A. Kirilenko (2010) 'High-frequency traders and asset prices', available at SSRN: http://ssrn.com/abstract=1569067.

Easley, D., M. M. L. de Prado and M. O'Hara (2011) 'The microstructure of the flash crash: Flow toxicity, liquidity crashes and the probability of informed trading', *The Journal of Portfolio Management*, 37(2), 118–128.

Egginton, J. F., B. F. Van Ness and R. A. Van Ness (2014) 'Quote stuffing', available at SSRN: http://ssrn.com/abstract=1958281.

ESMA (2012) 'Guidelines: Systems and controls in an automated trading environment for trading platforms, investment firms and competent authorities', ESMA/2012/122, February 24.

Frino, A. and A. Lepone (2012) 'The impact of high-frequency trading on market integrity: An empirical examination', a part of the Foresight project on The Future of Computer Trading in Financial Markets, UK Government Office for Science, May.

Gomber, P., M. Gsell, G. Pujol and A. Wranik (2009) 'Regulation and technology in equity trading – The impact of regulatory and technological changes on order execution and the trading venue landscape in Europe', in Engelen, P. and K. Lannoo, (eds) *Facing New Regulatory Frameworks in Securities Trading in Europe*, Antwerp, Intersentia.

Gomber, P., B. Arndt, M Lutat and T. Uhle (2011) 'High-frequency trading', Goethe Universität, Working Paper, http://dx.doi.org/10.2139/ssrn.1858626.

Hagströmer, B. and L. Nordén (2013) 'The diversity of high-frequency traders', *Journal of Financial Markets*, 16(4), 741–770.

Harris, L. (2003) *Trading and Exchanges: Market Microstructure for Practitioners*, New York, Oxford University Press.

Harris, L. (2012) 'Stop the high-frequency trader arms race', *Financial Times*, 27 December.

Harris, L. (2013) 'What to do about high-frequency trading', *Financial Analysts Journal*, 69(2), 6–9.

Hasbrouck, J. and G. Saar (2013) 'Low latency trading', *Journal of Financial Markets*, 16(4), 646–679.
Hendershott T. and R. Riordan (2009) 'Algorithmic trading and information', Net Institute Working Paper No. 09–08.
Hendershott, T. and P. Moulton (2011) 'Automation, speed and stock market quality: The NYSE's hybrid', *Journal of Financial Markets*, 14(4), 568–604.
Hendershott, T., T. C. Jones and A. J. Menkveld (2011) 'Does algorithmic trading improve liquidity?, *The Journal of Finance*, 66(1), 1–33.
IOSCO (2011) "Regulatory issues raised by the impact of technological changes on market integrity and efficiency', Final Report.
Jarnecic, E. and M. Snape (2010) 'An analysis of trades by high-frequency participants on the London Stock Exchange', 17th Annual Conference of the Multinational Finance Society MFS, Barcelona, Spain, 30 June.
Jarrow, R. A. and P. Protter (2011) 'A dysfunctional role of high-frequency trading in electronic markets', Johnson School Research Paper Series No. 08–2011, available at SSRN: http://ssrn.com/abstract=1781124.
Kirilenko, A. A., A. S. Kyle, M. Samadi and T. Tuzun (2011) 'The flash crash: The impact of high-frequency trading on an electronic market', available at SSRN: http://ssrn.com/abstract= 1686004.
Martinez, V. H. and I. Rosu (2013), 'High Frequency Traders, News and Volatility', AFA 2013 San Diego Meetings, available at SSRN: http://ssrn.com/abstract=1859265.
Menkveld, A. J., (2013) 'High-frequency trading and the new market makers', *Journal of Financial Markets*, 16(4), 712–740.
Moosa, I. (2013) 'The regulation of high-frequency trading: A pragmatic view', *Journal of Banking Regulation*, DOI: 10.1057/jbr.2013.22.
Riordan R. and A. Storkenmairm (2012) 'Latency, liquidity and price discovery', *Journal of Financial Markets*, 15(4), 416–437.
Sornette D. and S. Von Der Becke (2011), 'Crashes and high-frequency trading', Swiss Finance Institute Research Paper Series No. 11–63, available at SSRN: http://ssrn.com/abstract=1976249.
Stoll H. R. (2006), 'Electronic trading in stock markets', *Journal of Economic Perspectives*, 20(1): 153–174.
UK Government Office for Science's Foresight Project Foresight (2012) 'The future of computer trading in financial markets, final project report', UK Government Office for Science, May.
Zhang, (2010) 'High-Frequency trading, stock volatility and price discovery', Working Paper, http://dx.doi.org/10.2139/ssrn.1691679.

9

Islamic and Conventional Exchanges: A Performance Analysis and Governance Perspectives

Josanco Floreani, Andrea Paltrinieri, Maurizio Polato and Flavio Pichler

9.1 Introduction

Over the last two decades the securities industry has undergone a process of rapid transformation which has been accelerating over the last few years. The backbone of such a process is the demutualization and self-listing of a large part of stock exchanges around the world. Subsequently, a widespread consolidation process, which gathered speed at the beginning of the century, lead to the polarization of trading and gave rise to a very few large conglomerates operating on a transatlantic basis, with highly diversified business models, and managing vast pools of liquidity. Apart from these more dominant players, regional exchanges still exist (operating, however, with far lower levels of liquidity) and new rivals (electronic communication networks – ECNs) are prospering.

Integration of capital markets requires attention to be paid to the new exchanges that exist across the world; a great portion of these are located in Islamic countries, which, given their particular social and institutional features (Shariah institutions) contributes towards substantially differentiating them from conventional exchanges (CEs).[1] This raises the question whether such institutional and social features affect the development paths and performances of Islamic exchanges (IEs). Moreover, in recent years the consolidation process in the exchange industry has given rise to some convergence between major Western exchanges and Islamic market centres. In particular, we refer to the convergence between London Stock Exchange Group, the NASDAQ OMX Group and Borse Dubai.

However, Islamic exchanges are mostly still operating at the earliest stages of development with a reference market that is within their national boundaries. Liquidity levels are, in most cases, negligible.

The aim of this work is to take a glance at the functioning of CEs and IEs and to investigate whether, and to what extent, there are significant differences in business models, operational measures of performance and efficiency. From that starting point, we look at the specificities of the two clusters and explore the drivers of operational performances across them. Our main hypotheses are as follows:

> *Hypothesis 1*: Different social and economic environments lead to significant differences between business models, financial and operational structures across CEs and IEs.
>
> *Hypothesis 2*: Due to differences between business models, the two clusters are significantly different in terms of performance and efficiency and are sensitive to different drivers of profitability.

Our study is based on existing performance-related literature. The literature on the topic investigates the operational performances of CEs in concomitance with certain relevant events in the life of exchanges (i.e. changes in the legal status following demutualization and self-listing), in particular comparing pre-listing and post-listing performances with the ultimate goal of inferring the determinants of the decision to list. However, we take a different approach in the sense that we compare performances between two clusters of exchanges operating under very different jurisdictions and institutional arrangements. In our view, the issues we address could have relevant strategic implications, far beyond a matter of the industry's structure. On the one hand, CEs operate in a highly competitive environment, striving for new sources of revenue and new markets to exploit; major IEs seek to expand influence in the Western world. Should these developments prompt greater convergence between the two clusters, we expect significant effects on global capital flows, which implies major concerns for global governance.

Our study suggests that IEs are not substantially influenced in their operations and performances by social and institution-specific features.

The chapter is organized as follows. Section 9.2 provides a literature review and the theoretical framework. Section 9.3 describes the sample while Section 9.4 lays down the methodology. Then, Section 9.5 provides the main results. Next, Section 9.6 discusses the major implications. Finally, Section 9.7 concludes.

9.2 Literature review and theoretical framework

As it is widely recognized in related literature, the theoretical framework driving changes in the exchange industry is that of the network economies. More precisely, we can contextualize this framework within the theory of the exchange as a firm (see Di Noia, 2001). According to this view, management is concerned with efficiency and value creation; specific to the exchange industry is the relation between market liquidity and efficiency. The firm view emerged strongly, following the changing governance paradigms of exchanges, starting with demutualization and continuing with self-listing of major exchanges. Such transformations then naturally led to further transformations within the industry structure, through an intense consolidation process. Literature has dealt widely with the reasons for, and theoretical implications of, the aforementioned changes.

The main drivers that led stock exchanges to demutualize were increased global competition and advances in technology, rather than the mere need to raise capital (Steil, 2002). In the past there were floor-based exchanges: mutual organizations owned and controlled by their members, which enjoyed monopoly status in their domestic markets. In recent years, the background of the securities industry has changed. Technological transformations are the main drivers of competition, therefore contributing to a reduction in the costs of accessing exchanges' services and trading costs and prompting share cross-trading (Macey and O'Hara, 1999); by eliminating geographical barriers and fostering innovation (Domowitz and Steil, 1999) this eventually caused the monopolies to fall.

Falling national boundaries stimulated mobility on the listing side as well, reducing, at least in part, the home bias that prevents issuers listing abroad (Macey and O'Hara, 1999). These factors have also reduced the barriers to entry, encouraging direct competition between electronic communication networks (ECNs) and stock exchanges.

As a result of this process, academic literature was engaged, on the one hand, in comparing the relative efficiency of cooperatives and demutualized exchanges and, on the other, in establishing the effects of demutualization and self-listing on the performance of stock exchanges. Hart and Moore (1996) point out that outside ownership is becoming even more efficient than having a mutual organization, as the exchanges are facing greater competition and the vested interests of members are becoming more skewed. In particular, they argue that both the mutual model and the outside ownership model are inefficient; nevertheless, the more intense the competition and the greater the degree of member inconsistency, the more outside ownership emerges as relatively efficient. Moreover, demutualization qualifies as a typical feature of those exchanges located in countries which have higher levels of economic freedom and face greater competition (Brito Ramos, 2006). The link between governance and efficiency is further investigated by Serifsoy and Tyrell (2006): they show how a mutual exchange, facing competition from a for-profit, outsider-owned platform, can only survive by adopting a similar governance structure. As regards financial performances, the prevailing contributions in the field (Krishnamurti, Sequeira and Fangjian, 2003; Mendiola and O'Hara, 2003; Worthington and Higgs, 2005; Fleckner, 2006; Otchere, 2006; Otchere and Abou-Zied, 2008; Azzam, 2010) provide support for the idea that demutualization leads to increases in profitability, efficiency, and capital expenditure.

Among them, Otchere (2006) finds evidence of strong stock market performance for the listed exchanges (better than non-listed counterparts), and deduces a value effect of self-listing. Azzam (2010), analysing 11 demutualized stock exchanges from 1996 to 2008, shows that demutualization improves an exchange's financial performance, size and liquidity, while lowering its debt. Otchere and Abou-Zied (2008), performing an 'in-depth study' on the Australian Stock Exchange (ASX), document evidence of a strong stock market and operating performance, following the conversion from a mutual structure to a publicly traded self-listed structure. The same results are obtained by Aggarwal and Dahiya (2006).

Indeed, theoretically, envisaging changes in the ownership structure as a continuum ranging from mutual structures, demutualized but private exchanges and listed ones, the improvements in performances for listed exchanges may be attributable both to changes in the business model (the adoption of a for-profit objective function) or to the effects of market discipline. Oldford and Otchere (2011) find evidence that while publicly traded exchanges fare better than customer-owned exchanges, the comparisons between pre- and post-listing operating performances do not show relevant improvements in profitability.

All the factors previously examined have also affected the structure of the securities industry as a whole. In a more competitive environment stock exchanges are induced to pursue an external growth strategy. More precisely, the incentive to consolidate is grounded in the network economies theory. In the exchange industry, network economies are both direct and indirect. The more traders use the exchanges' platforms, the more traders are willing to join them (direct network economies). At the same time, as the liquidity increases the exchange becomes more attractive for issuers (indirect network economies): the application of the theory of network economies to financial exchanges is proposed by Economides (1993). Aside from (but related to) the theory of networks, another strand of theoretical research has developed. We refer, in particular, to the phenomena of economies of scale and scope. Stock exchanges operate, to a large extent, with a fixed cost structure (personnel expenses and investments in technology); therefore, we expect average costs to decline as the output increases. The issue has been investigated by Hasan and Malkamäki (2001) who accounted for the existence of significant scale economies, although with different magnitudes, across stock exchanges.

The Hasan and Malkamäki's study is relevant in that it represents one of the first attempts to gain insight into both cost and revenues of stock exchanges. It empirically investigates the productivity of stock exchanges over time, suggesting that both investments in technology and competition positively affect cost and revenue efficiency. Market size and quality, by contrast, seem to have a positive impact only on revenue efficiency.

Increasing consolidation leads to the rise of large conglomerates operating with a diversified business models which provide the opportunity for the exploitation of scale economies. Broadly speaking, we can envisage securities exchanges operating according to different business models spanning from a focalized model (an exchange which focuses on cash trading) to a model covering all trade-related services (trading on a variety of asset classes, dissemination of data information and post-trading activities). Polato and Floreani (2008) show that for large conglomerates the greatest parts of their total revenues are derived from complementary activities. In fact, a narrow business model is confined to smallest exchanges. From an economic point of view, the ability to provide a variety of related services using the same platform is expected to foster economies of scope (Macey and O'Hara, 1997).

Up to now, the effects of this consolidation trend on stock exchanges have not been fully analysed in the academic research. A particular strand of literature focuses on value creation in terms of mergers and alliances by investigating how changing ownership impacts on value. The main contributions in the strategic literature comprise those of Anand and Khanna (2000); Hasan and Malkamäki (2001); Dessein (2005); Gomes-Casseres, Hagendoorn and Jaffe (2006); and Hasan, Schmiedel and Song (2010).However, consolidation has mostly concerned the major stock exchanges so far. Claessens, Djankov and Klingebiel (2000) showed that

Eastern Europe's emerging market exchanges have not been involved in the consolidation process. If we also consider the first part of this century, the exchanges of developing countries appear to favour internal growth strategies, (Claessens, Klingebiel and Schmuckler, 2002), or other form of integration, such as linkages or alliances (Meera, Omar and Aziz, 2009).

As regards another subset of emerging markets, the Islamic ones, we find that in previous years there has been a strong preference for internal growth rather than for consolidation (Kabir and Suk-Yu, 2007). However, in the last couple of years, in a particular country of the Islamic area – the United Arab Emirates – a consolidation between their three stock exchanges has begun, as in 2009 the Dubai Financial Market bought Nasdaq-Dubai. Paltrinieri (2012) shows that the combined effects of market fragmentation, financial crisis and the collapse of trading values and market capitalization during the 2007–2011 period, could foster a full merger between Dubai Financial Market, Nasdaq-Dubai and Abu Dhabi Securities Exchange.

However, literature focusing on the relationship between the exchanges of developed and emerging markets is limited and has not been added to over time, despite the relevance of the issue in light of the high growth rates of Islamic finance over the last few years.[2] Major contributions are related to Islamic banks (Aggarwal and Yousef, 2000; Cihak and Hesse, 2010; Beck, Demirgüç-Kunt and Merrouche, 2013), dealing in particular with efficiency and stability of Islamic banks in comparison to conventional banks or mutual funds (Hayat and Kraeussl, 2011; Hoepner, Rammal and Rezec, 2011). Up to now, there has been no literature on Islamic stock exchange efficiency and performances apart some contributions dealing with business structures of IEs (Paltrinieri, 2012).

Nevertheless, Islamic markets deserve more investigation, in light of their particularities and the increasing convergence with CEs.

9.3 Description of the sample

We build on data of 31 exchanges. The sample comprises 17 listed exchanges and the 14 most relevant Islamic markets.

As regards to the Islamic subset, we consider stock exchanges of the countries belonging to Organization of Islamic Cooperation (OIC) for a total of 50 stock exchanges. We had to drop all stock exchanges that do not provide financial statements or market data. After applying these criteria, we obtained a sample of 14 Islamic stock exchanges. Unfortunately we were not be able to collect data for the two fully Shariah-compliant stock exchanges, namely the Teheran Stock Exchange, established in Iran in 1967, and the Khartoum Stock Exchange, established in Sudan in 1994.

Apart from listed exchanges (the Dubai Financial Market and Bursa Malaysia) which are obliged to comply with IFRS, other IEs in our sample are not required to disclose any information about their balance sheets. We are, therefore, aware that we could have a biased subsample. We have tried to homogenize information with that from our CEs subsample.

Regarding the other subset, the initial sample consists of 22 conventional stock exchanges and all of them are listed. For 4 out of 22 (namely, the Warsaw Stock Exchange, the Athens Exchange, the Santiago Stock Exchange and the Philippine Stock Exchange) we do not have complete and reliable data, so we ruled out them from the analysis, while the Malaysian exchange is included among IEs. Therefore, our sample at this stage consists of 17 conventional stock exchanges. We focus on conventional listed exchanges as they count for more than 89 per cent of WFE total revenues and trading volumes. In contrast, only two IEs are listed at this time.

On balance, our sample of CEs and IEs is quite heterogeneous in terms of governance structure, track record and market activity. Table 9.1 describes our sample of CEs and IEs reporting the legal status, date of incorporation and market capitalization.

Table 9.1 suggests that CEs have far higher market capitalization than IEs. Only a few Islamic exchanges (the Istanbul, Indonesia and Malaysian exchanges) have comparable capitalization to the smallest CE exchanges. Furthermore, differences also emerge on trading value and listed companies. Figure 9.1 compares CEs (upper panel) with IEs (lower panel), showing trading value and listed companies' compound annual growth rate (CAGR) for the period 2007–2011.

Both groups suffered during the crisis period through widespread declines in trading activity. However, it emerges that CEs fared relatively better (lower declines). IEs, at least some of them, show high declines in trading values. There is also greater volatility within the Islamic group. IEs, by contrast, proved to be more resilient as regards trends in listed companies.

Finally, we complete the analysis of our sample by reporting revenue composition across our two clusters. Table 9.2 below reports the breakdown of the exchanges' revenues distinguishing revenues from cash markets (listing and cash-trading revenues) and other sources (mainly, post-trading revenues, IT revenues, market data dissemination or investment activities).

Table 9.1 Sample characteristics: conventional (CEs) and Islamic (IEs) stock exchanges

Country	Stock exchange	Establishment*	Ownership structure	Market capitalization (billion $, 2011)
Germany	Deutsche Börse	1993	Listed	1184.5
Spain	Bolsas y Mercados Españoles	2003	Listed	1030.9
Great Britain	London Stock Exchange Group	2007	Listed	3266.4
United States	NASDAQ Omx	2007	Listed	4687.2
United States	NYSE Euronext	2007	Listed	14242.3
Canada	TMX	2008	Listed	1912.1
Japan	Osaka Stock Exchange	1878	Listed	215.3
South Africa	Johannesburg Stock Exchange	1887	Listed	789
Australia	Australian Securities Exchange	2006	Listed	1198.2
Brazil	BOVESPA	2008	Listed	1228.9
Mexico	Mexican Stock Exchange	1978	Listed	408.7
Singapore	Singapore Stock Exchange	2000	Listed	598.2
Hong Kong	Hong Kong Exchange and Clearing Ltd	1891	Listed	2258
Colombia	Colombia Stock Exchange	2001	Listed	201.3
United States	Chicago Mercantile Exchange	2007	Listed	–
United States	Chicago Board Options Exchange	1973	Listed	–
United States	International Continental Exchange	2000	Listed	–
Azerbaijian	Baku Stock Exchange	2000	Demutualized	–
Bahrain	Bahrain Bourse	1987	Demutualization in process	17
Bangladesh	Dhaka Stock Exchange	1954	Demutualized	50
Indonesia	Indonesia Stock Exchange	1977	Demutualized	270
Kazakhstan	Kazakhstan Stock Exchange	1993	Mutualized	33
Malaysia	Bursa Malaysia	1930	Self-listed	395
Morocco	Casablanca Stock Exchange	1929	Mutualized	63
Oman	Muscat Securities Market	1988	State-owned	27
Pakistan	Karachi Stock Exchange	1947	Demutualization in process	33
State of Palestine	Palestine Stock Exchange	1995	Self-listed	3
Tunisia	Tunis Stock Exchange	1969	Mutualized	9
Turkey	Istanbul Stock Exchange	1986	Demutualization in process	320
UAE	Dubai Financial Market	2000	Self-listed	49
Uganda	Uganda Securities Exchange	1997	Mutualized	5

*For CEs the year refers to the establishment of the last business combination (group or new entity).
Source: our elaborations on exchanges' annual reports and websites.

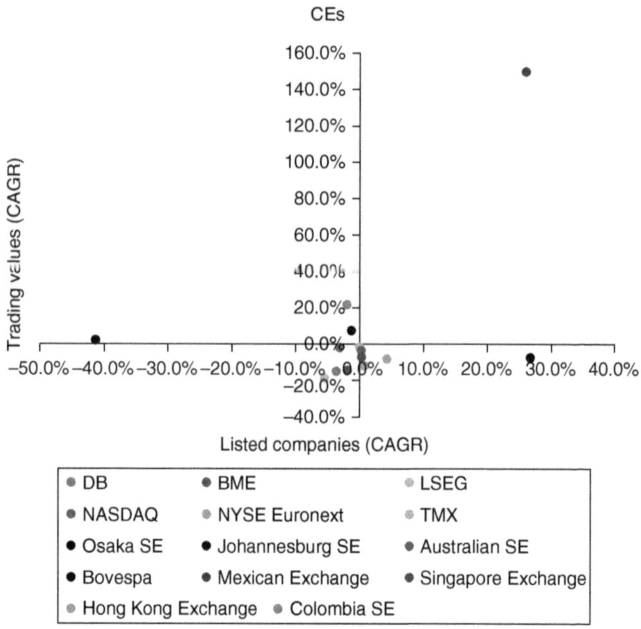

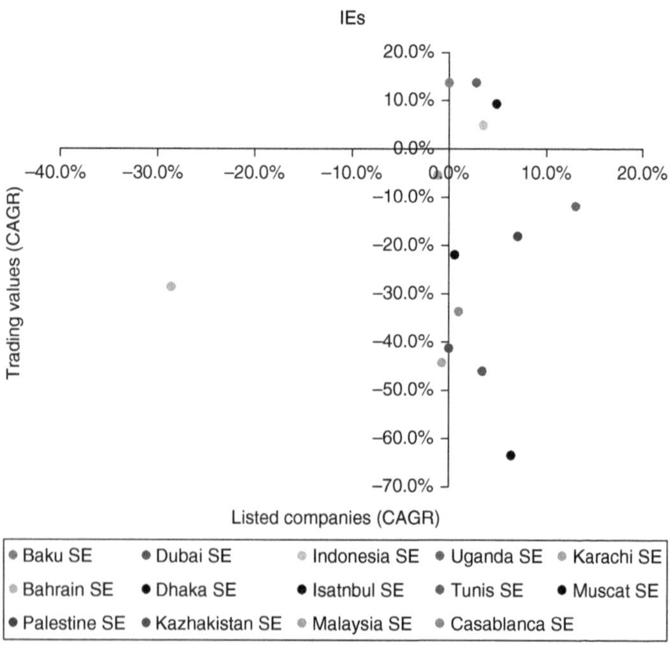

Figure 9.1 Trading values and listed companies (CAGRs)

Table 9.2 Revenue composition

	Listing (%)	Cash trading (%)	Derivatives trading (%)	Post-trading (%)	Info (%)	IT (%)	Investments (%)	Others (%)
Conventional exchanges	9.0	31.8	20.5	15.9	9.2	2.2	0.0	2.2
Islamic exchanges	6.1	58.3	0.8	2.8	1.3	0.1	1.9	11.0

Source: Our elaborations on exchanges' reports.

We find that on average CEs operate with highly diversified business models in comparison with IEs. While the fraction of cash-trading revenues is substantially lower in CEs, by contrast such exchanges have an increasing involvement in complementary business areas and, mainly, post-trading services and derivatives trading. In Section 9.5 we will study in more detail the distribution of revenues.

9.4 Data and methodology

We use financial and market data in order to compare economic and financial performances across CEs and IEs. We test out our hypothesis on a set of variables, which we group into four categories, which relate to: industry-specific variables, business and financial structure, operational performances and efficiency.

For each exchange we collect yearly financial and market data (trading values and listed companies) for a time frame spanning the period 2007–2011. We constructed our data set by drawing trading values and the number of listed companies from the statistical books of the World Federation of Exchanges (WFE) and the Federation of Euro-Asian Stock Exchanges (FEAS); we also collected information from the Arab Monetary Fund and reports from the exchanges in our IEs subsample. Financial data are drawn from the Bloomberg database for listed CEs and the annual reports for the exchanges from Islamic markets. We have 155 observations for our data set of both IEs and CEs. Table 9.3 summarizes the variables we employ in our analysis; then we provide a brief explanation of our variables.

We investigate trends in trading values and listed companies, and their impacts on financial performances, since they represent the core business of securities exchanges. It is obviously important to focus on industry-specific variables due to the well-known effects of network externalities.

Table 9.3 The variables

Tot_Ass	Total assets
Tot_Rev	Total revenues
Trad_Rev	Trading revenues
Inv_Rev	Investment revenues
Oth_Rev	Revenues other than cash market and investment revenues
Tot_Costs	Total costs
Trad_Val	Trading value (variation)
N List	Number of listed companies (variation)
Op_Lev	Operative leverage
Fin_Lev	Financial leverage
EBIT	Earnings before Interest and Taxes
Cost_In	Cost-to-income ratio
ROE	Return on equity
ROCE	Return on capital employed (EBIT/Tot_Ass)
Rev_Tv	Revenue per unit of value traded (Total revenues/trading values)
Trad_Int	Trading intensity (Trad_Vol/Tot_Ass)
Trad_Prof	Trading profitability (EBIT/Trad_Vol)

The distribution of liquidity across exchanges and macro-areas affects the efficiency of trading systems and determines competitive advantages in the exchange industry. Finally, mounting competition prompts us to investigate to what extent exchanges succeed in extracting profits from trading activity, which is expected to provide a first insight into the exchanges' efficiency. Ultimately, this has obvious implications for who will lead future developments in the industry.

Next, we investigate structure variables. We focus, in particular, on business and financial structure comparing CEs and IEs in terms of total assets, equity and revenue composition. There are several reasons for investigating the aforementioned variables, mainly related to the far-reaching consolidation process, which has reshaped the structure of the industry. Since M&As have mostly involved CEs, while IEs have not undergone a significant consolidation process, it is interesting to investigate whether there are significant differences between the two groups regarding dynamics in capital invested, business models, cost structure and how these impact on performances. First of all, consolidation in the exchange industry leads to an expansion of capital invested, particularly as a result of increasing goodwill. In combination with trends in trading values, this has implications for the efficiency of trading systems. Additionally, consolidation has a significant impact on revenues, generally leading to widespread business diversification and different business models. We compare CEs and IEs with the primary goal of assessing whether there are marked differences in business models and whether this implies different value drivers. Moreover, transformations in the industry might have an impact on financial leverage (for example, if we think about the use of debt to finance large M&As) and the cost structure of exchanges (thus impacting on the operational leverage).

In turn, differences in business models, cost structure and different exposures to competitive pressures might have wide impacts on efficiency. Apart from the standard cost-to-income ratio, we investigate industry-specific measures of efficiency, mainly related to the efficiency of the trading systems. Here, our relevant variables are the ratio of revenues on total trading value, to indicate the potential of each exchange to extract revenues from trading, and other two variables capturing the profitability of trading (Trad_Prof) and the efficiency of capital invested (Trad_Int), respectively. Trade_Prof and Trad_Int provide more insight into the drivers of the return on capital employed (ROCE).[3] This leads us to gain insight into whether exchanges compete on volumes (Trad_Int) or have some market power permitting to set prices (Trad_Prof).

Finally, the aforementioned developments are expected to have an impact on operational performances which we investigate in terms of ROCE, ROE and the EBIT margin.

For each variable we study the distribution (mean, median, 5th and 95th percentiles) across exchanges and point out the most significant differing paths in relation to our two clusters. We perform an analysis of variance as well, assuming CEs as the grouping variable. In particular, we perform Bartlett's test for the null hypothesis of equal variance. In addition, we analyse the differences in means between non-Islamic and Islamic markets by employing a two-tailed Student's t-test with a 0.05 significance level, to check whether CEs and IEs belong to different populations on different profiles. For those variables for which we reject the null hypothesis of equal variance we calculate the t-statistic recurring to Satterthwaite's approximation of the degrees of freedom.

We than expand our analysis by investigating the drivers of performances. We assume as dependent variable the EBIT margin (we follow, therefore, an approach similar to Otchere, 2006), and regress it against a subset of explanatory variables that we deem as having a significant impact on margins.

The variables we employ refer to trading values, listed companies, revenues, revenue composition and efficiency measures. Methodologically, we employ a generalized least square (GLS) panel model which we specify as follows:

$$EBIT\% = \alpha + \beta_1 Trad_{Val_{i,t}} + \beta_2 List_{i,t} + \beta_3 \%Oth_{Rev_{i,t}} + \beta_4 Op_{Lev_{i,t}} + \beta_5 Trad\_Int_{i,t} + \beta_6 Trad\_Prof_{i,t} + \varepsilon_{i,t}$$

We perform three regressions. The first one investigates the relation between the EBIT margin and the explanatory variables for the panel comprising both CEs and IEs in our sample. Then we perform two separate regressions, testing the relation between the EBIT margin and the explanatory variables for the clusters of CEs and IEs respectively.

9.5 Main results

9.5.1 Descriptive statistics

In this section we present the main findings of our analysis starting with some descriptive statistics. In general terms, the first step in the analysis of the business models and performances of exchanges is to investigate the correlations between variables. In particular, we expect there to be a positive correlation between liquidity measures and those measures expressing structure, performances and business risk. Moreover, should relevant differences across clusters emerge, this would allow for better insight into relations among variables.

Table 9.4 provides the matrix of correlations between basic measures of market activity, financial performances and business structure. Significant differences emerge among the two clusters. For CEs there is a strong correlation between trading values, revenues and operative performances. Islamic markets, in contrast, show a lower correlation

Table 9.4 The matrix of correlations

		Tv	N_List	Revenues	EBIT	Op. Lev
Non-Islamic markets	Tv	1				
	N_List	–0.0064	1			
	Revenues	0.9771	0.0338	1		
	EBIT	0.7464	0.0023	0.7352	1	
	Op. Lev	–0.1333	0.0955	–0.1608	–0.2088	1
Islamic markets	Tv	1				
	N_List	0.1838	1			
	Revenues	0.4865	–0.0857	1		
	EBIT	0.3141	–0.0956	0.2810	1	
	Op. Lev	0.3606	0.1996	0.2375	0.0741	1

among these variables. On the other hand, Islamic markets present a positive correlation of the operational leverage with trading values whereas the correlation is negative for CEs. While appearing straightforward, such results seem to point out the effectiveness of CEs (and, in particular, business diversification) in dampening operational risk. It is useful to note that IEs carry on substantial investment activities, beyond Shariah-compliant investment, that show a relevant difference with CEs. The higher weight of investment business, compared to non-Islamic exchanges, might, in turn, alter the relations between trading activity, revenues and margins providing a possible explanation of a weaker correlation between such variables for IEs.

Table 9.A in the Appendix provides descriptive statistics for all variables included in the model. In particular, we analyse the distribution of all variables for each stock exchange and for the two clusters as well. In this regard, we try to understand whether the two groups tend to behave differently by providing the number of exchanges for each group which lay above the median, above the 95th percentile and below the 5th percentile. Results are quite mixed.

As for industry-specific variables, CEs, on average, fare better in terms of Trad_Val CAGR. Looking at the distribution there is a greater proportion of CEs with values above the median. The pattern is different, however, for growth rate of listed companies.

In terms of business structure there are huge differences between the two groups, the most relevant in Tot_Ass and capital invested. Only Dubai, in the Islamic area, operates with a capital invested that is comparable to CEs. Financial structure, captured by financial leverage (defined as the debt-equity ratio), shows relevant differences as well. IEs, at a first glance, operate within a more fragile financial structure, with far lower levels of equity and higher leverage. Actually, when analysing Fin_Lev in more detail, there is a greater proportion of CEs with a higher leverage than the median value, nevertheless the IEs group contains two exchanges (those above the 95th percentile) with extremely high levels of leverage.

If we analyse the revenues of CEs there are, obviously, far higher levels than IEs because the group comprises the largest exchanges around the world. However, we did note that CEs' business models are substantially diversified, as they derive the largest portion of their revenues from business activities other than trading on cash markets. On average, the fraction of Oth_Rev on total revenues is higher for CEs compared with IEs. On balance, they tend to be distributed above the median value.

In contrast, only three IEs (Tunis, Muscat and Casablanca) operate with an incidence of Oth_Rev above the median value. IEs appear somewhat different as they have operated, so far, in a more segmented jurisdiction, with little pressure to consolidate, despite the expansion of certain Islamic financial centres (i.e. Dubai). From previous discussion, we know that a great part of IEs' other revenues come from investment activities, while businesses such as post-trading services or derivatives are quite negligible.

Institutional and religion-related factors, mainly connected to Shariah-compliant investments, are deemed to differentiate IE's. However, despite being a feature of Islamic exchanges, the magnitude of this phenomenon is quite limited. IEs derive roughly two per cent of their revenues from Shariah-compliant investments. Moreover, among the IEs, only the Dubai Financial Market is heavily engaged in such activities (which count for 27 per cent of total revenues). Overall, a greater part (11 per cent on average) of IEs' revenues is derived from other sources, which mainly comprise interest income. As for the operational leverage, conditions are quite different.

CEs, then, operate with lower values of leverage compared to IEs. There is a lower fraction of CEs with an operational leverage above the median value. Since they comprise major listed exchanges that carry on relevant investments (implying significant fixed costs), in light of the competitive struggle – which mainly affects large international players – one should expect their operational leverage to be higher. However, the results are largely influenced by the very low figures of NYSE Euronext (–4.22), the Johannesburg Stock Exchange (–2.49) and the Mexican Exchange (–2.89) which might seem quite unusual. This could depend on the cost structure of exchanges, and, in particular, higher fixed costs compared to contribution margins. However, such figures might also be influenced by structural transformations occurring within the securities industry which, supposedly, had some impact on the cost structure of exchanges: for example, costs related to the mergers which, during the last few years, have interested Western exchanges. Some stock exchanges, then, especially in American markets, bear significant costs of revenues. Excluding those figures, the average operational leverage for non-CEs is 0.84.

Looking at operational performances, we infer that the EBIT margin is quite normally distributed; moreover, we note that there are a similar number of CEs and IEs respectively above and below median value. However, only three Islamic markets (Dubai, Dhaka and Casablanca) have operative performances above 70 per cent, resembling those of most profitable Western exchanges. There is, therefore, room for improving efficiency among Islamic financial markets.

As regards ROA and the ROCE, there is no clear difference in pattern between the two groups and there is, at a first glance, no clear evidence of the superiority of CEs. However, there is a greater proportion of IEs which lie above the median value, although none of them falls above the 95th percentile. This might appear to be somewhat surprising given that CEs are all listed exchanges with, theoretically, the mandate to create value for shareholders. However, we count two CEs that have extremely high performances in terms of ROE and ROCE. Such exchanges are operating in fast growing areas (i.e. the Singapore exchange) or perform high growing derivatives business (i.e. the CBOE). Apart from the outliers, CEs do not outperform IEs.

Finally, we analyse efficiency measures. Trad_Prof and Trad_Int are the basic measures into which the EBIT margin breaks down. By employing such measures our aim is to establish a direct link between liquidity measures and economic measures. The measures we employ encompass both technical and economic efficiency.

We expected trading value to play a relevant role in determining trading revenues. However, depending on a variety of factors (the first and most intuitive being increasing competition) the ability for capturing revenues on trading values might be different across exchanges or jurisdictions. On average IEs fare much better than CEs in terms of Rev_TV. When considering overall distribution, IEs concentrate in the upper 50 per cent while CEs lie on the lower 50 per cent. This pattern, therefore, shows that our clusters form two distinct groups. Bartlett's test results suggest rejection of the null hypothesis of equal variance.

As we mentioned above, Trad_Int measures efficiency of a firm's assets (i.e. the magnitude to which assets produce trading values) and should be deemed as a measure of technical efficiency whereas Trad_Prof measures operational margins for each unit of trading value. Table 9.A in the appendix shows interesting results: while the distribution of the EBIT margin is quite close to a normal distribution, with similar behaviour for both clusters, things significantly change when looking at trading intensity and trading profitability. Both Trad_Int and Trad_Prof are quite skewed. But furthermore, it is worth stressing that there is different behaviour between the two groups. When looking at Trad_Prof we observe that the vast majority of IEs are above median value, while only one CE lies above the 50th percentile. In contrast, CEs are characterized by higher values of Trad_Int, tending to be distributed above median value, while almost all IEs (except two) are below the 50th percentile. Additionally, when looking at the distribution of the outliers, IEs are more likely to show extreme values.

These results imply that CEs are far more efficient in exploiting assets, while having poorer results as regards Trad_Prof than IEs. In contrast, IEs show higher levels of Cost_Inc. However, there are huge differences between market centres within Islamic world, with a few exchanges having ratios that are aligned (for example Dubai) with more reputable CEs and the majority suffering particularly high ratios (85 per cent of Islamic exchanges are above the median value against 29 per cent of CEs). The Palestine exchange has, on average, a 126.5 percentage ratio.

9.5.2 Analysis of variance and differences in means

Previous analysis demonstrates two different competition models. CEs are arguably more exposed to competitive pressures and are able to retain tighter margins from trading activity compared with the more closed IEs. They have, therefore, to compete on quantities by devoting large efforts to improving platforms.

Table 9.5 provides more insight by presenting average and relative standard deviations for our variables; subsequently, it performs variance analysis and tests the differences in means.

For those variables capturing business and financial structure averages and relative standard deviations are higher for CEs. When looking at industry-specific variables, CEs fare better, on average, than IEs regarding the growth rate of trading values with lower relative standard deviation. The opposite holds for the growth rate in listed companies. For efficiency of operational performances the results from the variables are quite mixed. For example, IEs presents higher average values and higher relative standard deviations for financial leverage, the EBIT margin, revenues per unit of trading value, cost-to-income ratio and trading profitability. The figures, therefore, show a higher riskiness for IEs. For other variables we find somewhat different pictures. ROE and ROCE, for instance, do not present relevant differences between the two groups.

The analysis of variance leads us to reject the null hypothesis of equal variance for almost all the relevant variables. It is only for the EBIT margin, cost-to-income ratio, ROE and ROCE that we accept, according to our results, the null hypothesis. Finally, Table 9.5 reports the Student's t-test and the p-value.

On grounds of the results described in Table 9.5, we summarize variables for which we reject and do not reject, respectively, the null hypothesis that the mean difference is zero. We perform a two-tailed t-test with a 0.05 significance level (Table 9.6).

Table 9.5 Islamic and conventional stock exchanges: a comparison

	Non-Islamic markets		Islamic markets		Bartlett's statistic		Student's t-test*			
	Average (a)	St.Dev/ Av	Average (b)	St.Dev/ Av	Statistic	p-value	Diff. (a–b)	t-statistic	p-value	DF
Tot_Ass	9121.18	11047.15	281.59	610.86	55.8606	0.000	8839.58	−3.1951	0.006	15.1
Equity	42578.45	158019.4	210.786	585.0533	123.6459	0.000	42367.66	−1.0725	0.3005	15
Tot_Rev	35841.21	112125.1	39.7363	53.9929	175.2256	0.000	35801.48	−1.3165	0.2066	16
Trad_Rev	16460.98	57572.81	27.7625	34.7137	167.1275	0.000	12564.01	−1.0283	0.3191	16
Oth_Rev%	80.26%	0.2247	40%	0.4509	6.5274	0.011	0.402586	−3.0431	0.0069	18.2
Trad_Val	−2.68%	0.1037	−19.49%	0.2465	9.3536	0.002	0.1680	−2.3737	0.0297	16.9
N_List	−1.23%	0.1348	3.07%	0.040	15.9592	0.000	−0.043	−1.0730	0.3001	15.1
Op_Lev	0.0982	1.6322	0.8809	0.4875	15.6728	0.000	−0.7826	1.8782	0.0755	19.3
Fin_Lev	29.75%	0.1677	47.17%	0.5420	16.9053	0.000	−0.1742	1.1543	0.2664	15.04
EBIT%	26.01%	0.2203	47.60%	0.3343	2.4084	0.121	0.3576	2.1565	0.0395	29
Rev_Tv	0.2798	0.9062	7.0408	14.3407	51.8861	0.000	−6.7610	1.7605	0.1016	13.10
Cost_In	27.53%	0.2334	67.23%	0.2780	0.04270	0.513	−0.3969	4.0954	0.0003	29
ROE	21.39%	0.1839	21.70%	0.1444	0.7723	0.379	−0.0030	0.0507	0.9599	28
ROCE	13.61%	0.1330	14.63%	0.1013	0.9733	0.324	−0.010123	0.2343	0.8165	28
Trad_Int	656.3051	561.5925	0.3860	0.5530	155.4209	0.000	655.919	−4.2111	0.0012	12
Trad_Prof	0.0145	0.0531	1.5570	3.0112	83.7287	0.000	−1.5424	1.9163	0.0776	13

Source: our elaborations on data collected from the annual reports of exchanges and the Bloomberg database. *Two-tailed test, with a 0.05 significance level.

Table 9.6 t-statistic test

	Accept H_0	**Reject H_0**
Liquidity and revenues	N_List	Trad_Vol
Structure	Equity, Op_Lev, Fin_Lev Tot_Rev, Trad_Rev,	Tot_Ass, Oth_Rev%
Operational performances	ROE, ROCE	EBIT %
Efficiency	Rev_Tv, Trad_Prof	Cost_In, Trad_Int

Results are based on a two-tailed Student's t test with a 0.05 significance level.

Evidence is quite mixed. We reject the null hypothesis of equal population in mean for a few variables. It is worth noting, at the first instance, the behaviour of Trad_Vol and Oth_Rev: apparently, there is a difference in the average compound annual growth rate of trading values across the two groups. The results account for a different pattern in market activity, with IEs that on average performed better. One of the assumptions of our work is that IEs and CEs operate with different business models. According to our results, the differences we found are significant. It is important to note that with a 0.1 per cent significance level the Op_Lev itself would present a significant difference in means. This would imply that the two groups are differently exposed to business risk (intended here as the risk of losing margins as a result of declines in revenues).

In our view the most interesting results are those related to operational performances and, above all, to efficiency measures. While there are no significant differences in ROE and ROCE, IEs fare better in terms of the EBIT margin and such differences are significant. As for efficiency measures, the results are ambiguous. We rejected the null hypothesis for Cost_Inc and Trad_Int; however, when assuming a 0.1 per cent significance level we had to reject the null hypothesis for Trad_Prof as well (and, Rev_TV would be just slightly below the critical t value). Therefore, we had to draw the implication that the two groups we analysed belong to two different populations as regards efficiency conditions.

These results are expected to have significant implications in relation to the competitive strategies of exchanges and we will discuss this point in the next section. The differences we have found lead us to delve into the determinants of margins in more detail. We expect the two groups to have different drivers of operating performance, given the differences in business structures.

9.5.3 Regression results

In order to analyse the determinants of the EBIT margin, we model a linear relation with a set of variables capturing market dynamics (variations in trading values and listed companies), financial variables (total revenues and revenues coming from activities other than cash trading), efficiency measures (Trad_Int and Trad_Prof) and operational leverage. We use a panel data analysis; more specifically, we apply a GLS model (see Table 9.7).

By regressing the EBIT margin to the explanatory variables for the entire sample, we obtain the result that the most significant variables are those expressing the weight of Oth_Rev on total revenues and variables of trading efficiency (Trad_Prof and Trad_Int).

Looking at r-squares, the overall effects are quite high for each of the two clusters while, when considering all the exchanges are far lower. Performing the regression on the two clusters separately, we obtain slightly

Table 9.7 Regression results

	All exchanges	Conventional exchanges	Islamic exchanges
Var. Trad_Val	0.0913(.) [0.028]	0.0913 [0.141]	0.0309(.) [0.607]
Var. List	–0.0421 [0.491]	–0.0074 [0.881]	–1.1570** [0.006]
Log Tot_Rev	0.0596* [0.046]	–0.0988 [0.123]	0.2639*** [0.000]
%Other Rev	–0.339 *** [0.001]	–0.5689*** [0.000]	0.0043 [0.971]
Op Lev	–0.0016 [0.896]	–0.0060 [0.548]	0.0488 [0.433]
Trad_Int	–0.00007** [0.010]	–0.00009*** [0.000]	0.1359* [0.026]
Trad_Prof	0.0116*** [0.000]	2.0142* [0.024]	0.0104*** [0.001]
Intercept	0.3845 *** [0.000]	1.0623 *** [0.000]	–0.0172 [0.879]
Chi 2	0.0000	0.0000	0.0000
R-sq within	0.3637	0.1805	0.6254
R-sq between	0.1470	0.7078	0.3536
R-sq overall	0.1844	0.6294	0.4377
Sigma_u	0.17518	0.08716	0.12924
Sigma_E	0.11530	0.08560	0.11443
Rho	0.69771	0.50902	0.56057
Number of observations	118	61	57

This table regresses the EBIT margin against our independent variables according to the following model:

$$Ebit\% = \alpha + \beta_1 Trad{+}Val_{i,t} + \beta_2 List_{i,t} + \beta_3 \%Oth\_Rev_{i,t} + \beta_4 Op\_Lev_{i,t} + \beta_5 Trad\_Int_{i,t} + \beta_6 Trad\_Prof_{i,t} + \varepsilon_{i,t}$$

We test the relation for the entire sample of both conventional and Islamic exchanges and for the two clusters separately. $Trad\_Val_{i,t}$ is a variable expressing variations in trading values for i-th exchange in period t; $List_{i,t}$ represents variations in listed companies for i-th exchange in period t; $\%Oth\_Rev_{i,t}$ represents the weight of revenues other than cash-trading revenues on total revenues for i-th exchange in period t; $Op\_Lev_{i,t}$ expresses operational leverage for i-th exchange in period t; $Trad\_Int_{i,t}$ is the trading intensity for i-th exchange in period t; $Trad\_Prof_{i,t}$ is the trading profitability (Ebit on trading values) for i-th exchange in period t. Significance codes: ***0.001; **0.01; *0.05; (.)0.1.

different results. In terms of chi square, the model seems to fit data with reference to each group. Looking at the regressors, different models emerge across the two groups. Market activity is generally positively related to margins, with the exception of variations in listed companies. However, market measures are not significant in explaining margins.

For CEs the percentage of other revenues is very significant in explaining margins. This is consistent with their business models (i.e. a high diversification of revenue sources). Surprisingly, the sign of the coefficient is negative. One explanation could be related to complexities arising from managing large conglomerates which would, in turn, reduce efficiency.

In contrast, for IEs we find total revenues have a great significance in explaining margins and, to a lesser extent, the variations in listed companies. We also note the relatively high value of Tot_Rev for IEs, compared with a negative value for CEs. These results are consistent with a more traditional business model and the strong relation between revenues and margins could be attributable to lower competitive pressures (weaker price elasticity) or to different cost structure.

If we consider Tra_Int and Trad_Prof, we find interesting results. Tra_Prof is particularly significant in explaining margins for IEs, while Trad_Int is more significant with reference to CEs. These results are consistent with the previous considerations. Interestingly a negative relation emerges between Trad_Int and margins for CEs. Expanding trading values, therefore, would put pressures on profitability. These results show that CEs operate at a more mature stage of the industry's development, making the case for seeking expansion in new markets. Finally, in both clusters there is a negative relation between the EBIT margin and operational leverage.

9.6 Strategic implications

The previous analysis performed a comparison analysis between the exchanges of CEs and IEs. The main results show significant differences, at least for certain profiles. While the main variables describing business structure do not seem to demonstrate relevant differences across the two groups, basic measures of efficiency apparently describe different patterns.

In our view, our results suggest relevant implications from the perspective of the further development in the global structure of the exchange industry. Arguably, despite the intense wave of consolidation that has been occurring during the last few years, there still remains room for improvement along the path of convergence among international financial centres.

In fact, relevant differences still remain between CEs and IEs. The differences we found in efficiency measures might be deemed as typical of different economic and institutional environments. In the meantime, such differences might constitute the economic and strategic rationale for increasing convergence between CEs and IEs. Although some consolidation took place among IEs, nevertheless they seem to favour convergence with CEs and, in particular, the largest Western exchanges. Such a pattern of development might seem somewhat surprising to those who would expect a consolidation within the Islamic world before expansion outside that area was to begin.

However, our analysis suggests that it is a cross-convergence (intended as the convergence between exchanges belonging to different economic, social and institutional areas) that is particularly beneficial to both Islamic and non-Islamic exchanges (at least to major exchanges in the two areas), permitting mutual leverage between their respective competitive strengths.

CEs are exposed to massive competitive threats: particularly the largest exchanges which suffer threats from new competitors, namely, economic communication networks. These networks are platforms similar to exchanges that offer trading facilities on large caps included in the main stock indexes. Their relevant market, therefore, tends to overlap with that of main exchanges, replicating the model of global platforms with thinner organizational structures than traditional exchanges. The latter react with an intense consolidation process which, while creating highly liquid, asset-efficient (as accounted by the higher values of Trad_Int) large pools, they give rise to complex conglomerates with heavy organizational structures. On the other hand, the jostle with ECNs leads to massive cuts in tariffs, putting pressures on margins.

IEs, in particular those controlled by sovereign funds, gain access to large liquidity pools by converging with the largest CEs markets and play a relevant role in international capital flows. On the other hand, convergence would be beneficial for CEs, allowing them to access new markets and diversify their risk exposure. Greater revenues and margins per unit of value traded suggest that elasticity of fees is lower in the Islamic world.

The considerations above do not necessarily imply, in our view, a further speeding up of the convergence process between IEs and CEs in the short run. The case for alliances mainly rests on strategic issues rather than pure financial considerations. So far, the deals involving CEs and IEs have been centred on the main exchanges in the respective areas and, namely, NASDAQ OMX and the London Stock Exchange on the one hand, and the Dubai Financial Market on the other. The latter is the major exchange in the Islamic cluster coming only after Bursa Malaysia and the Philippine Stock Exchange which, in our view, are diverse for geo-political reasons.

Actually, the Islamic world is quite heterogeneous in terms of financial conditions. Certain exchanges (in particular, the Istanbul, Palestine, Tunis and Kazakhstan exchanges) operate with fragile financial structures (low margins, high cost-to-income rations and high leverage) and low trading values (apart the Istanbul exchange). Arguably, some form of consolidation has to occur within the Islamic world.

Moving another step forward with the reasoning, such developments allow for reconsideration of the prevailing governance paradigm in the exchange industry. Formal mergers are not the only way to organize convergence. Recent experiences of cooperation between CEs and IEs follow a cluster model where convergence is built on a network of cross-shareholdings having the power to foster strategic coordination. We see relevant implications at this stage in the development of the exchange industry.

The governance paradigm as traditionally conceived is no longer appropriate to govern relations among different groups of shareholders. In other words, while theoretical literature and regulators have always regarded corporate governance as a way of governing relations within exchanges, recent developments prompt a refocusing of governance arrangements towards governing relations at an industry-wide level. Particularly challenging in this regard is how value is distributed among exchanges within the cluster. Considering them as different nodes of the cluster under the strategic direction of a common nucleus of shareholders, the rationale of value maximization is changing. The profit function carries the objective of maximizing value at cluster-wide level rather than at an exchange level. However, given the different competitive pressures on each node and the different price elasticity, this implies that certain exchanges in the node might serve to subsidize the others. An interesting point, at this stage, is how, and to what extent, this would eventually affect the flows of liquidity across economic areas. With increasing economic and market integration the point should be carefully addressed as it would imply relevant cross-externalities. Ultimately, the nature of the conflicting interests in the exchange industry might lead to change, opposing a core of large shareholders (mainly large international institutional investors) and investors, economic agents and communities who need fair and transparent capital markets to foster wealth creation.

Finally, there is the question of who will ultimately appropriate control over international liquidity flows. If clusters of exchanges under the direction of a few shareholders were to emerge they would concentrate power over a large bulk of liquidity. Floreani and Polato (2013) elaborated an index to measure the liquidity of exchanges as:

$$I_i = \frac{Vet_i}{Mcap_i} \cdot \left(1 + \frac{Ncr_i}{GDP_j}\right)$$

where I_i is the liquidity index of *i*-th exchange, which is the function of turnover (the ratio of value of share trading on market capitalization) and the ratio of new capital raised on GDP.

The sum of I_i's represents the liquidity index of the cluster. Suppose that the cluster comprises some of the large exchanges that are intermediating high trading values and relevant capital raised on primary markets, and that one, or a few, large shareholders have an α-percentage ownership. Those shareholders, in that case, would enjoy a fraction α of control rights over large international liquidity flows. Such a pattern is, for example, to be traced in the close links between LSEG, NASDAQ OMX and the Dubai Financial Market. In addition, such developments raise the issue of full transparency of ownership interests on clusters of internationally active exchanges, especially when belonging to different economic areas.

9.7 Conclusion

This chapter performs a comparison of the financial performances of Islamic and non-Islamic exchanges. We started by providing an overview of the main dynamics on market activity (trading values and listed companies). We then turned to an analysis of the main financial matters. We found some major differences among the two clusters of exchanges. The first pertains to the degree of diversification of the business model. We showed how Islamic markets have a substantially narrow business model, which is focused on cash markets, while non-Islamic markets are a step forward on the evolutionary process and are pursuing, in certain cases, consistent business diversification strategies. It is often maintained that a specific feature of Islamic exchanges are Shariah-compliant investments. However, what emerges is that such investments do not have a paramount relevance in Islamic markets (at least regarding revenue generation): it is only in the case of the

Dubai exchange that large revenues have been derived from such investments.

Efficiency results shows that IEs perform better in terms of operational margins and trading efficiency (revenues and margins per unit of value traded). CEs are better in terms of asset exploitation. It seems that the exchange industry, at least in certain non-Islamic countries (mainly Western countries), is beginning to show the features of a mature sector.

Our results elicit a few considerations regarding future evolutionary paths within the securities industry. On the one hand, we might conclude that there are only a very few Islamic markets which would, eventually, lead a possible consolidation process within the Islamic arena. On the other end, the figures might unveil further possible convergence between Islamic and non-Islamic markets. In this regard, there remains room for future research to investigate the governance implications. In our view, further research in that field should be focused at industry-level (rather than exchange-level) governance. The most challenging developments here are related to the distribution of value across economic areas and the appropriation of control over capital flows.

Appendix

Table 9.A Relevant measures of performance

	Tot_Ass	Rev_Tv	EBIT margin	Trad_ Prof	Trad_Int	Cost_In	ROE	ROCE	Op_Lev	Fin_Lev	Oth_Rev	Tr_Vol	List
DB	32039.2	0.0014	54.9%	0.00076	107.0934	57.5%	27.0%	5.4%	1.29	30.0%	84.4%	–15.0%	–3.7%
BME	23226.9	0.3040	68.1%	0.20567	0.1899	32.9%	33.6%	2.5%	1.38	21.9%	47.4%	–14.5%	–1.9%
LSEG	3100.5	0.0002	37.0%	0.00009	2553.5141	62.8%	4.1%	9.7%	0.15	27.6%	40.4%	–18.7%	–5.5%
NASD	11350.3	0.0003	13.2%	0.00004	1888.6428	58.4%	10.4%	6.4%	–0.51	42.6%	43.3%	–1.9%	–3.1%
NYSE E	14286.6	0.0003	12.8%	0.00003	1730.8319	66.3%	6.2%	5.3%	–4.22	28.2%	61.0%	–12.0%	0.8%
TMX	2849.1	0.0005	38.0%	0.00020	564.3424	31.5%	32.9%	10.9%	0.93	43.0%	63.0%	–1.7%	0.0%
OSAKA	623.2	0.1572	0.3%	0.00045	3.4823	0.5%	13.9%	14.0%	–0.22	18.3%	99.6%	–7.3%	26.7%
JOHANNESB.	258.8	0.0048	3.1%	0.00015	170.6087	7.0%	23.0%	18.8%	–2.49	49.7%	96.8%	2.0%	–41.3%
AUSTRALIAN	3609.9	0.0008	46.3%	0.00035	294.5808	19.2%	11.9%	11.2%	1.36	66.4%	68.7%	–3.5%	0.3%
BOVESPA	1349.7	0.0033	3.5%	0.00011	38.0755	1.9%	4.8%	5.4%	1.09	3.2%	97.8%	7.4%	–1.3%
MEXICAN	383.9	0.0219	2.3%	0.00049	18.4617	3.4%	8.1%	11.3%	–2.31	4.6%	98.2%	2.5%	8.0%
SINAGPORE	726.1	0.0031	32.4%	0.00102	297.3048	20.6%	51.5%	41.3%	0.69	25.1%	68.1%	–7.0%	0.3%
HONG KONG	2999.2	0.0056	7.9%	0.00044	68.9491	2.3%	63.2%	23.7%	1.31	19.0%	95.8%	–8.0%	4.3%
COLOMBIA EXCHANGE	–	3.4140	0.0%	0.00045	–	0.02%	–	–	1.23	19.0%	100%	21.6%	–2.0%
CME	28403.9	–	49.4%	–	–	31.1%	5.3%	6.2%	1.08	27.7%	100%	6.5%	–
CBOE	406.0	–	31.6%	–	–	42.2%	50.6%	52.5%	0.00	25.1%	100%	6.5%	–
ICE	20325.9	–	41.8%	–	–	30.4%	15.0%	4.6%	0.90	54.4%	100%	–	–
BAKU	3.3	0.3137	38.9%	0.10395	2.3743	61.0%	29.8%	29.4%	0.00	0.4%	0.5%	13.7%	0%
DUBAI	2324.8	3.8255	72.9%	2.77017	0.0210	49.3%	4.5%	5.0%	1.01	4.2%	7.1%	–46.1%	3.5%
INDONESIA	349.9	0.5670	49.0%	0.27760	0.3955	55.0%	26.6%	10.8%	1.28	163.7%	28.8%	5.0%	3.5%
UGANDA	1.3	53.760	12.3%	8.67274	0.0160	87.7%	19.8%	19.8%	1.00	4.6%	25.9%	–11.8%	13.0%
KARACHI	93.0	0.4382	34.4%	0.13362	0.4147	70.1%	12.7%	5.7%	1.35	148.2%	100%	–44.3%	–0.7%
BAHRAIN	13.5	19.6788	23.5%	4.02335	0.0715	76.5%	19.6%	15.9%	1.02	23.7%	43.3%	–28.6%	–1.0%
DHAKA	132.0	0.7511	78.0%	0.57404	0.2808	22.0%	35.7%	14.2%	1.04	50.2%	2.5%	–63.4%	6.4%

Continued

Table 9.A Continued

	Tot_Ass	Rev_Tv	EBIT margin	Trad_ Prof	Trad_Int	Cost_In	ROE	ROCE	Op_Lev	Fin_Lev	Oth_Rev	Tr_Vol	List
ISTANBUL	383.2	0.3175	27.8%	0.09259	1.0662	86.8%	16.7%	8.4%	1.13	37.9%	18.5%	9.3%	4.9%
TUNIS	11.1	2.7333	22.6%	0.65022	0.2224	77.4%	14.3%	14.8%	0.00	21.3%	100%	13.7%	2.8%
MUSCAT	20.1	3.5075	37.5%	1.11715	0.2984	62.5%	47.3%	40.1%	1.15	64.8%	11.6%	−21.9%	0.6%
PALESTINE	12.5	6.1398	−5.4%	−0.35269	0.0349	126.5%	1.1%	−1.1%	0.00	8.1%	14.7%	−18.1%	7.1%
KAZHAKISTAN	13.8	3.3102	25.9%	0.80252	0.3242	75.4%	13.8%	16.1%	1.09	10.3%	12.0%	−41.3%	0%
MALAYSIA	503.1	1.0708	51.5%	0.54914	0.2413	48.4%	19.5%	13.0%	1.16	104.2%	45.0%	−5.4%	−1.2%
CASABLANCA	80.0	2.1588	70.7%	1.49065	0.1478	42.6%	15.7%	19.5%	1.10	18.9%	100%	−33.6%	1.0%
Mean	4996	3.6603	31.67%	0.7541	286.7403	45.4%	21.3%	14.69%	0.4517	37.62%	62%	−10.5%	0.76%
Median	454.58	0.3155	32.37%	0.0468	1.0662	48%	16.2%	11.27%	1.0245	25.12%	62.95%	−7.2%	0.29%
P 5%	3.31	0.0002	0.01%	0.00003	0.0210	0	4.13%	2.53%	−2.4884	3.21%	2.49%	−46.1%	−5.46%
P 95%	28403.8	19.678	72.89%	4.0233	1888.643	88%	51.5%	41.31%	1.3589	148%	100 %	13.7%	13.04%
St.Dev.	9132.8	10.548	0.233	1.8115	662.2815	0.3110	0.1585	0.1224	1.2964	0.3873	0.3956	0.2002	0.1031
Skewness	1.899	4.1478	0.2464	3.3759	2.4777	0.2963	1.0116	1.5475	−2.2112	1.9871	0.0424	−0.814	−1.8851
Kurtosis	5.227	19.758	2.178	14.5137	7.7772	2.7354	3.2821	5.0247	7.4914	6.6056	1.996	3.1824	12.304
CEs above median	13	1	9	1	12	5	7	6	7	10	13	10	5
IEs above median	2	13	8	13	2	12	8	9	9	6	3	5	9
CEs above P 95%	2	0	0	0	1	0	2	2	2	0	0	1	1
IEs above P 95%	0	2	2	2	0	1	0	0	0	2	0	0	1
CEs below P 5%	0	0	0	0	0	0	0	0	2	0	0	0	2
IEs below P 5%	1	0	1	1	1	0	1	1	0	1	1	0	0

Notes

1. We use the locution 'conventional exchanges' (CE) to refer to all those exchanges which do not fall within the Islamic world. We include: Western (American and European exchanges) and Asian-pacific exchanges as far as the developing South African markets.
2. From 2006 to 2011 total assets in Shariah-compliant financial institution have doubled to reach $900 billion (Financial Times, 2011), though Shariah-compliant financial assets represent only 1.5 per cent of total global banking assets.
3. The return on capital employed, in fact, could be expressed as:

$$ROCE = \frac{EBIT}{Tot\_Ass} = \frac{EBIT}{Trad\_Val} \cdot \frac{Trad\_Val}{Tot\_Ass}$$

References

Aggarwal, R. K. and T. Yousef (2000) 'Islamic banks and investment financing', *Journal of Money, Credit and Banking*, 32(1), 93–120

Aggarwal, R. and S. Dahiya (2006), 'Demutualization and public offerings of Financial Exchanges', *Journal of Applied Corporate Finance*, 18(3), 96–106.

Anand, B. N. and T. Khanna (2000) 'Do firms learn to create value? The case of alliances', *Strategic Management Journal*, 21(3), 295–315.

Azzam, I. 2010) 'Stock exchange demutualization and performance', *Global Finance Journal*, 21, 211–222.

Beck, T., A. Demirgüç-Kunt and O. Merrouche (2013) 'Islamic vs conventional banking: Business model, efficiency and stability', *Journal of Banking and Finance*, 37(2), 433–447.

Cihak, M. and H. Hesse (2010) 'Islamic banks and financial stability: An empirical analysis', *Journal of Financial Services Research*, 38(2), 95–113.

Claessens, S., S. Djankov and D. Klingebiel (2000) 'Stock Markets in transition economies', Financial Sector Discussion Paper, 5, The World Bank, September.

Claessens, S., D. Klingebiel and S. Schmuckler (2002) 'The future of stock exchanges in emerging economies: Evolution and prospects', The Wharton Financial Institutions Center, University of Pennsylvania, 4 February.

Dessein, W. (2005) 'Information and Control in Ventures and Alliances', *The Journal of Finance*, 65(5), 2513–2549.

Di Noia, C. (2001) 'Competition and integration among stock exchanges in Europe: Network effects, implicit mergers and remote access', *European Financial Management*, 7(1), 39–72.

Domowitz, I. and B. Steil (1999) 'Automation, trading costs and the structure of the securities trading industry', Brookings Wharton Papers on Financial Services, 33–92.

Financial Times (2011) 'Islamic Finance', Supplement, 12 May.

Fleckner, A. M. (2006) 'Stock exchanges at the crossroads', *Fordham Law Review*, 74(5), 2541–2620.

Floreani, J. and M. Polato (2013) *'The economics of the global stock exchange industry'*, Palgrave MacMillan: Houndsmills.

Gomes-Casseres, B., J. Hagedoorn and A. B. Jaffe (2006) 'Do alliances promote knowledge flows?' *Journal of Financial Economics*, 80, 5–33.
Hart, O. and J. Moore (1996) 'The governance of exchanges: members' cooperatives versus outside ownership', *Oxford Review of Economic Policy*, 12(4), 53–69.
Hasan, I. and M. Malkamäki (2001) 'Are expansions cost effective for stock exchanges? A global perspective', *Journal of Banking and Finance*, 25(12), 2339–2366.
Hasan, I., H. Schmiedel and L. Song (2010) 'Growth strategies and value creation: What works best for stock exchanges?' Working Paper Series, European Central Bank, 1201, 1–61.
Hayat, R. and R. Kraeussl (2011) 'Risk and return characteristics of Islamic equity funds', *Emerging Markets Review*, 12(2), 189–203.
Hoepner, A. G. F., H. G. Rammal and M. Rezec (2011) 'Islamic mutual funds' financial performance and international investment style: Evidence from 20 countries', *The European Journal of Finance*, 17(9–10), 829–850.
Iqbal, M. and A. Mirakhor (2007) *An Introduction to Islamic Finance: Theory and Practice*, John Wiley & Sons (Asia) Pte. Ltd.
Kabir Hassan, M. and J. Suk-Yu (2007) 'Stock exchange alliances in organization of Islamic conference countries', Networks Financial Institute Working Paper, 18, July.
Krishnamurti, C., J. M. Sequeira and F. Fangjian (2003) 'Stock exchange governance and market quality', *Journal of Banking and Finance*, 27(9), 1859–1878.
Macey, J.R. and M. O'Hara (1997)) 'The law and economics of best execution', *Journal of Financial Intermediation*, 6(3), 188–223.
Macey, J. and M. O'Hara (1999) 'Globalization, exchange governance and the future of exchanges', Brookings Wharton Papers on Financial Services, 1–32.
Meera, A. K. M., M. A. Omar and H. A. Aziz (2009) 'Dynamic linkages among ASEAN–5 emerging stock markets', *International Journal of Emerging Markets*, 4(2), 160–184.
Mendiola, A. and M. O'Hara (2003) 'Taking stock of stock markets: The changing governance of exchanges', SSRN Working Paper, Cornell University.
Oldford, E. and I. Otchere (2011) 'Can commercialization improve the performance of stock exchanges even without corporatization', *The Financial Review*, 46(1), 67–87.
Otchere, I. (2006) 'Stock exchange self-listing and value effects', *Journal of Corporate Finance*, 12(5), 926–953.
Paltrinieri A. (2012) 'Stock exchange merger in the emerging markets: A case study of the United Arab Emirates', SSRN Working Paper, 1–37.
Polato, M. and J. Floreani (2008) 'Business diversification in the securities industry: Implications for the exchanges', *Transition Studies Review*, 15(2), 281–288.
Serifsoy, B. and M. Tyrell (2006) 'Investment behavior of stock exchanges and the rationale for demutualization – Theory and empirical evidence', Financial Institutions Center, Working Paper, no. 1
Steil, B. (2002) 'Changes in the ownership and governance of securities exchanges: Causes and consequences', Brookings Wharton Papers on Financial Services, 61–91.
Worthington, A. and H. Higgs (2005) 'Market risk in demutualized self-listed stock exchanges: An international analysis of selected time-varying betas', Working Paper, 1–2.

Index

ABS market, recovery of, 98, 102
'access to finance' as principal concern, 91–4
agency costs of equity and debt, 61, 65, 69
agency problems, 64, 65, 75
algorithm-driven traders, *see* high frequency traders
algorithmic trading, 152, *see also* high-frequency trading (HFT)
  definition of, 170
  impact on investors' confidence, 162
  MiFID II for managing risk of, 170–1
  regulation of, *see* high-frequency trading (HFT) regulation
  volatility with, 155
algorithms, mandatory notification of, 164
alternatives, 136, 148
  KIC geographical asset allocation in, 146
  KIC strategic asset allocation in, 143–5
Anglo-Saxon model, 81
anti-cyclical fiscal policy, 24, 30, 39
aseptic international organization, problems in creating, 54
Asian financial crisis of 1997–1998, *see* East Asian crisis of 1997–1998
Asia–Pacific region, KIC asset allocation in, 145–6, 148
asset allocation, 113
  geographical, 142, 145–6
  strategic, 141, 143–5
asset-backed securities (ABS), 43, 44, 98, 102, 103
asset management companies (AMCs), 6
  financial intermediaries, 111
  fund managers, *see* fund managers
  gains of, 110–11
  intermediation margin, 115
  portfolio companies and investors, relationship between, 111
  remuneration of, 112
assets and liabilities, 114
  changes in, 82
  maturity mismatching between, 44–5, 56
assets under management (AUM), 111
  of AMCs, 123, 127
  of KIC, 133, 134, 139, 144, 145, 147, 148
  of sovereign wealth funds (SWFs), 133–4
asymmetries of information problems, 64, 66, 75
austerity measures, 11
  and economic growth, controversy between, 38
  and hardship, 17
  recessionary impact of, 24, 27, 36
Australian equity markets, HFT market share in, 166, 167, 183
Australian government, proposals for curbing automated trading, 173–4
Australian Securities and Investments Commission (ASIC)
  new market integrity rules, 173, 181–2
  partnered with First Derivatives, 182
  report on dark liquidity, 174
Australian stock exchange (ASX)
  decline in average trade size of, 159
  FFI of Australian S&P ASX 200, 156
  self-listed structure of, 191
Austrian banking systems, liquidity crisis of, 47

BACH (Bank for the Accounts of Companies Harmonized) harmonized database, 85, 108n1
'bail-in' measures, bank recovery via, 11, 32, 34, 39
balance sheet
  analysis of AMCs and portfolio companies, 119, 121
  of EMU banks, 31
  of Italian AMC, 113–14
  of non-financial corporations, 82, 90, 95
bank-based financial systems, corporate governance of, 66
bank borrowing maturity, 5
  determinants of, *see* bank borrowing maturity, determinants of
  of firms with growth opportunities, 64
  and moral hazard problems, 73
bank borrowing maturity, determinants of, 63–6
  agency problems, 64
  choice of lender, 63
  civil-law/common-law origin, 63–4
  concentrated ownership, 65
bank CDS prices
  and sovereign CDS, spread between, 51–2
  and swap operations, 48, 50–1, 56
bank–company–market circuit, 101
bank debt maturity, *see* bank borrowing maturity
bank debt maturity choice, 75
  civil-law regime firms, 63
  common-law regime firms, 64
  external funds and ownership structure, 62
bank debt maturity choice, corporate governance regulations effect on
  in civil-law regime firms, 66, 72, 73
  in common-law regime firms, 72, 73
  empirical analysis of, 69–71
  short-term bank debt, 64–6
  substitution effect, 62
bank–firm relationship, 85, 86, 99, 101
bank indebtedness, 85, 105
banking crises, 37
banking-oriented financial system, 64
banking union, 24, 39
bank lending flows
  euro area, 86
  France, 86, 87, 89–90
  Germany, 86, 87, 89–90
  Italy, 83, 86, 87, 88–90, 89–90
  non-financial corporations and households, 86–7
  Portugal, 86, 87
  Spain, 86, 87, 89–90
  United Kingdom, 89–90
bank loans, 83, 85
  availability for euro area SMEs, 91, 93
  French SMEs need for, 91, 93
  German SMEs need for, 91, 93
  interest rates in euro area, 87–8, 95
  Italian SMEs need for, 91, 93
  need for Italian SMEs, 91, 93
  non-financial corporations preference for, 83
  preference of Italian firms, 83
  Spanish SMEs need for, 91, 93
Bank of England, 45, 48
Bank of Italy (Banca d'Italia)
  in-depth checks of banks, 89
  regulation of AMCs, 113
Bank of Japan, 45, 48
Bank of Korea, 137–8
  double-fee payment made by, 147
  withdrawal of financial resources from KIC, 138
Banque publique d'investissement, 103
BATS trading, 158, 179
behavioural distortions, costs of, 2
behavioural theories, 2, 3
Belgian banking systems, liquidity crisis of, 47
best execution regime, principles-based, 181–2

bonds, *see also* corporate bonds; mini bonds
KIC geographical asset allocation in, 146
KIC strategic asset allocation in, 141, 143
Brazil, foreign exchange reserves and swap of, 54
budget deficits, SGP rules for
3/60 criteria, 11, 14, 16
violations of, 17, 37–8

capital inflows, 10
to PIIGS countries, 10
to United States, 44
CDP ('Bank for Savings and Loans'), 97–8, 101, 103
central banks, 4, 132, 138, *see also* Bank of Korea; European Central Bank (ECB); Federal Reserve as ILOLR
financial statement indicators of SMEs, 85
central counterparty (CCP) operations, 163
China Investment Corporation, Linaburg–Maduell Index of, 141
Chi-X Australia, 181
circuit breakers, 164–5
civil-law countries, 62, 63, 69
civil-law regime firms
bankruptcy risk, 74
dependence on banks, 72
empirical analysis of, 69–71
growth opportunities, 72
growth rate of annual sales of, 74
non-debt tax shields, 74
ownership structure, 73
short-term bank debt, 62, 65, 72, 73
civil-law regime firms, corporate governance regulation of, 64
debt maturity structure, 65–6, 73
impact on bank debt maturity, 66, 72–3
institutional investors, 65
ownership concentration, 65, 73–4
and profitability, 74
supervision by banks, 70
transparency, 74
commodity funds and non-commodity funds, difference between, 133
Commodity Futures Trading Commission (CFTC), 173
report on March 2010 flash crash, 155
common-law countries, 62, 64, 69
common-law regime firms
bankruptcy risk, 74
corporate governance regulation of, 72, 74
empirical analysis of, 69–71
growth opportunities, 72
growth rate of annual sales of, 74
need for external funds (NEF), 73
profitability, 74
short-term bank debt, 62
competition, 8, 152
conventional exchanges, 209
ECNs and US stock exchanges, 156
and external imbalances, divergence of, 20, 21
Islamic and non-Islamic exchanges, 204, 206
price and wage flexibility, 25–6
and technological transformations, 190
and wage demands, 24–5
consolidated tape, 183
constructive ambiguity, policies of, 54, 56
contingency fund, *see* European Stability Mechanism (ESM)
contrarian strategy, 145
conventional exchanges (CEs), 8, 188, 215n1
and business models, 192
circuit breakers, 164–5
competitive threats to, 156, 209
consolidation trend on, 192–3, 208, 209
convergence with IEs, 193, 209–10, 212
cost and revenues of, 192
customer-owned, 191
decline in average trade size of, 159
demutualization of, 188, 190–1
external growth strategy, 191

conventional exchanges (CEs) – *Continued*
fixed cost structure of, 192
governance and efficiency, link between, 191
HFT flows, 158
internal growth strategies, 193
and Islamic exchanges, performance comparison of, *see* Islamic and non-Islamic exchanges, performance comparison of
jostle with ECNs, 209
kill switches, 165
liquidity of, 192, 211
listed exchanges, 191
operational performances of, 189
outside ownership model of, 190–1
publicly traded, 191
self-listing of, 188, 190–1
Convergence and Competitiveness Instrument (CCI), 29
core EMU members
capital transfer from peripheral to, 17
push for austerity measures, 16
corporate bonds, 97, 100, 106
corporate governance legislations
across countries, 66–8
Sarbanes-Oxley Act, 66
corporate governance mechanism, 64
bank-based financial systems, 66
common-law regime firms, 72, 74
short-term bank debt, 64–5
corporate governance regulation (CGR), 5, 69
bank debt maturity choice, *see* bank debt maturity choice, corporate governance regulations effect on
civil-law regime firms, *see* civil-law regime firms, corporate governance regulation of
goals of, 66
corporate investment trends in Europe, 90
corporate management division, KIC, 140
costs of production, 38
counterparty risk of HFT, 163
credit crisis, 2
causes of, 2, 55
and gross capital flows, 43
impact on European money markets, 10, 23
credit crunch, 16, 93, 95
and bank–firm relationship, 5, 80
strategies for eliminating, 5
credit crunch in Italy, 5, 80, 102
among all sizes of firm, 93–4
interest rates on loans, 95
linked to demand factors, 89–90
for smaller businesses, 93
credit crunch in Italy, exit strategies for eliminating, 96
CDP ('Bank for Savings and Loans'), 97–8, 106
corporate bonds, 97, 106
credit funds, 98–9, 107
crowdfunding, 99–100, 107
EIB and EIF, 98, 107
institutional investors, 99, 107
repayment of public sector's debt, 96
securitization and covered bonds, 98, 107
SME guarantee facility, 97, 106
venture capital and private equity, 99, 107
credit flows, negative trend in, 89–90
credit funds, 98–9, 103, 107
credit-rationed firms, 94
crowdfunding, 99–100, 107
currency reserves, *see* foreign exchange reserves
current account balance
of Germany and PIIGS countries, 28, 29
of United States, 44
Cypriot banks, 'bail-in' measures of, 34

dark trading venues, decline in average trade size of, 160
debt securities, 44, 83, 84
Decree for Growth, 100
demutualization, 188, 190–1

Deutsche Börse equities
automated trades *vs.* other trades on, 154
decline in average trade size, 159
direct market access (DMA), 169, 170
Dodd–Frank Act, 173
dollar shortage, 4, 43, 48, 53, 56
domestic demand bubbles, 26
Dow Jones Industrial Average
FFI of, 156, 157
May 2010 flash crash of, 153, 155
Draghi, Mario, 38
Dubai Financial Market
Nasdaq-Dubai and Abu Dhabi Securities Exchange, merger between, 193
Shariah-compliant investments, 202

East-Asian crisis of 1997–1998, 137
Economic and Financial Affairs Council of the European Union (Ecofin), 169
economic convergence, 25
economic divergence, 25
economic growth, 38
and institutional setting, link between, 72
model of South Korea, 7
electronic communications networks (ECNs), 8
competition with US stock exchanges, 156, 158, 179, 190, 209
emerging markets, 7
exchanges of, 193
KIC asset allocation in, 145–6
EMU, 39
adjustment problems, 13
competitiveness problem, 10, 20
'3/60' convergence criteria, 11, 23, 38
destabilizing factor for, 31
economic convergence policy measures, 25
external imbalances, 10, 20
fiscal transfers, 39
monetary transmission channels within, 35
national disaffection with, 13
as optimal currency union, 3, 9, 38–9
regional imbalances, 1
sources of stress within, 3
1999-2012 wage and productivity developments in, 20, 21
EMU banks
appetite for holding money at ECB, 36
difficulties in rolling over short-term liabilities, 43
failure of, 32
restructuring process, 34
EMU design flaws, 10–11, 38
euro crisis, 23–4
high inflation, 25
interest rates, 24
lack of policy coordination, 24–5
wage and price increases, 24–5
EMU, europhiles views on
monetory union benefits, 12–13
tackling high inflation, 13
EMU, eurosceptics views on
competitiveness problem, 13
external imbalances, 14
'one size fits all' problem, 13
zero budget deficit target, 16
EMU members, 4, *see also* core EMU members; peripheral EMU countries/PIIGS countries
asymmetric shocks to, 14
financial assistance to, 31–2
government deficits and government debt of, 14–15
structural reforms of, *see* Structural reforms, EMU members
equity
and bond markets for SMEs, development of, 100–1
KIC geographical asset allocation in, 146
KIC strategic asset allocation in, 141, 143–5
equity trading, *see also* financial markets
and conventional exchanges, *see* conventional exchanges (CEs)
factors influencing changes in, 152

euro adoption, consequences of, 3, *see also* EMU; EMU design flaws
euro area, *see also* EMU
  bank lending flows in, 86
  interest rates on loans in, 86–8
euro area SMEs, financial constraints for
  'access to finance' as principal concern, 91, 92
  availability of bank loans, 93
  need for bank loans, 91, 93
euro crisis, *see* euro sovereign debt crisis
Europe
  corporate investment trends in, 90
  HFT market share in, 166, 167, 183
  KIC asset allocation in, 145–6
  new liquidity landscape in, 178–9
European and US financial systems, interdependence between, 55–6
European Banking Authority (EBA), 32–3
European banking systems
  maturity mismatching, 44–5
  operations of, 57n2
  rollover problems, 44, 56
European banking union, 26, 35, 39
  moral hazard issues, 40
  reasons of creating, 30, 32
  smaller banks, 33–4
European banking union, stages of
  ESM, 33
  European Banking Authority, 32–3
  joint deposit guarantee fund, 33–4
  SSM and SRM, 33
European Central Bank (ECB), 17, 31
  efforts to restore monetary policy transmission, 88
  foreign exchange reserves and swap of, 54
  interest rate policy, 13
  as lender of last resort, 35–6, 40
  monetary policy stance, 24
  OMT program, 16–17, 18, 35–6
  provision of liquidity in dollars, 52
  as single supervisor of EMU banks, 33–5, 39
  survey on constraints for Italian firms, 91
  withdrawals on reciprocal currency arrangements, 45
European Commission (EC), 27, 172
  economic policy reforms, 29
  and EIB, 98
  FTT proposal, 169, 175, 177
  proposals for MAD II, 171–2
European countries and corporate debt securities, 44
European directives for HFT regulation
  MAD II and MAR, 171–2
  MiFID II and MiFIR, 170
European financial system
  as bank-based intermediation model, 81
  development trends of, 81–2
European firms
  financial structure indicators for, 85–6
  financing by size categories, 85
  liabilities of, 104–5
  performance comparison, 85
European integration
  functional, 9, 12, 35
  political, 9, 12
European Investment Bank (EIB), 98, 107
European Investment Fund (EIF), 98, 107
European money markets, 10, 35
European Parliament's Economic and Monetary Affairs Committee (ECON Committee), 171, 185n4
European Securities and Market Authority (ESMA)
  guidelines for HFT regulation, 168–9, 185n1
European Stability Mechanism (ESM), 11, 18, 22, 30, 33
  applying for support of, 31
  bank recapitalization, 31–2
  government-issued bond buying, 36
  mission of, 31
European Union (EU), 9, 11, 19–20, 32, 35, 39, 102
  fragmentation in, 156
  HFT in, 166–7
  legislation for HFT regulation, 170–2
  programmes to aid SMEs, 98, 107
  regulatory regimes for trading space, 181

euro sovereign debt crisis, 9, 23–4, 40
asymmetric shocks, 37
credit crunch, 10, 89
cut in credit ratings, 11
financial fragmentation, 86–8
from French perspective, 17
lending growth, 86, 87
policy response to, 18
rise in lending rates, 86
rise in NPLs, 89
eurozone, 40
economic recovery of, 26–7
spread between bank CDS and sovereign CDS for, 51–2
and US dollar swap lines, *see* US dollar swap lines
exchange industry
conflicting interests in, 210
governance paradigm in, 210
structure of, 191
theoretical framework driving changes in, 190
transformation of, 188
expansionary fiscal policy, 27
external financing, 65, 91
external funds, ownership structure, and bank debt maturity, relationship between, 62
external managers and KIC investment, 147

Federal Reserve as ILOLR, 43
drawbacks of, 43, 53
handling of dollar shortage, 4
moral hazard problems, 54, 56
net imbalances, 54–5
US dollar swap lines, *see* US dollar swap lines
Fidessa Fragmentation Index (FFI), 156–7
financial crisis of 2007–2008, *see* credit crisis
'financial innovation spiral,' 7
financial instruments, factors influencing choice between, 61–2
financial integration, 39
financial intensity ratio, 82
financial intermediaries, 64, 81, 111, *see also* asset management companies (AMCs)
financial liabilities, 61, 82–3, 85
financial markets, 24, 86, 102
consequences of deregulation of, 2
and high-frequency trading, *see* high-frequency trading (HFT)
integrity of, 157
internationalization of, 184
segmentation of, 11
SWFs in, 136
transaction costs, 178
volatility in, 144
Financial Services Modernization Act, 2
Financial Stability Oversight Council (FSOC), 173
financial surplus/deficit trend, 82–3
financial system design and institutional settings, 8
financial transaction tax (FTT), 169, 175, 185
fiscal backstop
ESM as, 40
permanent rescue fund as, 31–2
fiscal compact, *see* Treaty on Stability, Coordination and Governance
fiscal discipline, 26, 30, 37
fiscal fragmentation, 25
fiscal policy, 17
anti-cyclical, 24, 30, 39
counter-cyclical, 30
expansionary, 27
fiscal sustainability, 23
fiscal tightening, 16
fiscal transfer
countries, 22
homogeneity of, 22
fiscal union, 29
Maastricht Treaty, *see* Maastricht Treaty
scope and shape of, 30
SGP, *see* Stability and Growth Pact (SGP)
fixed income, KIC asset allocation in, 143, 144
flash crash of DJ index, 153
SEC and CFTC report on, 155
floor-based exchanges, 190

Fondo di Centrale di Garanzia (FCG), 97, 106
foreign exchange reserves, 4, 53, 138
  funding of non-commodity funds, 133
  and swap operations, link between, 45–7, 54
Foreign Exchange Stabilization Fund, 138
France
  approach to solving euro crisis, 17
  bank lending flows in, 89–90
  Banque publique d'investissement, 103
  corporate investment trends in, 90
  domestic FTT, 175
  flouting SGP rules, 16
  lending growth in, 86, 87
French SMEs, financial constraints for, 91, 93
FTSE 100, FFI of, 156, 157
'functional and structural finance' (FSF) paradigm, 5, 6
  and institutions, 1–2
  LLSV approach, 4–5
  neo-classical perspective of, 2–3, 7
fund managers
  exempted from regulatory obligations, 116
  fee waivers, 115
  manipulation of variable fees, 115
  performance of, 115–16
  private equity market, 112–13
  profitability of, 115, 116
fund managers and investments, performance comparison of
  hypotheses for, 117
  number of portfolio companies, 127
  OLS regression model, 120, 122–6
  specialization of investments, 127–8
FX swaps lines, *see* US dollar swap lines

geographical asset allocation strategies, KIC, 142
  in equities, bonds and alternatives, 146
  geographical areas, 146
  for period 2010–2011, 145–6
German corporations
  bank loan needs of SMEs, 91, 93
  lending rates for, 87
German government bond yields, 16
German reunification and labour mobility, 19–20
Germany, 10
  approach to solving euro crisis, 17
  bank lending flows in, 89–90
  corporate investment trends in, 90
  current account balance, 2000-2014, 28
  flouting SGP rules, 16, 17
  lending growth in, 86, 87
  regulation concerning HFT, 175, 177
  on smaller banks, 34
  unit labour costs of, 28
ghost liquidity, 165
global financial crisis of 2007, *see* credit crisis
governance structure of KIC, 139–40
government bonds
  investments in, 89
  rise in yield of, 16, 38
  sell-off, 38
  support-buying by ECB, 17
government debt
  EMU members in 2012, 14–15
  of short-term maturity, 36
government debts, 23
government deficits
  of EMU members in 2009, 18
  of EMU members in 2012, 14–15, 18
Government of Singapore Investment Corporation, Linaburg–Maduell Index of, 141
Gramm–Leach–Bliley Act, 2
Greece
  bailout of, 11
  current account balance, 2000-2014, 28, 29
  decline in unit labour costs in, 28, 29
  lending growth in, 86, 87

HFT firms
infrastructure of, 161
market maker obligations on, 164, 171
higher risk/return relationship, 144–5
high-frequency traders, *see also* high-frequency trading (HFT)
information disclosure requirements for, 172–3
market making *vs.* opportunistic, 155
reactions to changing market conditions, 158
as subset of large traders, 172–3
trading strategies used by, 153, 157–8
high-frequency trading (HFT), 1, 7, 183
challenges to regulator of securities markets, 153
commission schemes, 166
definition of, 152
factors contributed to birth of, 152, 183
impact on market integrity, 7–8, 157, 183
impact on market quality metrics, 154–5, 183
infrastructure, 161
low latency for, 161
market share in Australia, 166, 167, 183
market share in US and Europe, 166, 167, 183
minimum resting time, 165–6
policy measures to mitigate risks of, 163–6
regulatory challenges related, 168
revenues generated by, 158
technical glitches, 153
UK Foresight Committee report on, 155
high-frequency trading (HFT), market factors contributing to rise of
electronic communications networks (ECNs), 158
fragmentation of order flows, 156–7
maker-taker pricing model, 158
MTFs, 156, 158
regulatory changes, 156
slicing of orders, 159
high-frequency trading (HFT) regulation, 176, 184–5
Australian government, 173–4
ESMA guidelines, 168–9
European directives, 170–2
financial transaction tax, 169, 175, 185
German HFT Act, 175, 177
IOSCO recommendations, 167–8
levels of disclosure, 172–3
MAD II, 171–2
and market structure, *see* market structure and HFT regulation, relation between
MiFID II, 170–1, 174, 184
MiFIR, 170
SEC approach, 172–3, 184
at supranational level, 167–70
high-frequency trading (HFT), risks associated with, 161
counterparty risk, 163
low investors' confidence, 162
market risk, 163
operational risk, 163
permanent instability, 162
systemic risk, 162–3

illiquid assets, KIC asset allocation in, 141, 145
IMF, 11, 17, 96
'impossible trinity principle' theory, 10
indebtedness
bank, 85, 105
of non-financial corporations, 82
institutional investors, 65
corporate equity acquisition role of, 99
sovereign wealth funds as, 132
institutional isomorphism, 2
institutional rigidity, 7
institutional settings and financial system design, 8
interest rates, 24
differentials between peripheral and core countries, 88
on loans in euro area, 87–8, 95

interest rates, – *Continued*
'one size fits all' problem, 13–14, 22, 24
rise in, 38
intermediation margin, 115
internal political bias analysis, 142, 146
external managers, 147
rise in-house investments, 147–8
international lender of last resort (ILOLR), 1, 4, *see also* Federal Reserve as ILOLR
invested companies, return on, 119–20
investment firms, 169
controls relating to, 170
obligation to implement best execution regime, 181
total exposure limit for, 165
investment management division, KIC, 140
investment process and 'internal political bias,' 6
investors
AMCs and portfolio companies, relationship between, 111
demand for funds, 115–16
rights protection, 73
IOSCO report
on HFT regulation, 168
on market fragmentation, 157
Ireland
bailout of, 11
current account balance between 2000–2014, 28, 29
decline in unit labour costs in, 28, 29
lending growth in, 86, 87
Islamic and non-Islamic exchanges, performance comparison of, 8, 189, 205, 211–12, 213–15
business and financial structure, 198–9, 201
competitive strategies, 204, 206
consolidation, 201–2, 208–9
EBIT margin, 202, 203, 204, 206–8
efficiency measures, 199–201, 203–4, 206, 209
financial and market data, 197
financial performances, 200
industry-specific variables, 197–8, 201, 204
institutional and religion-related factors, 202
liquidity measures, 200
market activity, 200–1
operational leverage, 202, 204
operational performances, 199–201, 204, 206
revenues, 201–3, 207
ROE and ROCE, 203, 204
sample characteristics, 193–7
Student's t-test and the p-value, 204–6
trading intensity and trading profitability, 203, 208
t-statistic test, 206
Islamic banks, 1, 193
Islamic exchanges (IEs), 8, 188
consolidation process in, 188, 210
convergence with CEs, 193, 209–10, 212
liquidity levels, 189, 209
Italian AMCs and portfolio companies, performance comparison of
balance sheet analysis, 121
descriptive statistics, 2008–2011, 118–19
hypotheses for, 116–17
number of funds managed, 127
number of portfolio companies, 127
OLS regression model, 120, 122–3
OLS regressions dependent variables, 124–6
PE fund size and economic performance, link between, 127
performance indicators, 122–4
private equity-backed companies, 118, 121
private equity funds, 117, 121–2
probit model, 122
profitability of fund managers, 119–20
profit, total assets, ROA and equity, 126
research limitations, 128
return on invested companies, 119–20
revenues, 118
specialization of investments, 121, 122, 127–8

Italian AMCs, balance sheet of
income statement, 114
structure of, 113
Italian asset management companies (AMCs), 110
earnings analysis, 6
gains of, 113
income statement for, 114
investment portfolios of, 113
portfolio management services, 113
Italian banking system, 96
credit crunch, *see* credit crunch in Italy
restructuring of, 102
Italian banks, 80
establishing bank–company–market linkage, 101
lending volumes and interest rates, 88–9
provisions for default, 89
rise in NPLs of, 89
Italian companies
credit-rationed, 94
firm size and access to credit, 94
interest rates on loans to, 87–8
preference for bank loans, 83
reluctance towards outside investors, 99
Italian financial system, 100
financial surplus/deficit trend, 82
indebtedness of non-financial corporations, 82
Italian firms, financial constraints for
access to finance, 91, 92
cost of funding and firm size, 95
credit crunch, 93, 95
ECB survey on, 91
lending and creditworthiness, link between, 95–6
Italian government
'Decree for Growth,' 97
reluctance towards OMT program, 36
Italian private equity industry, 6
Italian SMEs
mini bonds, *see* mini bonds
need for bank loans, 91, 93
Italy
bank lending in, 83, 89–90
corporate investment trends in, 90
domestic FTT, 175
lending growth in, 86, 87

joint deposit guarantee fund, 33–4

Kenen, Peter, 20
kill switches, 165
Knight Capital, 165
Korea Investment Corporation (KIC)
acting as asset management company, 138
aims of, 137–8, 141
AUM of, 133, 134, 139, 144, 145, 147, 148
financial resources for, 138
governance structure, 139–40
legal personality, 138
Linaburg–Maduell Index, 133, 141
performance, 147–8
problems with, 135
statutory auditor, 140
Truman scoreboard, 133, 141
withdrawals from, 138
Korea Investment Corporation Act, 137, 140
Korea Investment Corporation (KIC) investment strategies, 6–7, 135, 148–9
benchmark analysis, 141, 142–3
geographical asset allocation, *see* geographical asset allocation strategies, KIC
home bias analysis, 142, 145–6
internal political bias analysis, *see* internal political bias analysis
strategic asset allocation, *see* strategic asset allocation strategies, KIC
Korean Won depreciation, 137

labour markets and wage increases, 24–5
labour mobility criterion, 19–20, 38
lending and creditworthiness, link between, 95–6
lending volumes and interest rates, 88–9
life insurance market, 3

limited partnerships, 111–12
Linaburg–Maduell Index, 133, 141
liquidity
of exchanges, 192, 200, 211
and high-frequency trading, 154
and market making obligations, 170–1
market structure and HFT regulation, relation between, 178–9
provisionig in dollars, *see* US dollar swap lines
and US equities with HFT, 154
LLSV approach, 4–5
London Stock Exchange, decline in average trade size of, 159
long-term refinancing operations (LTROs), 88

Maastricht Treaty, 37
'3/60' convergence criteria, 11, 14
maker-taker pricing model, 158, 159
Market Abuse Directive (MAD), 168
MAD II, 171–2
market fragmentation
concerns raised by, 157, 168
consolidation of exchanges and, 193
levels of development of, 156–7
negative effects of, 88
of order flow, 156
of trading, 156, 178
Market Integrity Rules, 156
market making obligations, 113, 164, 170–1
market-oriented financial systems, corporate control in, 64
market risk of HFT, 163
Markets in Financial Instruments Directive (MiFID), 156, 168
MiFID II, 170–1, 183
principles-based best execution regime, 181
revision of, 170
market structure
characteristics of, 182
definition of, 178
fragility of, 184
market structure and HFT regulation, relation between, 178–83
Australian market surveillance system, 181–2
complex systems, 179–80, 184
consolidated audit trail, 179–80
liquidity flows, 178–9
NBBO calculation, 180
principles-based best execution regime, 181
trading venues, 179
market timing, 113
market volatility, 51
CD prices impact on, 52
financial markets, 144
and high-frequency trading, 154–5, 157, 173, 174, 183
of stock exchanges, 194
maturity mismatching between assets and liabilities, 44–5
maturity transformation, 44
MiFIR, 170
mini bonds, 97, 103, 106
development of, 100–1
obstacles to, 101
prerequisites for issue of, 100, 103
minimum resting time, 165–6, 171
monetary policy, common
conflict of national interests with, 10, 22
and solidarity criterion, 22
monetary transmission channels and OMT program, 35–6
monetary union, *see also* European banking union
building blocks for, 4
pillars for viable, 25–6
preconditions for fulfilling role of, 14–18
moral hazard problems, 36, 40, 54–7, 64–5, 72–4
mortgage markets, 2

national best bid best offer (NBBO), 180
neo-classical theory, 2–3
neo-institutional theory, 2
Netherlands, lending growth in, 86, 87
net imbalances between countries, 55–6

network economies, 190–2
non-commodity funds and commodity funds, difference between, 133
non-debt tax shields (NDTS), 74
non-financial corporations, Italian
  breakdown of liabilities, 83, 84
  financial liabilities/GDP (amount outstanding), 82
  financial surplus/deficit of, 82, 83
  and households, growth in lending for, 86–7
  lending rates for, 86
  preference for bank loans, 83
non-Islamic exchanges, *see* conventional exchanges (CEs)
non-performing loans (NPLs), 89
NYSE equities, automated quoting facility for, 154–5
NYSE Euronext and NYSE Euronext US, decline in average trade size in, 159

OECD economies, 62
  US banks short-term claims on, 47
OLS regression model, 120, 122–3
OLS regressions dependent variables, 124–6
'one size fits all' problem, 3, 13–14, 22, 24
openness criterion for OCA, 20
operational risk of HFT, 163
optimal currency area (OCA), 3, 4, 9, 39
  adjustment known in, 38–9
  criteria for, 10, 38
  preconditions for becoming
    fiscal transfer homogeneity, 22, 39
    labour mobility criterion, 19–20, 38
    openness criterion, 20, 38
    policy preference homogeneity, 22
    production diversification criterion, 20
    solidarity criterion homogeneity, 22
  socio-political criteria for fulfilling role of, 22
optimal currency unions, 3
order-to-trade ratios (OTR), 166
Organization of Islamic Cooperation (OIC), 193
outright monetary transactions (OMT) programme, 16–17, 18, 35–6, 88
ownership structure (OWN)
  external funds and bank debt maturity, relationship between, 62
  and short-term bank debt, substitution effect between, 73–4
ownership structure, concentrated, 76n3
  common-law regime firms, 73, 75
  as mechanism of corporate governance, 62, 65, 73

PE fund size and economic performance, link between, 127
performance indicators, 122–4
peripheral EMU countries/PIIGS countries, 41n1
  credibility gap, 16
  current account balance of, 28
  default consequences, 17
  economic boom and burst in, 10, 23, 25
  net imbalances, 55
  unit labour costs of, 28
  wage rates in, 20
permanent rescue fund, *see* European Stability Mechanism (ESM)
policy preferences, homogeneity of, 22
political bias and investment process, 6, *see also* Korea Investment Corporation (KIC)
portfolio companies, 127
  AMCs and investors, relationship between, 111
  and Italian AMCs, performance comparison of, *see* Italian AMCs and portfolio companies, performance comparison of

Portugal
bailout of, 11
current account balance, 2000–2014, 28, 29
decline in unit labour costs in, 28, 29
flouting SGP rules, 16
lending growth in, 86, 87
price discovery, 154–5
private debt, 23, 24
private equity-backed companies, 118, 121
private equity funds, 117, 121–2
private equity investments, 6, 111, 115, 118–19, 121
probit model, 122
production diversification criterion, 20
productivity development in EMU,1999–2012, 20, 21
profitability, 74
profit, total assets, ROA and equity, 126
public debt, 63

real wage costs, 20
Regulation National Market System (Reg. NMS), 156
codified NBBO, 180
trade-through rule, 180
Regulation SCI (systems, compliance and integrity), 173
reserve investment corporations, 132
retirement system, 6
revenue, 118
of conventional exchanges (CEs), 192
of Islamic and non-Islamic exchanges, 201–3, 207
of Italian AMCs and portfolio companies, 118
risk management division, KIC, 140

Sarbanes–Oxley Act, 66
savings funds, 132
Securities and Exchange Commission (SEC), 165
approach concerning HFT, 172–3, 185n1
and CFTC report on flash crash, 155
Regulation SCI, 173
reliance on 'consolidated tape,' 183
securities information processor (SIP), 180
securities market programme (SMP), 88
securitization of firms' loans, private and public guarantees for, 98
self-listing of CEs, 188, 190–1
settlement failure risk, 163
Shariah-compliant investments, 8, 201–2, 211, 215n2
short-term bank debt
civil-law regime firms, 62, 65, 72, 73
common-law regime firms, 62
maturity choice and corporate governance, 64–5
and ownership structure, substitution effect between, 73–4
short-term bank debt to total bank debt (SBDBD), 69
short-term US dollar refinancing, 43
Singaporean SWF, 133
Singapore, foreign exchange reserves and swap of, 54
single currency adoption, 25
benefits of, 10
consequences of, 37–8, *see also* credit crisis
single resolution mechanism (SRM), 33
single supervisory mechanism (SSM), 33
small open economy, domestic prices for goods in, 20
SME guarantee facility, 97, 106
SME operations, financial variables affecting, 82–3
social security reserve funds (SSRFs) *vs.* sovereign wealth funds (SWFs), 149n2
solidarity criterion, homogeneity of, 22
South Korea
economic growth model, 7
foreign exchange reserves and swap, 54
foreign reserves of, 137

sovereign-bank nexus, 33, 39
Sovereign CDS
  and bank CDS, spread between, 51–2
  and swap operations, 50–1
sovereign debt purchase scheme, *see* outright monetary transactions (OMT) programme
sovereign pension reserve funds (SPRFs), 132
sovereign wealth funds (SWFs), 7
  asset allocation by, 136
  case studies on, 133, 135
  classification of, 132
  definitions of, 132
  impact on target firm's performance, 136
  as institutional investors, 132
  investment strategies, political motivations in, 136, 137
  Korea Investment Corporation, *see* Korea Investment Corporation (KIC)
  objectives of, 135
  portfolios of, 135, 136
  regulatory framework for supervising, 135
  vs. social security reserve funds (SSRFs), 149n2
  top twenty, 134
  total assets under management of, 133
Spain
  bank lending flows in, 89–90
  corporate investment trends in, 90
  current account balance between 2000-2014, 28, 29
  decline in unit labour costs in, 28, 29
  lending growth in, 86, 87
  reluctance towards OMT program, 36
Spanish SMEs, bank loan needs of, 91, 93
special investments, KIC asset allocation in, 144
specialization of investments, 121, 122, 127–8
Stability and Growth Pact (SGP), 13, 29, 30
  EMU's inability to enforce, 25
  fiscal 3/60 criteria, 16
  penalties for excessive deficits, 16
stabilization funds, 132
statutory auditor, 140
stock exchanges, *see* conventional exchanges (CEs)
stock pricing, 113
strategic asset allocation strategies, KIC, 141, 143–5
  in alternatives, 143–4
  in bonds, 141, 143
  contrarian strategy, 145
  in equity, 141, 143–5
  in fixed income, 143, 144
  higher risk/return relationship, 144–5
  illiquid assets, 141, 145
  shift in, 143, 145
  in special investments, 144
  time horizon and, 141
structural reforms, EMU members, 26, 40
  and austerity, 27
  cross-border labour mobility, 19
  ECB as lender of last resort, 35–6, 40
  European banking union, 32–5
  financial assistance for, 29
  fiscal discipline and coordination, 29–31
  institutional change, 27
  permanent rescue fund, 31–2
  prices and wages, 27
  real wages costs, 20
  to restore confidence, 38
surveillance databases, 168
systemic risk of HFT, 162–3

technological transformations
  and competition, 190, *see also* competition
  impact on market structures, 152, 168
tick size, limitations on, 165
tight fiscal policy measures, 27
time horizon and strategic asset allocation, 141

too-big-to-fail banks (TBFBs), 2
Treaty of Maastricht of 1992, 9
Treaty of Rome of 1957, 9
Treaty on Stability, Coordination and Governance, 29
troika rescue programs, 11, 18
Truman scoreboard, 133, 141

Underinvestment and asset substitution problems, 63
United Arab Emirates, consolidation of stock exchanges in, 193
United Kingdom
  bank lending flows in, 89–90
  foreign exchange reserves and swap, 54
  re-examination of HFT tax, 177
United States
  current account balance of, 44
  HFT market share in, 166, 167, 183
  HFT regulation in, 172–3
  increase in gross capital flows to, 44
  KIC asset allocation in, 145–6
unit labour costs, 28, 29
US banking system
  contagious effect on, 53–4, 56
  short-term claims on OECD economies, 47
US dollar funding gap of European banking systems, 44
US dollar swap lines, 43, 57n3, 57n5
  advanced and emerging countries, 54
  announcement timeline, 49
  effects on CDS prices, 48, 50–1
  granting of, 46, 48
  impact on exchange rate, 57n7
  on official reserves, 46
  provided by Federal Reserve, 48–53
  rollover risk reduction, 48
US dollar swap lines, demand for, 44–7
  Bank of England, 45
  Bank of Japan, 45
  ECB, 45
  in financial crisis, 53–4
  variables affecting, 45–7
US equities with HFT
  and liquidity, 154
  low trading costs, 154
US firms, debt maturity of, 72
US money market, 44–5

variable definitions and data sources, 129–30
venture capital and private equity, 99, 107

wage demands and competitiveness, 24–5
wage development in EMU, 1999–2012, 20, 21
wage flexibility and labour mobility, 19, 38

zero agency cost base case, 65

Printed and bound by CPI Group (UK) Ltd, Croydon, CR0 4YY